P9-CSC-249

"This takes, wisely, a humble approach: instead of trying encapsulate the entirety of India's changes, it follows a few lives along the idiosyncratic ways they develop. For people who savored Katherine Boo's *Behind the Beautiful Forevers*."

—Evan Osnos, NewYorker.com

"[A] lucid, balanced new book . . . Kapur is determinedly fair-minded, neither an apologist nor a scold, and he is a wonderfully empathetic listener, willing patiently to visit and revisit a large cast of men and women over several years to learn how they are bene-fiting from—and being battered by—the change going on all around them."   —*The New York Times Book Review*

"Impressively lucid and searching . . . In his clarity, sympathy, and impeccably sculpted prose, Kapur often summons the spirit of V. S. Naipaul."   —Pico Iyer, *Time*

"There are many virtues of Akash Kapur's beautifully sketched portrait of modern India. . . . The book inhabits parts of India we do not explore often enough, the India of the south and of the transforming countryside. Mostly, it takes us into the minds and hearts of Indians seeking to adapt to a society changing at discon-certing speed. The book reads like a novel . . . Kapur's skill is to get people talking and to weave their stories into a necessarily messy debate about India's future."   —*Financial Times*

"Readable, acutely observed, and crammed with well-drawn char-acters . . . Kapur's strength is in letting his characters display the ambiguity that many feel about the ongoing change. . . . Kapur offers a corrective to a simplistic 'new, happy narrative' of a rising India."   —*The Economist*

"A gripping book [that] describes the dark side of the boom—and the opportunities."
                                                              —*Der Spiegel*

"Kapur himself, with one leg in the East and one in the West, is an excellent ambassador to explain the dynamic of change in India, what the nation is becoming. Any reader who would like to understand the country better would do well to give him a read."
                                                              —*The Daily Beast*

"[Kapur] has a fluency that outsiders—even those of us who claim some genetic tie—lack."   —*The New Republic*

"A fascinating look at the transformation of India, with broader lessons on the upside and downside of progress."
                                                              —*Booklist* (starred)

"[A] lively, anecdotal look at the people who have been vastly changed by the entrepreneurial explosion in India. . . . An honest, conflicted glimpse of a country."   —*Kirkus Reviews*

"This is a remarkably absorbing account of an India in transition—full of challenges and contradictions, but also of expectations, hope, and ultimately optimism."   —Amartya Sen

"Marvelous . . . Kapur shows how the old rural cycle of the south Indian village depicted and romanticized by R. K. Narayan is fracturing and breaking apart to reveal a very new, more unstable world where the old certainties are disappearing and everything is up for grabs. Sharp-eyed, insightful, skillfully sketched and beautifully written, *India Becoming* is the remarkable debut of a distinctive new talent."

                              —William Dalrymple, author of *Nine Lives:*
                                  In Search of the Sacred in Modern India

"Akash Kapur lives in and writes out of an India that few writers venture into. Curious, suspicious of received wisdom, and intellectually resourceful, [Kapur is] one of the most reliable observers of the New India."

—Pankaj Mishra, author of *Temptations of the West:
How to Be Modern in India, Pakistan, Tibet, and Beyond*

"Through a series of deft character sketches, Akash Kapur captures the contradictions of life in modern India—between city and country, technology and aesthetics, development and the environment, greed and selflessness, individual fulfillment and community obligation. His writing is fresh and vivid; his perspective empathetic and appealingly nonjudgmental."

—Ramachandra Guha, author of *India After Gandhi*

"Beautifully written . . . Akash Kapur celebrates the gains and mourns the losses, conveying a complex story through the ups and downs of the lives of some fascinating individual women and men."

—Kwame Anthony Appiah, author of
Cosmopolitanism: Ethics in a World of Strangers

"India today is in the midst of profound change and Akash Kapur captures the impact of that change on the lives of ordinary Indians with a narrative that avoids all clichés, platitudes, and simplifications."

—Gurcharan Das, author of *India Unbound*

india becoming

A Portrait of Life in Modern India

AKASH KAPUR

RIVERHEAD BOOKS

NEW YORK

RIVERHEAD BOOKS
Published by the Penguin Group
Penguin Group (USA) Inc.
375 Hudson Street, New York, New York 10014, USA

Penguin Group (Canada), 90 Eglinton Avenue East, Suite 700, Toronto, Ontario M4P 2Y3, Canada
(a division of Pearson Penguin Canada Inc.) • Penguin Books Ltd., 80 Strand, London WC2R 0RL,
England • Penguin Ireland, 25 St. Stephen's Green, Dublin 2, Ireland (a division of Penguin
Books Ltd.) • Penguin Group (Australia), 707 Collins Street, Melbourne, Victoria 3008, Australia
(a division of Pearson Australia Group Pty. Ltd.) • Penguin Books India Pvt. Ltd., 11 Community
Centre, Panchsheel Park, New Delhi—110 017, India • Penguin Group (NZ), 67 Apollo Drive,
Rosedale, Auckland 0632, New Zealand (a division of Pearson New Zealand Ltd.) • Penguin Books
(South Africa), Rosebank Office Park, 181 Jan Smuts Avenue, Parktown North 2193, South Africa •
Penguin China, B7 Jiaming Center, 27 East Third Ring Road North, Chaoyang District,
Beijing 100020, China

Penguin Books Ltd., Registered Offices: 80 Strand, London WC2R 0RL, England

While the author has made every effort to provide accurate telephone numbers,
Internet addresses and other contact information at the time of publication, neither the
publisher nor the author assumes any responsibility for errors, or for changes that occur after
publication. Further, publisher does not have any control over and does not assume
any responsibility for author or third-party websites or their content.

Copyright © 2012 by Akash Kapur
Cover design by Gabriele Wilson
Book design by Susan Walsh
Frontmatter map by Jeffrey L. Ward

Grateful acknowledgment is made to the Estate of Ryszard Kapuściński
for the permission to reprint a quote from his work *Szachinszach* (*Shah of Shahs*),
copyright © 1982 by Ryszard Kapuściński.

First Riverhead hardcover edition: March 2012
First Riverhead trade paperback edition: March 2013
Riverhead trade paperback ISBN: 978-1-59448-653-1

The Library of Congress has catalogued the Riverhead hardcover edition as follows:

Kapur, Akash.
India becoming : a portrait of life in modern India / Akash Kapur.
p.   cm.
ISBN: 978-1-59448-819-1
1. India—Economic conditions—21st century.   2. India—Social conditions—21st century.
3. India—Rural conditions.   4. Social conditions—India.
HC435.3.K36   2012   2011047588
330.954—dc23

*Penguin is committed to publishing works of quality and integrity.
In that spirit, we are proud to offer this book to our readers;
however the story, the experiences and the words are the author's alone.*

Auralice, Aman, Emil

History shows that where ethics and economics come in conflict, victory is always with economics. Vested interests have never been known to have willingly divested themselves.

—B. R. Ambedkar

Development is a treacherous river, as everyone who plunges into its currents knows. On the surface the water flows smoothly and quickly, but if the captain makes one careless or thoughtless move he finds out how many whirlpools and wide shoals the river contains.

—Ryszard Kapuściński, *Shah of Shahs*

Life does not agree with philosophy.

—Anton chekhov

CONTENTS

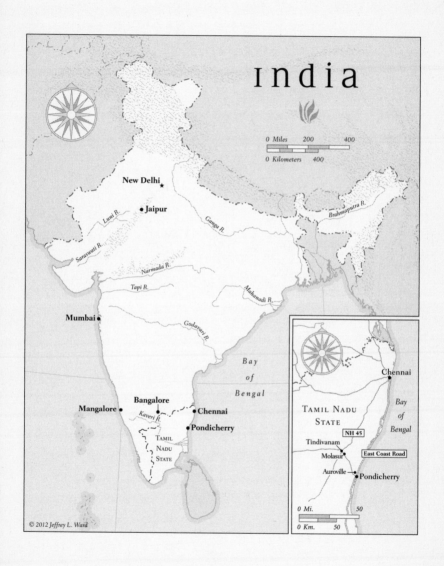

PROLOGUE

The East Coast Road has changed. Twenty-five years ago, when I was a child growing up at its edge, it was a potholed tar road that meandered across the South Indian countryside, cutting through rice fields and coconut plantations and sleepy fishing villages. The views were stunning—a rippled ocean, the gray waters of the Bay of Bengal, shimmering under the harsh coastal sun.

Sometime in the nineties, government contractors descended upon the road. They surveyed neighboring fields and farms, they bulldozed surrounding huts. Villages were cut in half, families were uprooted. Hundreds of ancient trees were brought down. Activists protested, but they were told the social and ecological disruption was the price of progress.

By the time I moved back to India, in the winter of 2003, after more than a decade in America, the country road I knew as a child had become a 160-kilometer highway. Politicians extolled it as a model for modern India—an ambitious collaboration between government and private companies, the kind of infrastructure the country needed to develop its economy.

The surface of the East Coast Road is now a smooth mix of tar and powdered rock. The road is adorned with dividers that glow in the dark, signs for emergency services, and toll counters that light up the night with their halogen lamps and bright metal booths. Some of the rice fields remain, and the views are still beautiful. But much of the countryside has given way to the promised development—beach resorts, open-air restaurants, movie theaters, and scores of small tea shops catering to the tourists that throng the road on weekends.

At the top of the East Coast Road, outside the city of Chennai, the capital of the state of Tamil Nadu, tourist attractions lead into urban congestion. Traffic is denser, the crowds swell off the sidewalks and onto the streets, and the ocean breeze is obstructed by tightly packed shops and office buildings.

The East Coast Road joins Rajiv Gandhi Salai, Chennai's technology corridor. The change here is even more striking. Twenty-five years ago, Rajiv Gandhi Salai was itself a country road, a little-used path that carried tourists from Chennai to the seaside town of Mahabalipuram. Like the East Coast Road, it was bordered by farms and plantations; well into the nineties, when the software and outsourcing companies began setting up shop, you could see the occasional tractor, maybe even a bullock cart, on the road.

Today, Rajiv Gandhi Salai, also referred to as the Old

Mahabalipuram Road—as if to distance it from the present, to demarcate it as a relic from a different moment in the nation's history—is a showcase of the new India. The farmland has become fertile terrain for steel-framed and glass-paneled office buildings. These buildings house the technology companies driving India's economic boom—the Yahoo!s and PayPals and Verizons that have rushed into the country over the last couple of decades, but also local upstarts like Infosys, Satyam, and Wipro that have for the first time put India on the map of global business.

Employees of these companies—men in tightly tucked shirts and khakis, women more likely to be dressed in pants than saris—swarm to work in the mornings, jamming the highway with their motorcycles and scooters. At noon, they break for lunch on well-maintained gardens, expansive lawns adorned with transplanted palm trees, like something out of Southern California. These are the foot soldiers of India's surging economy; with their confidence, their enthusiasm, their willingness to work long hours, they are driving the emergence of a new nation.

*It was to this new nation—this country where rice fields were giv-*ing way to highways, farmland to software complexes, and saris to pants—that I returned in 2003. I was coming home, but in many ways it was to a home I didn't recognize anymore.

I landed in Chennai on a December morning. It was just before dawn. The sky was a dark blue, the air was cool but heavy. I remember being surprised by the humidity.

Outside the airport, amid the touts and baggage handlers, the commotion of a crowd whose crush I had almost forgotten, I caught an air-conditioned car. I was going to Auroville, the town where I had grown up, about a three-hour drive from Chennai.

I took the East Coast Road. In Chennai, I crawled through congested streets where traffic had once flowed easily, and I drove past the towers of Rajiv Gandhi Salai, their cubicles lit up even at that early hour. Outside the city, with the ocean gleaming on the horizon, I passed through the urban sprawl of gated communities and plotted-out fields.

In the village of Kadapakkam, about an hour and a half from the airport, I stopped for a coffee in a tea shop by the side of the road. The owner of the tea shop was a skinny, garrulous man. He stood over a kerosene stove and told me about his life. He said he was born poor, the son of a landless laborer. The road had changed everything for him.

He talked about the taxis and buses that stopped in at his tea shop, about the new house he had built, about the motorcycle he had bought himself. He talked about the private school where he sent his children.

He talked and talked and then, while he was talking, an older man sitting in front of me, a customer, interrupted. He told the owner he was wrong; the road had ruined many lives. He spoke about families that had lost their houses to government acquisition, about all the development that had spoiled the area, about the accidents.

Just last month, the customer said, a boy, the relative of someone he knew, was run over and killed outside this village.

Their conversation turned into an argument; a few others joined in. I listened for a while, and then I turned away. I was jet-lagged, still taking in the familiar yet strangely unfamiliar sounds and smells of my childhood. But I heard enough to know that I was with the owner: I welcomed the change. I found what was going on in India exciting, even intoxicating.

In America, I had been living in New York. I loved New York— loved the nightlife, loved the parks, loved the diversity of the city—but increasingly, I had found life there stifling. America, I felt, was in a kind of fog. The war in Iraq was turning sour, the economy was sputtering. The country was depressed, consumed with forebodings of decline.

India was so different. India was emerging from its depression, a centuries-long misadventure of colonialism, poverty, and under-development. Now, on its way to what was surely a better future, the country was giddy, exuberant. Bookstores were filled with titles like *India Arriving, The Indian Renaissance*, and *India Booms*. Newspapers and magazines regularly ran surveys showing that India was the most optimistic country in the world.

In America, my friends were worried about losing their jobs; they held on to what they had. But in India, people I knew were quitting their jobs, casting aside the safety of well-established careers for the excitement—and potential riches—of starting their own business. Every other person I met dreamed of being an entrepreneur; they were willing to take a bet on the future.

It was as if my world had come full circle. I had grown up between India and America, the son of an Indian father and an American mother. I always considered both countries home. In

1991, at the age of sixteen, I moved to America in search of better education and more opportunities. Like so many before me, I was escaping the economic and social torpor of India—the austerity imposed by the nation's socialist economy, the fatalism and bureaucracy that blocked all creative impulse and even a hint of entrepreneurial energy.

The India of my youth felt cut off, at the edge of modernity. When I boarded that plane in Chennai, trading the heat of coastal South India for the bitter winters of boarding school in Massachusetts, I felt like I was entering the world.

Now, twelve years later, India was at the center of the world. It was India, with its resurgent economy, high savings rates, and young, educated workforce, that beckoned with the sense of a brighter future; it was India that offered the promise of a country and an economy on the upswing. Einstein once wrote of America that its people were "always becoming, never being," but it was in India now that I felt that sense of newness, of perpetual reinvention and forward momentum that I had felt when I first moved to America.

Almost half a century ago, R. K. Narayan, that great chronicler of Indian life in a slower, less complex time, traveled through the United States. In a book he later wrote about his journey, he noted the apparently irreconcilable gaps that separated the two nations. "America and India are profoundly different in attitude and philosophy," he wrote. "Indian philosophy stresses austerity and unencumbered, uncomplicated day-to-day living. America's emphasis, on the other hand, is on material acquisition and the limitless pursuit of prosperity."

Indians, Narayan added, cultivate a certain "otherworldliness."

Americans have "a robust indifference to eternity." A typical American "works hard and earnestly, acquires wealth and enjoys life. He has no time to worry about the afterlife."

By the time I returned home, India was determinedly shedding the abstemiousness and detachment that had defined it since independence. "Material acquisition" was no longer the preserve of Americans. The "otherworldliness" of an earlier era—a certain apathy, a charming if ultimately unproductive indifference—was being replaced by the energetic (and often ruthless) ambition of a new generation.

A great reconciliation was taking place. As a boy, my two worlds had often felt very far apart. India and America were literally—but also socially, culturally, and experientially—on opposite sides of the planet. Now, for better and for worse, in ways that both excited and at times frightened me, I felt as though India was co-opting the very qualities that defined America.

India's transformation began in 1991, when a financial crisis forced the government to lower import barriers, ease foreign exchange controls, and allow a greater degree of private investment. These reforms unleashed the nation, spurring economic growth from an anemic 3.5 percent or so (what economists derisively referred to as "the Hindu rate of growth") to around 8 or 9 percent. They transformed a closed, socialist—or at any rate semi-socialist—nation into a country that was far more willing to accept and even embrace global capitalism.

The change was most evident in the cities, in urban metropolises like Chennai and Bangalore and Mumbai, which were the first to feel the impact of the reforms. On the green lawns of software parks, in the corridors of new shopping malls, crowded with young consumers clutching cell phones and bags of cosmetics and DVDs, and in the bars and clubs where men and women mingled freely, I felt that India was being redefined. The nation was widening its horizons, experimenting with fresh ideas and ways of living.

But even in rural India, where I had grown up, and to which I was now returning, the reinvention was palpable.

Auroville is in the countryside; it is surrounded by five villages. In the fields around me, farmers who had once gone to work in bullock carts without tires now drove shiny tractors. Down at the beach, fishermen were trading catamarans for diesel-powered motorboats. Satellite dishes were ubiquitous, and even a couple of ATMs had sprouted up between the older thatch huts and the new concrete buildings.

In both city and country, in shopping malls and on farms, what struck me most about India was not so much the cell phones and satellite dishes and other physical manifestations of change. I was impressed by something less tangible, something in the spirit of the nation.

Middle-class children, sons and daughters of parents who had aspired to nothing so much as a secure government job, were planning careers as software entrepreneurs; they envisioned themselves as the next Bill Gates. Farmers and fishermen were setting up restaurants and guesthouses; their ambition challenged the social order that had for so long pinned them to poverty and illiteracy.

For the first time—the first time in my life, but arguably in India's history, too—people dared to imagine an existence for themselves that was unburdened by the past and tradition. India, I felt, had started to dream.

Later, after I had spent more time in the country, when I had traveled around and met more people, I began to question aspects of that dream. The self-confidence I began to see as a kind of blindness, an almost messianic conviction in the country's future. The unrelenting optimism was often delusional, a blinkered faith that ignored the many problems—the poverty, the inequality, the lawlessness, the environmental depredation—still facing the nation.

I grew less impressed with the shopping malls and shiny office complexes, with the fancy bars and the variety of cocktails they served. I began to feel that the country was being engulfed in its encounter with capitalism, swallowed by a great wave of consumerism and materialism that threatened to corrode the famous Indian soul.

Nothing is free. The more time I spent back home, the more it became apparent to me that India would have to pay a price for its prosperity—that new money was being accompanied by new forms of inequality, that freedom and opportunities were opening the floodgates, too, to disorder and violence.

Millions of Indians have risen out of poverty since the nation's economic reforms. But millions more remain in poverty, and millions, too, are being subjected to the psychological dislocation of having their world change, of watching a social order that has given meaning to them—and their parents, and their grandparents before them—slip away.

Development, I came to understand, was a form of creative destruction. For everyone whose life was being regenerated or rejuvenated in modern India, there was someone, as well, whose life was being destroyed.

This book really contains two stories. One is a story of progress, of the sense of purpose and direction that rapid economic growth can bestow on a nation that had in many ways lost faith in itself. The other is a darker story; it tells of the destruction and disruptions caused by the same process of development.

One process, two outcomes. India is a complex country. Sometimes the creativity and the destruction, the good and the bad, were hard to disentangle.

I didn't see this complexity when I first came back. My understanding of the country I had known only as a boy was superficial. When I landed on that winter morning in Chennai and took the East Coast Road back to Auroville, I saw just the optimistic side of India.

I suppose I saw what I wanted to see. After years of feeling alienated, never quite belonging in America, I was desperate to find a home. This book is in part a story of that homecoming—of how I embraced and found myself revitalized in the new India, of how I rejoiced in the nation's economic progress; and then of how, after a few years, I learned to see the many edges, more than a few jagged, of that strange phenomenon called development.

Most of all, this book is the story of the people I met after returning to India. These people allowed me to glimpse, and at least partially understand, the complexity and nuance of this exceptionally layered country. I have come to know India again through the men and women who shared with me their life stories, who allowed me into their families and their homes. Many of these people have become friends; their friendship has allowed me to write this book.

I have been back in India, now, for a little over nine years. A lot has happened in my life during that time. I have built a house, married, had two children. Sometimes I watch my boys—Aman, age six, and Emil, age four—play in the same forests I did as a child, run through the same fields and villages I knew when I was just a little older than they are. It makes me happy, warms me in a place that I didn't know I had until they were born, that their childhood memories will occupy the same landscape as mine.

But I know, also, that that warm feeling is a little bit of wishful thinking—that though the forests and fields and villages remain, and though my children are growing up, as I did, in rural India, nothing is really as it was. The world I knew as a boy doesn't exist anymore.

Most of the time, I'm at peace with that reality. I celebrate the new India. But there are moments when all I can focus on is the sense of loss—the memory of a time before software parks and shopping malls, the sobriety and moral purpose of a country before it succumbed to the bland homogenizations of twenty-first-century capitalism.

I know that the great transition under way now is inevitable, and probably even desirable. I know, too, that it is unstoppable. The forces at work in modern India are part of the great sweep of history. All I can do is watch them, understand them, and maybe, through understanding, learn to accept them.

I'd like to think of this book as a step in that direction. It represents my effort to come to terms with the forces remaking my home.

part 1

GOLDEN TIMES

"We used to ride across these fields on horses," R. Sathyanaray-anan, or Sathy, as he called himself, told me.

"I remember it so well. We'd ride from that mountain over there, where my uncle lived. My father had a gun, a Webley & Scott pistol from Birmingham he'd inherited from my grandfather. He'd shoot it in the air to announce our arrival. The whole village knew we were coming. Our cook would warm up the food."

We were standing in an empty field outside Sathy's village of Molasur. It was summer. The land was hard and dry. Sathy was dripping with sweat.

He pointed to the gray mountain on the horizon by which his uncle still lived. He said all the land between that mountain and where we were now standing, thousands of acres, had once belonged to his family. They were zamindars, feudal lords. Not too long ago, just a few decades, they had ruled over the land and the villages on it like country nobility.

We walked through the flat fields, along irrigation channels, up an embankment overlooking a village reservoir. The reservoir was empty. Ancient granite steps led down the embankment. Sathy sat on one of the steps and talked about fishing and swimming in the reservoir with his brothers when they were boys.

Back then, he said, the reservoir was always full. Now it was full only after the rains, when the monsoons brought muddy water from the fields and surrounding hills. But Sathy never went swimming anymore, and he never let his children fish in the reservoir. It was too dirty, he said; villagers used the area as a toilet. They lined up in the mornings, crouched around the reservoir, and used the water to clean themselves.

"It's disgusting," Sathy said, and he shook his head and wrinkled his nose. The reservoir had been built a thousand years ago. For a thousand years, it nurtured the village—irrigated the fields, provided bathing and drinking water to homes. People had forgotten all of that, Sathy said; now they defecated in the water.

"People don't care anymore," he said. "Before, there was respect, there was decency. Now all that's gone. Who knows what people believe in anymore?"

He wiped the sweat from his brow. He pressed down on his mustache, flattening it with the sweat off his palms. Sathy had a big mustache. It curled up at the corners. Sometimes, when he pressed on it, settled it down, I thought he was trying to maintain a degree of control.

I met Sathy about a year after returning to India. He was forty-one years old. We were introduced by a relative of mine who ran an equestrian academy not far from Molasur. Sathy brought his children—his son, Darshan, age eight, and his daughter, Thaniya, age seven—to learn from her. He no longer kept horses in the village, but he wanted his children to know the old ways.

When my relative first told me about Sathy, she said he was a talkative man. She knew I was writing a book. She thought I might find some of his stories interesting.

So we met, one afternoon, in Pondicherry, a former French colony near Auroville, an elegant town of tree-lined streets and high-ceilinged villas by the ocean. We met in the courtyard of a hotel. We had coffee under a mango tree. Sathy talked a lot. He seemed jittery. I thought he was trying to impress me.

He told me all about his family at that first meeting—about their noble background, about the land they had owned, about the way they had dominated Molasur and the roughly seventy-five villages around it. He said they were Reddiars, members of a warrior caste that had migrated from the north some eight centuries ago and become the biggest landowners in the area.

He told me about a childhood of status and privilege. One of his ancestors, he said, was a famous chief minister of Madras Presidency, an amalgamation of South Indian states during colonial rule. He had grown up in the biggest house in Molasur. His family owned the only car in the village. Whenever they left home, villagers would line the roads and bow their heads in respect.

For centuries, the Reddiars had ruled over the countryside, making a comfortable living off agriculture, extracting labor and taxes from semi-indentured workers. They had proven to be adaptable rulers. Wave after wave of invaders—the great Chola dynasties, who controlled much of South India until the thirteenth century; the Mughals, who swept down from the north around the seventeenth century; and the British—came through. But the Reddiars always managed to hold on to their power.

Sathy talked a lot about his family's land that afternoon—about the fields and forests that were their main source of wealth, about the hundreds of acres he still cultivated with rice and peanuts. Farming was in his blood, he said, and I could see he was excited, exuberant in a way that was almost childish, when he remembered the times he had spent with his father in the fields, burning under the sun or soaking in the rain, planting and plowing and reaping from their land.

It was harder to make a living off farming now, Sathy said. He leaned forward, as if he was letting me in on a secret. He emptied his third cup of coffee. He said that the land around Molasur was less fertile; it had been poisoned for too long by chemical fertilizers and pesticides. The water table, overextended and overpumped, was in decline.

"Agriculture is a difficult business these days," Sathy said, and for the first time since we met, his confidence seemed to sag a little. He said it was a challenge to keep the farm running. He hinted that the family's financial position wasn't quite what it had once been.

It was just a little crack in the façade. There would be many more. But on that afternoon, Sathy pulled back quickly. He started talking about real estate. He said he'd been thinking about developing his land. There were fortunes to be made.

He'd been considering building some homes, maybe selling them to technology workers from the cities looking for country retreats. Or maybe he'd build a golf resort. He asked if I knew people with money; he invited me to join him in the resort project.

"People in Chennai and Bangalore are big into golf these days," he said. "It's the new fashion. I'm sure they'd travel to my village if I had a world-class resort."

I wasn't interested in building a golf course with Sathy. But I was interested in knowing more about his world. Sometimes Sathy seemed excited about the changes in Molasur, all the wealth and opportunities presenting themselves to "my people" (as he always referred to them). Other times he seemed less positive, even downcast. He worried about his loss of status, about the way the social order he had known as a boy was disappearing. He said that villagers were losing their values, succumbing to the temptations of money, turning into liars, cheats, and murderers.

"People are lost," Sathy said to me one time. "They no longer know who they are. All the money has taken them away from themselves."

I thought Sathy was himself a little lost. He seemed disoriented, maybe confused. I knew that his discomfort was in many ways cause for celebration, part of the great emancipatory wave sweeping across India. The old feudal order was crumbling; as the fortunes of the Reddiars declined, thousands of men and women in and around Molasur were rising.

Still, I couldn't help feeling a little sympathetic. Molasur was around thirty kilometers from Auroville. My childhood was very different from Sathy's, but I grew up in the same rural landscape. By the time I met him, it had become apparent to me that the world I had known was also disappearing. The change was overwhelming—and, in many ways, bewildering.

Once, the villages around Auroville had been a jumble of thatch huts, fetid ponds, mud roads, and cashew plantations. Malnourished children, their bellies bloated and their skin pulled tight against their faces, so that they looked like old men, played naked by the side of the road. Few houses had running water or electricity.

Now, a little more than a decade later, the villages were transformed. Mud roads had been tarred, and cashew plantations turned into restaurants, coffee shops, and yoga centers. Streets were jammed with mopeds and motorcycles and even cars. In the evenings, the restaurants were busy, buzzing. The prosperity, the sense of progress, was hard to deny.

But I knew, also, that below the shine of new money, below the easy confidence and optimism, the villages around my home were wounded places. The wealth that had flowed into the area had swept away existing hierarchies and power structures. It had led to new resentments, and new feelings of entitlement. It had demolished a long-standing social structure that held the villages together.

In the years before I returned to India, the villages in my area were wracked by gang warfare. More than ten people were killed. One of them was pulled off his motorcycle and hacked up in broad daylight. Another was chased through the streets, into a home where he took refuge, and cut into pieces. Someone I knew was kidnapped, bound with his son for several days before ransom was arranged.

Once, the *panchayat*s, traditional assemblies made up of village elders, would have been able to control the violence. They functioned as local courts and law enforcement bodies. But young men in the area, flush with new money and a sense of empowerment, no longer feared their elders. The *panchayat*s still met, under banyan trees and in temple courtyards, but they were mostly toothless. The village elders were intimidated by their youth; they didn't dare assert their authority.

There was a woman I talked to sometimes from one of the villages. She was in her fifties. She lived a humble life, but it was less humble than it had been. She lived in a single-room house with a concrete roof, running water, and electricity. Her son drove a motorcycle. I spoke to her one day, not too long after a murder, the latest in a series of tit-for-tat killings in her village. There were policemen on the streets. Shops and restaurants were closed, boarded up in anticipation of further violence.

"This is what all the money has brought to us," the woman said to me. "We were poor, but at least we didn't need to worry about our lives. I think it was better that way."

I saw all this happening around me. I watched a great transformation unfold, unfurl like a heavy, crushing carpet over fragile societies and cultures. I knew that something momentous was happening, but I didn't know what to make of it. I was on the outside. I felt I needed Sathy to help me understand it.

Auroville is in rural India. But it is not of rural India. It is an intentional community, with around two thousand members from more than thirty countries. These men and women—dreamers, searchers—had come together in the late sixties and carved out a dry, barren corner of South India to build a new world. They were motivated by a quest for human unity; they were inspired by the idea of a place without hierarchy and class.

What they made was like no other place I know. Auroville isn't really a town. It is a collection of small communities, spread across hundreds of acres of beautiful land, colored red from the iron oxide in the soil. Growing up, I was surrounded by rural India. But I lived in a world apart: an aspiring utopia of Americans, Germans, Belgians, and Swedes, a unique population of doctors and engineers and teachers and architects.

So Auroville was a good place from which to see South India, watch it evolve. But it wasn't a place from which to really know it.

In the months after I met Sathy, after that initial encounter under a mango tree in Pondicherry, I found myself increasingly drawn to his life. The stories that had seemed long-winded, a little tiresome, now seemed fascinating; Sathy's loquaciousness was full of insight.

We would meet for coffee or tea, usually in Pondicherry. Sometimes he would visit me at home. We would have lunch together, in one of the new restaurants or coffee shops that had come up in the area.

I started spending time in Molasur. I would take the forty-minute drive from Auroville, along a bumpy road bordered by villages and market towns. The road was narrow, badly maintained, but there were rumors that the government was going to widen it, turn it into a national highway, and the real estate activity was already evident.

All along the road, in neat little compounds between rice and sugarcane fields, colleges and shopping centers and gated communities were coming up. Their developers gave them names that captured the spirit of a people who knew their children would have better lives than their own. My favorite, attached to a residential development, was "Rich India Dream City."

Molasur was a few hundred meters off the main road, on a crumbling village track that hadn't been tarred in decades. Sathy's house was at the head of the village. It was a traditional house, built in the nineteenth century, with whitewashed walls, a sloping tile roof, and cement floors that stayed cool even in the summers.

Sathy always served me coffee when I visited. It was delicious coffee, filtered in the South Indian style, made with fresh milk from a cow tied to a post in a courtyard at the back. Sathy's mother sat just off the courtyard, surveying the kitchen, in a cane chair positioned at the edge of the sunlight—close enough to get the light, but not the heat.

Sathy lived in that house with his mother, a sister, and various other relatives. His room was upstairs, by a veranda that overlooked the village. It was usually unkempt, clothes and books and sometimes a comb strewn across an unmade bed. It was a bachelor's room. Sathy's wife and children lived in Bangalore.

His wife was originally from the city. Her name was Banushree Reddy, or Banu. After marrying Sathy, Banu had moved to Molasur for a while and tried to adjust to the village. But it hadn't worked out. Village life was constraining; it was tough for a modern woman like Banu—someone with engineering and business degrees, brought up to believe that women could work and have careers—to fit in. She moved back to Bangalore, and she started a consulting business. She trained new recruits at the city's technology and outsourcing companies.

His family's absence was a constant source of tension to Sathy. He talked a lot about his children; he saw them only on weekends, when he drove or took the bus to Bangalore. Banu told him he should move to the city, that his children needed their father. But Sathy was too attached to his ancestral land—to the fields he walked every day, and to the villagers whom he still seemed to consider his charges if not his subjects.

"What can I do, Akash?" he asked me once. "This is my place. This is my village, and these are my people. They need me, all these people depend on me. What would happen to them if I left and moved to Bangalore?"

I loved going for walks in the fields around Molasur. Sathy and I would start in the village, on narrow lanes lined with thatch huts and tile-roofed houses. The lanes felt crowded; more than five thousand people lived in Molasur. We'd pass by a sandy children's playground, and then an ancient temple, its turret blackened by the years, which stood at the edge of Sathy's land.

The land was wide open. It was always exhilarating, like a breath, to step from the congested village into the open fields.

Sathy carried a bamboo stick whenever we walked. He swung

it in big back-and-forth motions, up and down, sometimes passing it horizontally between his hands. He said the stick was to protect us against jackals, but I never saw any jackals. I thought the stick was a way of asserting his authority.

There was a gray afternoon in November, an interlude between monsoon showers, when Sathy said he wanted to show me something on his land. He said we would be going farther than he had ever taken me before—past the fields, past the reservoir, to what he called his "forest land." It was almost one hundred acres of wild, uncultivated property. He said it had been used in the old days—by "the Britishers"—to hunt for rabbits and pheasants.

We began outside his house. As we passed through Molasur's winding streets, people ran up to greet Sathy, many of them with folded hands, some of them bowing a little. Sathy was paternalistic. He inquired after their education or health, he asked how their jobs were going. He chided one man who worked in Chennai, reminding him to send money home for his ailing father. He scolded another who had been without a job for several months.

One man jumped off his cycle, ran up to us, and began grinning somewhat deliriously. "Get lost," Sathy said, playfully, and when the man was gone, Sathy told me the cyclist had been indebted to him ever since he'd saved his marriage. The man's wife was going to leave him because he didn't make enough money in his job as a watchman. Sathy had found him a new job, as a stone crusher on a road project. He was paid twice as much at the new job; his wife stayed with him.

"These days, women are fussy," Sathy said, and he chuckled.

We came across a group of young men standing around a motorcycle. They were dressed in polyester shirts and dark pants, with synthetic belts wrapped tight around the narrowest hips I had ever seen. They were sharing a cigarette, and when Sathy saw them, he shouted, demanded that they drop it.

The men looked straight at Sathy. They laughed, kind of a sneer, and Sathy, taken aback, kept walking. "It's just something that matters to me," he said. "It's from the old days. People would never smoke in front of my father."

When Sathy's father died, of a heart attack at the age of sixty-three, Sathy had been attending law school in Pondicherry. He was forced to return to Molasur to tend to the family's property. He tried to fill his father's shoes, but it was the early nineties, and people in the village were developing new ideas about their place in the world. Young people, in particular, were no longer in awe of the Reddiars.

As Sathy walked me around Molasur that afternoon, he talked about the social reconfiguration he had come up against when he moved back home. Partly, he said, this reconfiguration was driven by the new sense of self-esteem that was transforming villages across the country. But it was also driven by the dwindling fortunes of agricultural families like the Reddiars. Throughout India, agriculture was in crisis. Farm yields were down, input prices (the price of labor, fertilizer, and pesticides) had soared, and people were abandoning the profession. While India's overall economy was growing at 7 to 9 percent, agriculture was growing at below 3 percent.

Sathy acknowledged that his family was better off than many. Smaller farmers, unable to achieve the necessary economies of scale, too poor to buy tractors and other mechanized tools, had been decimated. Many small farmers were swallowed by debt:

tens and perhaps hundreds of thousands of farmers committed suicide in the decades following India's economic reforms. Still, Sathy said, even families like his had felt the pinch. They could no longer rely on the vast fortunes they had used to build patronage and buy loyalty in the village.

"It was really a shock for me when this started happening," Sathy said, speaking of the difficulties his family faced in keeping the farm running. "We were never poor—we didn't suffer as badly as so many others. But I remember how freely my family used to spend. I never imagined that we would have to worry about money. It was something new, a new challenge we had to face."

"I don't need the money for myself," he went on. "I'm happy to live simply. But it's true that people see us differently now. Everybody knows the Reddiars aren't as rich as they used to be. And the sad truth is that even in the village, money buys respect. People admired us for our status, but I'm not so simple to think they weren't also impressed by our family's wealth."

We came upon an old man in a loincloth. He, too, was smoking, a beedi nestled discreetly in the palm of his hand. Sathy yelled at him to drop it, and the man did, immediately and without hesitation. Sathy was satisfied. He told me that the young men who had refused to stop smoking probably weren't from the village; they must have been daytrippers from the city.

"Most people in Molasur still remember the old ways," he said. "They know who I am, and they know how to behave. They know how to give proper respect."

Respect was one of Sathy's favorite words. It cropped up all the time in our conversations. Sathy said his wife mocked him for using the word so much. She told him he was a fool, that he was so hung up on the past, so intent on maintaining a semblance of his family's old dignity, that he cared more about respect than the practicalities of life.

"Can you eat respect?" she would ask him. "Will respect educate your children?"

"In a way, she's right," Sathy said. "But she doesn't understand. Banu is from the city. She doesn't know what matters in the village."

It was late afternoon as we walked through Sathy's fields. The sun was low. It had just emerged from gray clouds, into a narrow band of blue stretched over the horizon. It was a gentle, blurry, winter sun; it hung like a butter ball over the land.

Sathy talked, kind of babbled, as we walked. He seemed preoccupied. He had just returned from a trip to Bangalore. One of Banu's relatives, an uncle who had made a fortune in real estate, had given a party to celebrate the purchase of a large property. He invited six thousand guests; they were served a lavish meal, with hundreds of dishes, and live music for entertainment.

After the party, Darshan, Sathy's son, asked him if they could give feasts like that, too. Sathy said: "I told him, 'Never. Never. Don't expect these kinds of extravagances from me. I'm just a farmer. I can't rise to that level. But I get good respect, everyone knows who I am, and I can give you a good life. That's all you can expect from me.'

"People are so superficial in this country nowadays," Sathy said. "All they care about is showing off. I go to Bangalore and it's full of all these IT workers—all these young kids with their cell phones and money and all that. They've become like Americans: they have wallets full of credit cards, and pseudo-feelings. You meet them and they say hi, and then they say bye. They might even say they love you, but there's no real feeling. It's just like America. We want everything big and quick.

"The thing is, I understand why it's like that in America. Americans need everything big because they have nothing old. But why does it have to be that way with us? The other day I was driving past a new temple. It was huge. I turned to my driver and I asked him, 'What, are we building temples like the Americans now?' It's not necessary, Akash. Look at the idols in our old temples—they're tiny, they're ancient, and they have all the power. We're losing sight of what really matters: our history, our past.

"Don't get me wrong," he went on. "I'm happy for my people. I want them to develop, I want them to get rich. Development is good for them. It's educating them, making them more confident. People stand up for themselves. Even the women—they're so bold. My mother never dared to raise her voice with my father, but look at Banu: she does what she wants. She moves to Bangalore with my children, and what can I do? I can't say anything."

I said: "You sound like you're contradicting yourself."

He said: "No, I'm not contradicting. I know it's good for the country. I know things have to change; they should change. Some people rise, and others have to fall. My family was high for so long. I know my status can't stay the same forever. But still, the ego is there—the ego clings to what it had."

He told me that some nights, lying in bed, he woke up thinking about how different life in Molasur had become. He thought of the farms that were turning fallow, and of the old country road running by the village that was becoming a highway. He knew things would change even more; he figured he had about five years before the village became unrecognizable. His kids would never live in Molasur. They would never be farmers; he would have to sell the land.

He woke up in the middle of the night, and the knowledge of all this change, of a way of life he'd never share with his children, would seize him. He'd feel a tightness in his chest. He would think of how his father had died, and the tightness frightened him.

He would sit outside his room, on the veranda. He took deep breaths. The village would be quiet, the lights off. It was something like the way it used to be, before everyone got motorcycles and televisions and electricity, and the silence would calm him, give him strength. At moments like that, he felt like he could handle anything.

"We have to learn to let go, Akash," Sathy said, swinging his stick as we walked through the fields. "We have to learn to accept. It is difficult, of course, but we have to accept."

He read a lot; that helped him. He read spiritual books. He quoted a line from the Indian philosopher J. Krishnamurthi, his favorite author: "There are no solutions; there are only problems, and the resolution of each problem lies in the problem itself."

There was another book that helped him: *Who Moved My Cheese?* by Spencer Johnson. I laughed when he told me that, and he seemed surprised. He told me I should read the book. It would help me accept the fact that nothing stayed the same. He said it would help me understand what was going on around Auroville.

He'd given the book to his son. Darshan had read it several times. "He knows all the characters' names by heart," Sathy said. "He knows them even better than I do."

Sathy's forest land wasn't really a forest at all. It was, in fact, quite barren. Sathy said it had once been covered with mango, neem, and palmyra trees. Now all that remained was a thin line of palmyras, their trunks encased in an ancient carapace of spikes, their leaves rustling in the monsoon wind.

The forest had been cut down, chopped away one branch at a time by villagers foraging for firewood. It had been reduced to a flat—if wild and beautiful—stretch of shrubs and thornbushes. "We lost control of the land," Sathy said. "Before, no one dared to cut on our property. But when our status went down, I couldn't manage things as well as my father. I couldn't stop the villagers around here from killing our forest."

My legs were tired from the walk. I crouched on the ground, on the slippery gray clay, above a stream. The stream flowed fast and strong. The rains had been heavy; it was a successful monsoon. "Quite a downpour," I said to Sathy, and he agreed, and said it was good for the farmers. But then he shook his head and said it was nothing compared to some of the rains he remembered.

He remembered standing on this land in the pouring rain, his face flat in the gusting wind, with his father when he was a boy. They had come to inspect a dam. The rains had been ferocious, the strongest Sathy had ever seen. The dam was in danger of breaching. The village could have been flooded. Sathy's father gathered more than five hundred men. He called, and they came, and they worked in the rain, strengthening the dam with bags of sand and logs from cashew trees. They worked for three days, under the supervision of Sathy's father. They saved the village.

Sathy told me that story, and he told me how proud he had felt of his father. "He had so much control, so much charisma," he said. "Everyone obeyed him. Sometimes I wish I could imitate him. But I don't have his looks, and I don't have his charisma. I never had the same control that he had over the village."

"Do you think that the village would have stayed the same if your father was still alive?" I asked him.

"No, no, I wouldn't say that," Sathy said. "That's going too far. Even my father couldn't stop modernity. Even he couldn't block what's happening in this country now. Sometimes, to tell you the truth, I think it's good he died. He wouldn't want to see everything that has happened."

Sathy told me a story about a meeting that took place in the village near the end of his father's life. The meeting was held outdoors, under a banyan tree. His father was late; everyone stood up when he arrived. Everyone, except for one man—a Dalit youth named Raju. Raju had spent some time working in the cities. He had fancy, modern ideas; he was defying the Reddiar.

Sathy said his father's face turned to stone when he saw Raju sitting. He didn't say anything at the meeting, though, and he didn't say much the rest of the day. He was silent at dinner. Later, when Sathy was massaging his father's feet in the bedroom he shared with his parents, his father looked straight at him and said: "I don't know how you will manage. I don't know how you will cope."

Sathy told his father not to worry. He said times were changing, and the family had to change with them. He said he would learn to adjust; they all had to adjust.

Now, Sathy told me, when he visited places like Bangalore and Chennai, when he saw what was going on in the cities, he wondered if maybe his father was right. "Sometimes I think that maybe I goofed up my life," he said. "Why did I stay a farmer? It's silly to be a farmer these days. We landlords missed the industrial revolution, and now we're missing the technology revolution. Sometimes I ask myself why I'm struggling to keep the farm running while so many kids are making millions. Maybe my father had a point—we didn't know how to cope."

Sathy didn't say anything for a while after that. The land, too, was silent. We felt far away from the village, far from the road that was becoming a highway, and farther still from the cities that would be connected by that highway.

Dragonflies hovered above the stream. A group of mynah birds dug at the ground. A kingfisher exploded in a burst of blue.

Sitting there, the stream gurgling below me, the chirp of crickets in the air and a mongoose pawing nervously at a clump of wild berries, searching maybe for prey, I could just about remember the way my rural home had felt so many years ago, when I was a boy. Sathy's forest land felt untouched. I felt alone, which in India, with its crowds and commotion and constant churning, was something to cherish.

"I love this land," Sathy said. "It's that old feeling, something that hasn't been lost."

Sathy always talked about how people in Molasur were moving up in the world. He talked about children of landless laborers who had moved to the cities, gone to college, gotten jobs in software or technology companies, and sent money home. He talked about men and women whose parents had once worked for his family as agricultural laborers, but who had now gotten rich, bought plots of land.

He was ambivalent and occasionally distressed about his place in the changing social hierarchy. Sometimes, his obvious sense of entitlement, the way he clung to the feudal past, made me cringe a little. But his dismay was always balanced by a broader recognition—and appreciation—of the more general movement toward meritocracy in the nation. I respected Sathy for holding these two competing perspectives together. I saw a kind of poise, even wisdom.

Sathy talked, in particular, about the changing condition of Molasur's Dalits, the caste formerly known as untouchables. For much of India's history, Dalits had been at the bottom of the social order. They were condemned to menial positions—toilet cleaners, butchers, garbage collectors, leather workers—that were considered polluting. They were subjugated and cowed, and, for the most part, bore their repression meekly. Now, Sathy said, everything was different. Dalits were staking their claim to the new India. They weren't afraid to demand rights and privileges for themselves.

"Dalits are no longer so timid," he said to me once. "They stand up for themselves. We used to dominate them, but now they dominate us. No one dares challenge them anymore."

I was a little skeptical. For all India's progress, for all the government's very real efforts since independence to erase the stigma of caste, I knew that caste discrimination was still rampant. In the media, I saw stories about tea shops that refused to serve Dalits from the same cups as other castes, and about so-called honor killings in which families murdered Dalits (and sometimes their own children) for daring to elope across caste lines.

When Sathy told me that the Dalits of Molasur were no longer oppressed, I suspected a bit of landlord bias. I thought Sathy was painting something of a rosy picture.

Sathy told me that if I didn't believe him, I should come see for myself. He said he would introduce me to a Dalit man named M. Das. Das had been born into poverty; no one would have bet on his future. Now, Sathy said, I should come and see what he had made of his life.

I met Das on a wet January afternoon. He was forty-two years old. He was standing outside Sathy's house, in the rain. His shirt was drenched. Sathy was inside, and when he came out to introduce us, I asked Das why he hadn't gone in. He looked at Sathy, questioningly. "Speak, speak freely," Sathy said. "Be honest with him. Tell him everything."

Das said he was standing outside out of respect for the elder members of Sathy's family. They were from a different generation. They might not be comfortable with the idea of a Dalit in their house. I asked Das how he felt about that, and he laughed, but without bitterness. He said: "How do you think it makes me feel? Still, they are old, and I have to respect their feelings."

"Come on, come on, show him your house," Sathy said, and he pulled Das by the arm. He opened an umbrella. He gave Das and me shelter. He led us through the village.

Like most villages in the state of Tamil Nadu, Molasur's geography was historically delineated by caste. The village was traditionally divided in two—the *ur*, where upper castes lived, and the colony, where Dalits lived. Now, Sathy told me, these distinctions were breaking down. Dalits were moving out of the colony, into parts of the *ur*. Even on his street, traditionally reserved for Reddiars, the highest caste in the village, there was talk of a Dalit moving in. The old geography was blurring.

"It's true," Das said to me, in Tamil. "When I was a boy, I could never be on this street. I had to push my cycle around the village to avoid the *ur*. We took back roads. We were terrified. Our parents told us we would be punished if we stepped in here."

We walked through the *ur*, past the houses that had traditionally been occupied by upper castes, past the concrete structures and tile roofs that suggested relative wealth. I tried to imagine Das scared to walk these streets. It all felt so natural now.

At the edge of the *ur*, beyond the last tile-roofed house, we entered an open field. It was like a no-man's-land, extending about two hundred meters between the *ur* and the colony. The road that led into the colony was muddy. The mud was mixed with human feces. It was hard to tell mud from shit.

Houses in the colony were smaller, less solid, than in the *ur*. Signs of poverty were evident: more malnourished-looking children, fewer motorcycles and satellite dishes, and a general air of dilapidation, exacerbated by the recent rains.

But as we walked around, got deeper into the colony, Das pointed out several new constructions, concrete blocks, many in bright colors, some rising two stories. "These people have sons and brothers and cousins working in the cities," Das said, running his hand along a street that was almost all concrete buildings. "Many of them are educated, or their children are. It doesn't look at all like it did when I was growing up here."

Das himself had a degree in history, from a college in Chennai. He had moved there at the age of eighteen, and studied for a three-year undergraduate degree. While he was in college, he started thinking about the plight of Dalits in Molasur. On his visits home, he would be reminded of the insults he had taken for granted as a child—the way Dalits were refused entry to temples, the way they had to cross the road when a higher caste walked toward them. At his school, Dalit children weren't allowed to drink water from cups; the teachers would pour water into their hands. Dalits weren't even allowed to touch the vessels used to pour water, for fear of contamination.

Chennai was very different. There, in the cauldron of urban anonymity, caste didn't play such a big role. No one knew about Das's background; they didn't know who his parents were or where he lived. In college, Das was astonished to find himself friends with members of higher castes. His best friend was an Ayar, a member of the Brahmin caste. He and his friends would sit around for hours, talking, eating together, sharing bottles and utensils—activities that would have been unimaginable in Molasur.

Das remembered standing outside a temple on one of his visits home. While the higher castes streamed in, offering flowers and sweets to the deity, Dalits had to pray from outside. Das was hit by the injustice of it all. "Let people do whatever they want in their homes," he told me, years later. "But a temple is run by a government trust—it's a public space. Before moving to Chennai, I didn't understand that. But now, after my education, I understood enough to question that—how could we be restricted from public spaces?"

When Das returned to Molasur, he moved in with his family, into the thatch hut where he had grown up. It was a single-room hut, without electricity or running water. Twelve people lived in it—Das's parents, Das and his wife and their three children, and his brother and wife and their three children. Das was determined to do something about the condition of his people. He and some of his Dalit friends, many of whom had also spent time in the city, demanded change. They started standing up for themselves, coming together as a group and retaliating against other castes when they felt insulted.

In the late eighties and early nineties, the area around Molasur was hit by a series of often violent caste clashes. Once, after the statue of a Dalit leader in a nearby town was found garlanded with slippers, thousands of Dalits took to the streets, blocking traffic, breaking the windows of passing vehicles, and even burning a few buses. The police were called out; they charged the crowd, swinging sticks and firing in the air.

Another time there was a scene on a bus when a Dalit from Molasur accidentally touched a passenger, a member of a higher caste from a neighboring village. The higher caste took offense and accused the Dalit of contaminating him. That evening, several higher castes showed up in Molasur and started beating Dalits. When they were gone, the Dalits regrouped and decided to send a gang of young men to the neighboring village to teach the higher castes a lesson.

On their way to the village, the gang came across a man walking on the road. They didn't know the man; they didn't know if he had anything to do with the scene on the bus or the subsequent violence. But the gang stabbed the man in his stomach. They stabbed him so deep that his intestines poured out. There was blood all over. They left the man on the road.

Das stopped and looked at me when he told me that. He was well groomed, with dark hair that might have been dyed, and a comb in his back pocket. His eyes were bloodshot, red from dust or fatigue, and I thought there was something defiant in them. He wanted to see how I would react to his story.

"Why did your people attack an innocent man?" I asked him.

"We wanted to instill fear," he said. "We wanted to show their community not to play with our community. We wanted to show them that they couldn't control us."

Sathy said it was a "useless thing to do." Das looked at Sathy and nodded. "Yes, you are correct," he said. "But we were young. We had to show that we weren't weak."

Das's house was a two-story concrete structure, with whitewashed walls that had somehow kept from peeling despite the rains. By the side of the house, overlooking a covered veranda, was the thatch hut where Das had grown up, and to which he had returned when he came back from Chennai. It had a low entrance, about a meter high. It was around fifteen square meters in size. I couldn't really imagine twelve people squeezed into it.

Das's wife, dressed in a blue sari, with a welcoming smile on her face, set up some plastic chairs on the veranda. Das told me about his childhood. He said his parents had been poor, illiterate, but that he had a good childhood, playing in the fields, picking tamarind from the groves that surrounded his hut.

Even as a boy, though, he knew that his parents' life was tough. His father worked as a farmer and a cow broker. He didn't make a lot of money. During the monsoons, their hut would leak, and his parents would stay up at night, catching the drops in metal plates. His father was a frustrated man. Das said he drank heavily.

Das said that things were so much more promising for his children than they had been for him. After returning to Molasur, he'd done some work in real estate. He started with small plots in the fields around Molasur. But he worked hard, he moved on to bigger pieces of land, and he had made some money.

Now two of his children were in a private college in Chennai, studying engineering. When they visited home, he could afford to send a taxi to pick them up. His youngest son went to an English medium school near Molasur; it was the same school where one of Sathy's nieces was enrolled.

"Can you imagine that?" Sathy said. "Going to the same school as the zamindar's children!"

Das gave me a tour of his house. Downstairs, in a kitchen set behind the veranda, he showed me his washing machine and television. Upstairs, he showed me his bedroom, with an air-conditioning unit in the window, a treadmill in the corner, and another television, this one with a cable box.

We stood on a balcony outside Das's bedroom, looking over the colony. The rain had stopped; there was a cool breeze. The sounds of the village—screaming children, a few motorcycles, some devotional music—were muffled.

Sathy pointed to the no-man's-land between the *ur* and the colony. He showed me some property he had sold there a few years ago. The land was being plotted out now by a group of developers from Chennai. They were selling it for fifty times what Sathy had sold it for just five years ago.

"I'm a fool," Sathy said. "I sold too early."

He said that anyone with land now was rich. He said Das was a rich man. Das flinched when Sathy said that, and he started to deny that he was rich. But Sathy cut him off, and Das didn't argue.

I asked Das how it felt to have money. He said it made him feel like he was someone. He said his father had recently been diagnosed with cancer; he'd paid 1 lakh, 100,000 rupees, for his treatment. His wife had needed an operation; he'd paid 50,000 rupees for her. It gave him satisfaction to be able to afford things like that.

Das said: "To tell you the truth, when I think of my situation, when I think of how much things have changed, I feel that it is one of the wonders of the world. I'm telling you this from my heart, not my head: My life is a miracle. It's a miracle that Sathy comes to my house, that he and I can sit side by side like this, that we share water from the same bottle. It's a miracle that I can go into the temples around here and no one can stop me. My father was always at someone's mercy. I don't have to depend on anyone.

"You know, in the past, when Dalits went to a village meeting we were forced to stand with our arms crossed while the other castes sat and talked. Even if there were seats available, we weren't allowed to sit. Now when we go to meetings, even if there aren't enough chairs, the other castes stand up for us and give us their chairs. You ask me about change? This is the change I have seen in my life; this respect, this dignity that I have gained. I don't know who to thank or how to thank him for it. But I know that my life is a miracle, and I am grateful for that."

"It's true," Sathy said. "Well put, well put," he said, shaking his head with something that looked like wonder.

On the way back to the ur, *with the rain picking up a bit, falling* in a warm drizzle, Sathy was full of stories. He opened his umbrella again; he talked a lot. I thought our time with Das had affected him, brought out old memories and his conflicted emotions about change.

At the no-man's-land between the *ur* and the colony, Sathy put his hand on my shoulder. He wanted to show me the land he had sold all those years ago. The ground was muddy, slippery. I was reluctant, but Sathy dragged me across the wet fields.

He showed me the yellow stones marking the plots being sold by the developers from Chennai. He showed me a house they had already started building, a concrete shell where work had stopped, presumably because of the rain. "Look how ugly it is," Sathy said. "Is this a house? Can you even call this a house?"

He said that in a few years, the whole field would probably be full of ugly buildings like that. There would be no gap between the *ur* and the colony. Molasur would be just one big stretch of houses. Outsiders would come in, people from Chennai looking for second homes, maybe even people from as far away as Bangalore. Probably, Sathy said, he wouldn't know half the villagers anymore.

He told me a story about hunting in the tall grass that used to grow where we were standing. That was at a time when farming was still a viable profession. Sathy said he had grown rice and *varagu*, a millet, in these fields, but that pigs from the village kept breaking in, destroying his crops. He hired a gypsy to shoot the pigs.

The gypsy showed up one evening with his rifle. Sathy and the gypsy made their way across the fields, got on their stomachs in the grass, and the gypsy started shooting at the pigs. He fired shot after shot, but he kept missing. "Ayo," the gypsy would say. "What's wrong with me today? Ayo, I'm missing everything."

Sathy said he couldn't figure out what was going on. He knew the gypsy was a good shot. He used to hunt owls for Sathy. Sathy couldn't understand how he could hit a small owl but keep missing a pig. It didn't make any sense. Sathy was upset—perplexed and annoyed by the gypsy.

Later, he told some of his friends what had happened, and they laughed at him. They told him the pigs belonged to the gypsy. They said the gypsy had been pulling his leg. He'd missed his shots intentionally.

"They all mocked me, they said I was a fool," Sathy said. "I went after that gypsy fellow. I caught him and slapped him. I literally beat him. He was begging for mercy. He said, 'What can I do? Those pigs are my living.'"

Sathy paused. He laughed at the memory of the gypsy who had cheated him.

"His name was Kuppam. He's no more. He became head of the state gypsy association. He was fighting for his rights, always standing up for his people. A nice chap, actually. I used to have to stand in line with him during election time at the Collector's office. We had to surrender our weapons during the elections—he had his rifle, and I had my pistol. We used to stand together and he used to feel bad about it. That idiot was so embarrassed standing next to me, worried that he was bringing down my status. I told him not to mind, I said it was like that now. It was fine, it didn't bother me."

Sathy kicked at a crab shell on the ground, and I asked him what it was doing there. He said the crab had been eaten by a jackal. He said jackals put their tails down crab holes, and when the crabs latched on to their tails they pulled them out of the ground, turned around, and grabbed the crabs in their mouths.

"All these stories about jackals," I said. "Do you really have them here?"

"Of course," he said, and he told me that just a couple months ago he'd taken his son out to the fields, in the tractor, and they'd been surrounded by jackals, at least fifty of them. The jackals were running around, barking and howling, and Sathy made his son get off the tractor and chase them with a stick. His son was terrified, but Sathy wanted him to learn. He wanted his son to know country life.

"I used to do it as a kid," Sathy said. "I enjoyed it so much. He's such a city boy now, I wanted him to enjoy this, too. It used to be so much fun, chasing away those jackals across the fields."

Sathy talked about working the fields as a young man—planting, watering, clearing irrigation channels, keeping pigs and birds at bay. He said that the very land we were standing on now, the land that was dotted with yellow stones, used to be piled high with rice and millet. The whole area would have been crowded with semi-naked laborers, shirtless, dressed only in loincloths. Everyone would be out in the fields. Molasur was still a farming village then.

"How can I tell you about this, Akash?" he asked, and he held his palm up, as if requesting a pause. "How can I explain to you what it was like? They were the golden years of my life. Those were golden times."

DEMOGRAPHIC DIVIDENDS

There was a sunny morning in Bangalore, not too long after I returned to India. I was in the offices of an American software company, in a cafeteria overlooking one of the city's main thoroughfares.

It was mid-morning. Below me, sunlight glinted from the hoods of cars, off the chrome handlebars and helmets of motorcyclists. The road was jammed. I knew it was miserable in that traffic. But from where I sat, several floors up, behind tinted glass and air-conditioning, Bangalore was gleaming.

I was visiting the American company because I thought they might have a job for me. I didn't really know what I wanted to do, and, looking back, I can't imagine how I could have been useful. But technology was driving India's economic surge, and Bangalore was India's technology capital, and I guess I wanted a piece of the excitement.

I had tea in the cafeteria with a young man who worked at the company. I'll call him Harsh. He was square-jawed, clean-cut, and well dressed. He had graduated from one of the country's top business schools. He had a good job, and now he was weighing his next step. He told me he'd been offered positions in America and Europe. They were well paid; they'd look great on his résumé.

Once, he said, he would have leaped at the opportunities. He always assumed he'd work abroad, at least for a while. But now he was reconsidering. He'd started thinking it would be silly to leave India. Europe and America were the past, he said. The future was in places like Bangalore—in cities that heaved with ambition and entrepreneurship and opportunity.

"This is where it's all happening," Harsh said, pointing around the room. I remember bright colors on the walls and the furniture, and the silver surface of a serving counter. I remember the sun pouring through the windows, lighting up a corridor on the table between us.

Harsh leaned into that corridor. He told me, with light on his face, that everywhere in this city, people his age were building high-powered careers. Many were getting rich. They had their own apartments, their own cars, and some even had chauffeurs. He knew he could have all of that. Anything was possible.

"Whenever I think of leaving India, I remind myself: 'I can make it here,'" he said. "This is the time to be in India. I can make whatever I want of myself."

He asked me where I lived. I told him. He asked how long the drive was from Auroville to Bangalore. He laughed. He asked: "But why would you want to live so far from the action?"

Harsh was confident, very confident. That's what I remember most about him. I remember thinking he was maybe a little too confident. His faith in the future was self-congratulatory, his self-assurance bordered on arrogance. But of one thing, he was right: the action was in the cities.

I didn't end up taking a job in Bangalore. I chose to stay in Auroville. My wife and I built our house there, and we had our children there. The house was by a forest, at the edge of a canyon that filled with muddy water and cacophonous frogs during the monsoons. It was a good life. I thought of the canyon like a moat—it kept the world, the roar of motorcycles and cars, the disruptions of commerce that were tearing at the villages, at bay.

Change in the villages around me felt complicated. Modernity in the countryside was layered with ambivalence. The present carried all the baggage of the past. It was hard to disentangle the old from the new, and harder yet to separate the positive from the negative.

The cities were so much simpler. In the cities—and especially in metropolises like Bangalore and Chennai, Mumbai and New Delhi—there was little ambivalence about wealth and development. Like Harsh, the cities were self-confident, brash and unshakably optimistic. The twenty-first century had come to them like a party, a celebration of the nation's potential; they embraced modernity unhesitatingly.

Gandhi famously wrote once that the soul of India was in its villages. That was still true when I was growing up, when the pastoral world around me—the hand plows, the windmills, the bicycles, the catamarans and bullock carts—contained all the charm and simplicity (and the backwardness) of the nation. Cities were little more than dusty, unhappening centers of business and government.

Now the center of gravity was shifting. Although around 70 percent of the population still lived in the countryside, they were migrating by the millions to the cities. A study I read predicted that between the turn of the millennium and 2030, India's urban population would increase by around 300 million people—roughly equivalent to the entire population of the United States. That same year, more than 70 percent of the nation's GDP would be generated in the cities.

India's traditional agricultural economy was becoming a relic. Cities—with their software parks and service-sector jobs and armies of young, independent workers—were building a new economy. Cities were chaotic, messy, and to my mind often unlivable. But they were also dynamic and euphoric. The Indian political scientist Sunil Khilnani called them "bloated receptacles of every hope and frustration"; cities were crucibles of a new nation.

I lived in the countryside. And I loved the countryside. But my first few years back in India, I spent a lot of time in the cities. I traveled around the nation. I visited New Delhi, Mumbai, Chennai, Bangalore, Hyderabad—all places that had flourished in recent years, metropolises transformed by new money. I visited smaller towns, too, places like Cochin and Panjim and Madurai, where the gold rush was just beginning, where the buildings were less sparkly but the streets just as clogged and the sense of opportunity as palpable.

I spent most of my time in Chennai, the nearest big city to home. I would get up early in the mornings, drive up the East Coast Road, the sun still soft, its reflection diffused across the ocean, and wander around all day. I had a few friends in Chennai; I made up errands. Mostly, I was directionless. I came to Chennai because I wanted to feel connected. Being in the cities made me feel like I was part of something.

Every time I drove up Rajiv Gandhi Salai, Chennai's technology corridor, I saw a new software complex, each bigger and shinier than the last. Sometimes I watched as the excavators dug up the earth and the cranes lifted a glass panel above the coconut trees, and I would feel a rush of excitement, a stirring in my heart. "This is the new India," I would think. "A new country is being built, brick by brick, before my eyes."

In the Park Hotel, a hip, flamboyant place near the center of town, I hung out in the Leather Bar and drank mojitos and martinis. A DJ in black spun music (too loudly, I thought) at his table. Well-dressed, cosmopolitan men and women leaned into each other, touching, sometimes doing more.

I spent many days in Spencer Plaza, the largest shopping mall in Chennai, a hulking red building on one of the city's main roads. The old wings of the mall were dowdy; their souvenir shops and cheap jewelry stores were throwbacks to an earlier era. But the new wing sold Nike and Reebok and Nokia, and the young men and women who passed through its corridors, texting and trailing large shopping bags, were decidedly of a new era.

These young Indians were like no Indians I had ever known. I didn't see myself in them; my generation never had the casualness, the comfort with consumerism or easy modernity that they seemed to possess.

※

*It was on one of my visits to Chennai, during my aimless wander-*ings around the city, on an interlude between malls and bars and software parks, that I met T. Harikumar, or Hari. He was twenty-seven years old. He was the friend of a friend, a man named Leo. They had recently met in an online chat room.

Leo and I went out to dinner one night. I started talking about India's new generation. I said that I didn't get them; sometimes, I told Leo, India's youth made me feel like a stranger in my own country. Leo suggested I meet Hari. He introduced us, Hari and I spoke on the phone, and we met a few days later in a coffee shop up the road from Spencer Plaza.

The coffee shop was a comfortable place, with soft music, strong air-conditioning, and thick glass that kept out the heat and dust from the road. Chennai could be oppressive, especially in the summers, right before the monsoons, when the air was pregnant with rain but the streets still brutally dry. The coffee shop was a welcome oasis.

Hari and I started meeting there regularly. We'd meet in the afternoons, before he started the evening shift at his firm, a multinational business that outsourced research to India. He would order coffee, maybe a piece of chocolate cake. I usually had tea. We'd lean back in synthetic leather chairs, watching the autorickshaws pass outside in a blur of yellow, and Hari would tell me about his life.

He was from Tindivanam, a market town about 120 kilometers south of Chennai, not far from Sathy's village. Hari's father ran a small provisions store there; he was illiterate. Hari's mother worked as a clerk in the local court.

Hari grew up with his parents, his brother, and his two sisters in a rented single-bedroom apartment in Tindivanam. The apartment didn't have a television, telephone, or fridge. His father cycled to work. Hari said his mother's family had once been wealthy, but her father drank and gambled their fortune away. When Hari was a boy, his grandmother would walk with him in the villages around Tindivanam and point out pieces of land that used to belong to their family.

Hari left home at the age of seventeen. He studied for a business degree at a college in Chennai. He didn't much like his college. It was full of rules; it felt like a jail. But he liked living in Chennai: it was a world away from Tindivanam. I knew Tindivanam. It was a crowded, dreary place, with vegetable vendors that encroached on the roads, blocking the cars and buses and trucks that idled in black clouds of exhaust. I knew the town mostly as a traffic jam on the way to Chennai.

Hari interviewed at more than a hundred companies when he graduated from college. It took him six months to find a job. Finally, after he got an interview through a friend, he was offered a position at the company where he now worked. It was a good job, with reasonable hours, and good pay. Three years into the job, he was earning 15,000 rupees a month—more than either of his parents made after twenty years of work.

When Hari called his parents to tell them he'd found a job, he expected them to be overjoyed. They'd invested a lot of money in his education. They'd been worried that it was taking him so long. But then, when he told them, they didn't say much. His father just handed the phone to his mother. She said: "You are earning more than us, but be careful. You're still young. Don't spend it all."

Hari wasn't offended; he knew it was their way. He told me about a time, shortly after he'd started his job, when his parents visited Chennai. They came to see how he was doing, and Hari wanted to impress them. He wanted to show them how he might live one day. So he took them to an expensive hotel for a meal.

They went to the hotel in a white Ambassador car. Hari sat in the front, with the driver, and his parents sat in the back. The restaurant was crowded, and Hari could see his parents were a little uncomfortable. They were humble people. His mother had grown up in a hut; his father had worked at construction sites to support his parents and siblings.

When Hari had invited them to dinner, his parents were worried because they didn't have anything to wear. Hari bought them some clothes—a blue shirt for his father, a green sari for his mother, made from the finest Bengal cotton. Now, at the hotel, he held his mother's hand and he told his parents to relax. He told them not to feel intimidated. Without acknowledging that they were, they smiled at him.

Hari later told me: "They were very new to this. I had to guide them through the buffet. I told them, 'This is good for you,' 'This is bad for your health,' 'This is too spicy.' I explained it all to them. I told them what they were having. My mom only had fried rice and roti, and then some dessert. But my dad, he tried everything. I told him, 'This is how you do it, how you eat this,' and he tasted everything."

After dinner, in the car home, his parents complained about the evening. His mother said the food lacked taste, it wasn't spicy or salty enough. His father said it was too expensive, a waste of money. But, Hari said, even while his mother was complaining, she gave him a look that was full of happiness. She said something to him; he wouldn't tell me what it was, but he knew his mother was overjoyed that her son had taken her out to a nice dinner.

Later, he heard from one of his sisters that when his father got back to Tindivanam he went around town boasting about the evening. He told everyone that the food was delicious. He talked about his new clothes and the car in which they'd driven to the hotel. He said the atmosphere at the hotel was wonderful, so calm and peaceful. It was the first time Hari knew his father was proud of him.

*Hari had lots of plans. He was always taking calls from headhunt-*ers, negotiating for a higher salary, considering new job offers. Like so many young Indians I met, he had great faith in the future. He felt he was living in the right country at the right time, working in the right field—what people called India's ITES sector, or Information Technology Enabled Services.

"Life is full of opportunities. I can do whatever I want," he told me one of the first times we met. "I work in IT. It's for me to decide what I want to do, and then just do it."

"You're lucky," I told him. "Do you think your parents had the same opportunities?"

"Maybe not the same," he said. "But opportunities are always there—in any country, any generation. It's up to us to see them, grab them, and make something of them."

It was sometimes hard, amid all the talk about new jobs and opportunities, to know what Hari really wanted to do. He talked about starting a clothing store, a fast-food chain, and occasionally a hotel.

Hari's ambition was large, but I felt it was vague, undirected. It seemed motivated less by his specific circumstances than by a general mood in the country—a mood that exalted entrepreneurship and the entrepreneur's lifestyle, that venerated capitalism and wealth accumulation in the same way India had once venerated public service or spiritual renunciation.

We were surrounded by fabulous rags-to-riches stories. We heard and read all the time about India's rising population of billionaires, about the way the founders of Infosys, India's best-known software company, worth billions of dollars, had started in 1981 with just a few hundred dollars of investment. These stories had seeded themselves in the country's imagination; they were part of an emerging national mythology.

One of Hari's goals was, indeed, to be an entrepreneur. He had seen others do it—he had seen them raise capital, acquire customers, get rich. He had seen people around him buy cars and houses and take foreign holidays. He wanted these things for himself.

For a while, he was shopping around a business plan he had put together with two friends for a fast-food franchise. They figured it would take 57 lakhs, about $120,000, to get it off the ground. It was a lot of money. Hari talked about it for a bit, and then he moved on to other ideas.

Another one of Hari's dreams was to be a fashion designer. He talked a lot about fashion. He berated me for what he felt was my poor choice of clothes. He was especially disappointed by my inability to color-match. He obviously spent a lot of time (and money) on his own appearance.

He wore pretorn jeans, dark sunglasses, and tight, brightly colored T-shirts. He was often in the city's shopping malls; he was always up on the latest deals. Almost all his clothes had an imported designer label. He wore an earring, and often had what looked like a carefully cultivated stubble. He was tall, with delicate eyes and an angular face. I thought he was quite handsome.

I saw a picture one time of Hari from his Tindivanam days. He must have been about sixteen. He was skinny, dressed in cotton pants and a baggy shirt. The shirt was untucked; it hung down to his thighs. He had a thin, pencil mustache. His hair was oiled to his scalp.

City life had been kind to Hari. In the picture, he looked like a country boy.

*Hari had a wide circle of friends. He was gregarious and gener-*ous, and people liked him. I met some of his friends. They were mostly in their twenties. They all worked in some kind of technology or outsourcing business. Like Hari, they were hardworking, ambitious, and self-confident. They were part of what India called its "demographic dividend."

The demographic dividend was a remarkable feat of alchemy, really. It referred to the nation's large population of young people, a result of high fertility rates. Those high fertility rates were for so long considered a liability, one of the main reasons for the country's backwardness. Now, suddenly, they offered hope. In comparison with the aging economies of Europe and Japan—and even China—a much larger share of Indians were of working age, and thus potential contributors to the nation's economic output.

A lot of India's hopes rested on its youth. They offered a pathway to what politicians and the media kept calling "economic superpowerhood."

At the same coffee shop where I met Hari, I met Nikhil, who worked as a programmer for a software company on Rajiv Gandhi Salai. His skills were in great demand. Over the course of a coffee one afternoon, he received several calls from headhunters. "Everybody wants me," he said, laughing.

In Adyar, one of Chennai's more upscale and pleasant neighborhoods, I met Peter, another friend, who told me about his dream of starting an online public relations firm. He'd recently attended an advertising conference in New Delhi. He believed there were fortunes to be made in the industry. He planned to make a fortune.

Outside Chennai, in Sholinganallur, a once-nondescript suburb that had in recent years been transformed into a neighborhood of young technology workers, I met a woman named Selvi. She was twenty-one. She lived with four other women in a two-bedroom apartment. They all worked at the same call center, a company that handled credit card queries for American customers.

I met Selvi through her landlord, a man named Murugan. The first time he took me to see his tenant, I told her I had recently returned from America. She said she knew something about

Americans. She spoke to them on the phone every day at her job; she wasn't impressed.

The men flirted with her—"They call me honey," she said, raising her nose a little—and the women sometimes shouted at her. She tried her best to help them, she said, but often, they seemed more interested in berating than listening to her.

"I used to have very high opinions of Americans until I started mingling with them over the phone," she said, when we'd known each other for about fifteen minutes. "Now I think they're rude. Rude, and also quite stupid."

Selvi was opinionated. She told me she was "independent-minded," a trait she got from her father, a businessman who had fallen on hard times when he got into a dispute with his partners.

She had a thin, bony face, and eyelids that sat heavily on narrow eyes. She was short and slight and dark; her neck was wiry, almost emaciated.

Selvi had moved to Chennai just a few months before I met her. Like Hari, she was from a small town, a village really, in the hilly western part of the state. But she was rawer, less adjusted to city life. Most of her friends were still in the hills, in or around the village where she'd grown up. She had never really planned to move to the city. But she was ambitious, and her parents were ambitious for her, and one day, when she heard about a job fair being held in a town about four hours from her village, she skipped class and jumped on a bus.

She went on a whim. She didn't know what to expect; she wasn't even sure what job she was applying for. When she got to the job fair, there were about a thousand applicants, split into groups of fifty, waiting in a hall. Eventually, Selvi was taken into a room and played cassettes of Americans talking in strong accents. A woman said: "Hi, Johnny, how are you doing?" and Selvi was supposed to tell her interviewers whether the woman had been addressing someone named Joannie, Johnny, or Jenny. There was a lot of talk on the cassettes about shopping at Walmart, and credit card transactions.

Selvi said she understood only about half of what was said on the tapes. But she did well on the second part of the interview, where they asked her what her motto was in life. She said it was: "If you rest, you rust."

She got the job. It was a big deal for her. She would make 10,000 rupees a month, and she would be moving to the city. Some of her relatives weren't thrilled with that prospect. They were worried that her "character would get spoiled." They told her about women who had moved to the city and gotten involved with men. One aunt told her the story of a young woman who was recently murdered in Bangalore. She, too, had worked for an outsourcing company, and there were rumors that she had been romantically involved with her murderer. The aunt warned Selvi that "the city will divert your mind."

Selvi was confident that wouldn't happen. She said she would remain "faithful" to her parents. It was true she was different from her aunts, and from her mother, who had never worked outside their homes. But she told me she was "very pet" to her father, by which I guess she meant that she was loyal. "I know that my father wants only good things for me," she said. "Whatever he says, I'll go with it. He will never do something that is not good for me."

When Selvi's aunt came to see her before she left home, she reiterated her warnings about city life. Selvi told her: "Auntie, don't worry. I am a good girl. I am strong. I know where I come from. I may have more opportunities than you did, and I want to take them. But I will always be true to this place."

Selvi worked the night shift. She usually got home past midnight. She would be tired, hungry, in need of a shower. Often, there was confusion over the two keys she shared with her roommates. Selvi would be locked outside, frantically working her cell phone until she could find someone with a key.

One time, two of the roommates were locked out all night. They waited, sitting around the corridors of their apartment block, wandering the children's playground and the pathways of their sprawling complex. They tried to get a neighbor to force the door. Finally, at six-thirty in the morning, they got into an autorickshaw and went to their landlord's house.

They asked him for a spare key. They asked for some tea. They asked him, too, if they could use his bathroom. The girls were too modest to go to the toilet at work; they'd been holding it in all night.

I generally visited Selvi late in the morning, around eleven. She would just be getting out of bed. Her eyes would be puffy, and her hair would be unkempt, hurriedly bundled. But she always made sure to dress up for me, even when it was clear she hadn't found the time to shower or brush her teeth.

I felt the dressing up was a form of reserve, a way of keeping me at a distance. We met only at her apartment; she refused to meet anywhere else. She was friendly and polite, a little formal.

She'd ask if the neighbors had seen me. She wanted to know if the security guard had asked what I was doing with her.

Once, she told me about going to the beach with her friends, hanging out by the water and buying cotton candy, and I told her I would love to go with them sometime. She got nervous. She said she'd have to ask her roommates, and also her "uncle," a distant family member who was acting as her guardian in the city. She never mentioned it again, and neither did I.

She seemed to be enjoying city life. She and her roommates hung out in the shopping malls. They watched the crowds, maybe bought some clothes or costume jewelry. On weekends, she often went to the movies. But first, she always telephoned her mother, even if it was in the middle of the afternoon—not to get permission, she said, but to let her mother know where she was going to be.

On workdays, Selvi got home late. But on her days off, she never stayed out past nine p.m. She said that some of her office-mates liked to go to clubs, dancing, maybe even drinking. They went with boys; they flirted with them. But, she insisted, she wasn't like that, and she never would be.

Her aunt was still worried about her. She called Selvi all the time, asked her what she was doing, warned her not to get too close to any men. Selvi told her aunt about her schedule. She said she worked from lunchtime to past midnight every day, with only a half-hour break for dinner. She didn't have time to meet men.

She said: "Auntie, you have to trust me. I won't start any other life. If I meet anyone, if I like any boy, I'll come and inform you all and you can help me decide. Before anything happens, I'll inform my dad, because it's so important that he should like anyone I meet. Don't worry, I'll never fall in love."

"You have to understand, Akash," she said to me. "I'm not a city girl. My background is different. I was brought up in a different way. I wasn't brought up to stay out late and do those kinds of things."

We were sitting in her living room when she said this to me. It was a cloudy morning. It had rained hard the night before, and Selvi had gotten drenched on her way back from work. She seemed tired, under the weather. She had a bit of a cold.

"Yes, but lots of people come to the city with different backgrounds and then change," I said.

"No, not me," she said. "I believe the day is for working, and the night is for sleeping. I'll never change."

She seemed a bit irritated. She blew her nose into a tissue. She got up and started packing a bag for work. Then she put the bag down and looked right at me. "I'm still exactly the same person I always was," she said. "I told you already: I'm not one of those girls whose minds can get swayed. I know who I am."

She had a sharp, direct manner that often made me feel like I was saying or doing the wrong thing. She was schoolmarmish. I thought from the first time we met that there was something determined, even ferocious, about Selvi.

Hari was telling me one day about how he learned to speak English. He hadn't spoken it at home; both his parents spoke only Tamil. He said he had learned English from watching television, and from reading books and pamphlets at his mother's workplace. From a young age, he was determined to be fluent; he knew that English was his ticket out of Tindivanam.

He told me that when he was a boy, he was teased a lot at school for always speaking English. His classmates would taunt him. They would say *"Rumbo Peter vidurai,"* which, with its reference to an English name, was a way to mock someone for putting on airs by speaking a foreign language. Hari said he didn't care. He'd always been different. He'd always felt apart from other people his age.

It was true that Hari's English was pretty good, especially for someone who had grown up in a small town. But when he talked about being different, I wasn't convinced that he was just talking about his affinity for a foreign language. In the time I had known him, I had noticed a few things about Hari. I noticed that he wore pink a lot. I noticed that he waved his hands when he was making a point, in a whimsical, wristy kind of way. Whenever I asked about marriage, he changed the topic, saying his parents were eager to marry him off, but that he wasn't interested.

I had noticed some things about the coffee shop where we met, too. I noticed that its regular clients were almost all male. They would order a coffee or a tea, and sit around for hours, sometimes with their laptops open, messaging, or hanging out in chat rooms. Many of these men seemed to recognize each other, although they weren't necessarily friends. They would nod their heads or maybe smile, but they rarely sat at the same table or even spoke.

One day I was there with Nikhil, Hari's friend, when a well-built man walked in. He sat behind a counter at the other end of the room. Nikhil went over, they chatted a bit, and when he came back he told me he'd had a one-night stand with the man. He said he met the man online. They communicated for a few months, and then later, when they were comfortable with each other, they met at a coffee shop. They went back to the man's house. They watched some porn on his laptop; they made love.

Leo, the friend who had introduced me to Hari, told me that he thought Hari was gay—although he wasn't sure that Hari would acknowledge that, or indeed that he even knew it himself. Hari might just consider his feelings about men to be an extension of normal adolescent behavior, Leo, who had a wide circle of gay friends, said. It wouldn't be all that unusual for boys in college, brought up in a conservative society where they were denied female interaction, to experiment with each other.

But in Leo's opinion, Hari was a little different. Hari and his friends, men like Nikhil, seemed more conventionally homosexual. Their relationships with other men weren't just a matter of adolescent experimentation.

I decided to broach the topic with Hari. We went shopping one day for a cell phone together. The phone was for me; I had asked Hari, whom I now considered an expert shopper, for advice, and he told me he'd take me to his regular dealer, who sold out of a small shopping center in the crowded north of the city.

Hari showed up, in a pink T-shirt and a blue Adidas baseball cap, on his scooter. He led me down a flight of stairs to a basement store stacked with cell phones and other electronic gadgets. I picked a phone, and we came back out. It was hot. We were thirsty. We decided to find a shop where we could get a bottle of mineral water.

On the way to the shop—crossing the street, navigating traffic that seemed determined to kill us—I mentioned to Hari that I had seen someone using a chat room in the coffee shop where we met. I asked Hari if he spent a lot of time in chat rooms. He told me that, in fact, he was the moderator for one. "But I hardly use them," he said. "They're full of fakes."

"What do you mean?" I asked.

"They're full of crooks pretending to be gay men. Sometimes old men act as young men. Sometimes I heard they're not even gay—they just pretend to be gay, and they use the Internet to trick young men and steal from them or even blackmail them. Personally, I don't know anything. I just moderate the rooms. I don't have any experience of this. But I've heard about it from my friends."

Hari asked me if I was happy with the phone I'd just bought. Then he started talking about the war in Iraq. He said it was a disaster; he asked how America could have been so foolish to get involved. He wondered about the British, too; he'd always thought they were smarter. He seemed to want to change the topic.

Walking back to Hari's scooter, I asked him about marriage. Then he told me that his parents were harassing him. They wouldn't leave him alone. He kept telling them he wasn't ready, but they wouldn't give up. In fact, he said, there had just been a huge scene at home recently, when he went there for a long weekend.

It happened in the morning, while Hari was relaxing in his old bedroom. Some guests showed up and Hari's mother called him out of his room. She told him the visitors were the parents of a prospective bride. She'd found them through a matchmaker.

Hari got worked up. He threatened to pack his bags and take the next bus to Chennai. His mother managed to cool him down. She convinced him to come out and meet the parents. They showed Hari a picture of their daughter. She was slim and fair-skinned and, he said, not unattractive. But she was too young, just a student, and anyway, he knew for sure he wasn't interested.

Hari's mother forced him to sit and make small talk. The girl's parents were full of questions—about Hari's job, about his salary, about his life in Chennai. His father started telling them Hari's life story. Hari interrupted. "Father, please," he said, and his father stopped. There was silence.

After the guests had gone, Hari shouted at his parents. He threatened to leave home. He said if they ever tried to trick him like that again, he would go away and never come back. His mother started screaming. She said the moment had to come; Hari couldn't put it off forever. "No, the moment will never come," Hari told her, and he stomped out of the room.

The whole ride back to Chennai, in the bus, Hari felt anxious. He was upset about all the questions, and he was upset that the guests had been so inquisitive. He valued his privacy; he didn't want people from home, people who knew his parents, digging around his life in Chennai.

One evening not too long after that episode, Hari's office received some visitors looking for him. Fortunately, it was on Martin Luther King Jr. Day, so he had the day off. But the visitors spoke to the company's security guard, and later the guard told Hari they'd asked a lot of questions about him. They told the guard they were there "about an alliance."

Hari called home right away and asked his parents what they thought they were doing. He told them that if anything like that ever happened again, they would lose their son. His parents told him he was being unreasonable; they said he was holding up the line, that his younger sister couldn't get married because of his stubbornness. They said he would ruin the family's reputation.

Hari shook his head when he told me that story. We were

standing at his scooter. He said that he had been really, really upset. "I don't want people coming to Chennai and finding out about me," he said. "I don't want them to know who I am."

"Why?" I asked. "What don't you want them to know?"

He didn't say anything. I asked if he liked men. "No," he said. "I love women. I grew up surrounded by women—my mother, my cousins, my sisters. I was very close to my grandmother. I love girls."

He fiddled with his handlebars; he played with his hat. "The only thing is," he said, "that maybe I like both men and women."

I wasn't at all surprised by Hari's reticence. Tindivanam wasn't exactly a hospitable environment for a gay man. Hari would have grown up with parents and friends to whom the very concept of homosexuality would have been alien. Nobody at home knew about his sexual orientation, and he had no intention of telling them. He said his father would never accept him; he'd probably ask him to leave the family. And it would devastate his mother; he couldn't do that to her.

Technically, homosexuality was illegal in India. Section 377 of the Indian Penal Code, dating from British times, criminalized "carnal intercourse against the order of nature." The law was rarely applied, though, and when it was used, it was usually as a form of harassment or blackmail—an attempt to extort a bribe, perhaps, or to settle an unrelated score.

The media was full of reports about a budding gay scene, especially in urban India. I had several gay friends, but they had all either spent time in the West or were born into Westernized families. I had never met an openly gay person who had grown up, like Hari, in a small town, with traditional parents.

On a summer day in Chennai, I visited Dr. Narayana Reddy, a leading sex therapist—or "sexologist," as he referred to himself, eschewing what he felt were the insufficiently holistic labels usually applied to his profession. I thought he might be able to help me better understand Hari and his conflicted feelings about his homosexuality.

Dr. Reddy was a short, bald man, with a soft-spoken manner. He worked out of a first-floor office in a residential building on a quiet side street. It was an unflashy setup, just the kind of place, I thought, where someone would go if they had a problem they wanted to keep private.

He had been in practice since 1982. In a way, he was at the front lines of India's cultural transformation. In an office adorned with lifetime awards from sexual organizations around the world, and with a couple nervous men sitting outside in his waiting room, he told me that his profession had changed beyond recognition.

When he first started, he said, people thought he was crazy. Friends and family wondered why he didn't go into a respectable profession like cardiology. The media wouldn't write about his work (once, a newspaper referred to a conference of sexologists simply as a meeting of doctors), and the medical fraternity didn't take him seriously. Dr. Reddy knew he would have to attach himself to a hospital—people would be too shy to visit a stand-alone sexual health clinic—but no one would give him a position or a place.

When he was finally given an office, on the premises of one of

Chennai's leading research hospitals, it was in the maternity block. He was asked to refer to himself only as a reproductive biologist. He spent the first eight months without a patient. He would sit around his office all day, reading magazines. It was a difficult time. His family's finances were precarious; his wife was frustrated with him.

Then one day a patient finally walked in. Dr. Reddy said he was so relieved that he was ready to garland the man. His joy was short-lived, though, because it turned out the patient had strayed in only by accident. He and his wife had been having trouble conceiving, and his wife was with a gynecologist in the adjoining office.

Dr. Reddy and the man started talking. The man told Dr. Reddy that he and his wife had been trying to conceive for thirteen years. They had traveled around, tried all sorts of tests, visited doctors in Mumbai and Singapore, but no one could tell them what was wrong. Dr. Reddy asked the man if he and his wife were having regular sex, and the man said they were.

Dr. Reddy thought maybe he'd talk to the man's wife. She was in the room next door. She was a conservative woman and refused to talk to him. So Dr. Reddy had to find a nurse to act as an intermediary. The wife told the nurse that yes, her and her husband's sex life was perfectly normal. She said her husband lay down regularly on her, moved around, and then got up.

"But do you feel any penetration?" Dr. Reddy asked the woman, through the nurse, who blushed when he asked the question.

"I don't know anything about that," the wife said, and she refused to continue the conversation.

The couple's doctor had scheduled laparoscopic surgery to see if she could determine the reason for their infertility. But Dr. Reddy, operating on a hunch, convinced the doctor to postpone the surgery. He said he wanted to conduct a postcoital exam on the patients. He asked them to have sex in the hospital. A nurse took a swab from the woman's vagina. The test was usually done to determine the health of semen in the vagina; this time, there was no semen. For thirteen years, the husband had been ejaculating between his wife's thighs.

Dr. Reddy laughed when he told me this story, but he was making a serious point: he was trying to show me how far the country had come in its awareness about sex and sexual issues. He said that in the nineties, when satellites started broadcasting Western soap operas into people's living rooms, and as Indians became more exposed to Western cultures and ways of living, the country started shedding its sexual hang-ups.

People became more open, and more aware. The younger generation, in particular, was very liberated. Although not as prevalent as in the West, premarital sex was no longer taboo. It would be hard to imagine a couple today not knowing even how to have sex.

Dr. Reddy said he started noticing a change in his practice around the mid-nineties. Patients were more informed, and they were less shy about seeking help. Women would come into his clinic and complain about their inability to have an orgasm. Young men would talk freely about their homosexuality, and housewives—women from respectable middle-class families—would speak openly about their extramarital affairs.

Dr. Reddy showed me his appointment book. It was crawling with names. He said that often, he saw more than thirty patients a day. He felt he couldn't do justice to their needs, but he couldn't bring himself to turn them away.

We talked about Hari, and about the pressure his parents were putting on him to get married. "That's always the biggest challenge," Dr. Reddy said. "They have the most difficulty dealing with the marriage problem."

He said that in some ways, things were easier for gay men today than they had been a decade before. Then, he said, he used to see a number of patients who had already been pressured into marriage. They would come to him, sometimes with their wives, complaining about their inability to perform. They would say: "Somehow help me get a child so I can worry less." Before the advent of Viagra, he had few options. He could advise the man to fantasize, but if that didn't work, it often led to serious marital and family discord.

Now, Dr. Reddy said, he saw fewer gay men who were already married, and more men like Hari: men who knew they were gay, whose families were putting pressure on them, but who were facing up to the problem before getting married. Sometimes the men would bring their parents to him. It would be his job to explain why their children were resisting marriage. The news would come as a shock; parents would cry, they'd demand psychological counseling for their children.

Often, even if they were forced to acknowledge their children's homosexuality, parents would still insist on a marriage. "You know how it is in India," Dr. Reddy said. "When you meet somebody in a wedding, the first thing they say is, 'Hello, how are you?' then, 'How is your business or practice?' and then they ask how many

children you have. And if you say, 'Our son has finished his education and is working,' then they ask right away if he's married. It's
our way of picking a conversation. Parents feel really pressurized."

He told me that if parents kept insisting on marrying their gay
children, he would warn them that things weren't as simple as
they used to be. If the bride's family found out after marriage that
their son-in-law was gay, they could register a criminal case, for
cheating, against the groom and his parents. They'd demand their
dowry back, and they could even demand a jail term for the damage to their daughter's reputation. He'd seen it happen. In the old
days, divorce was unheard-of; now families didn't hesitate anymore to undo a bad marriage.

"So what would you advise someone like Hari to do?" I
asked him.

He sighed; he said there was no easy solution. Even though
things were better, more open, India was still a difficult country
for homosexuals.

"Well, at least he moved out of his small town," I said. "I imagine it's a lot easier for him here than in Tindivanam."

Dr. Reddy said it probably was. But he added that ultimately,
the important thing was for someone like Hari to face up to the
fact of his homosexuality and accept it. Otherwise, he said, the
city could pose its own dangers. He'd seen many men—and
women—who had moved to the city with unaddressed issues.
They lost their way. They turned to drugs or alcohol or pornogra-
phy; they couldn't control their shopping, they got into debt. They
succumbed, he said, to "compulsive masturbation."

"It's not easy for these people to move to a place like Chennai,"
he said. "The city changes people."

"Does it always?" I asked. I was thinking, now, of Selvi.

"In my opinion, yes, it will always have some effect. People have to adjust; they have to adapt to the city."

He went on: "It's true that some people resist change. They refuse to change. I may have a bias, but my sense is that they have a personality disorder, and ultimately, they will get damaged.

"See, in India it's considered a virtue to be rigid, to resist change at any cost. Most politicians cry themselves hoarse about 'culture, culture, culture' without understanding the meaning of the word. Today, where is Indian culture? Even in small villages you find hundreds of restaurants serving Chinese, Tandoori, Mughlai dishes. The Chinese have taken over India through gastronomy more effectively than they ever could through political or military might. And today so many girls, even in the villages, wear *salwar kameez* in Tamil Nadu even though it's supposed to be North Indian attire. So where's our culture?"

Dr. Reddy's phone rang, to the tune of Michael Jackson's "Beat It." He excused himself, and when he came back, he continued: "People who resist change do it at a detriment to themselves. It produces tremendous conflict—frustration, depression, jealousies, sexual problems. If you don't change with the times, you will ultimately pay a price for that."

Where, exactly, was Indian culture? It seemed like a fair question. When I visited the cities, when I met people like Harsh or hung out with Hari and Selvi, it was hard not to wonder what it meant to be Indian at the turn of the twenty-first century. Their worlds were so different from the one in which I had grown up, and indeed from the one in which I was still living. For all the change—all the troubled modernity—in the countryside around me, the villages sometimes seemed to exist in a different nation than the cities.

When I first started spending time with Hari and his friends, I did so because I was drawn to what I didn't know. Like an anthropologist (or like a writer), I found myself studying their lives, hoping to understand the country in which I was trying to build my own life. Slowly, the sense of unfamiliarity lifted. I started having little flashes of recognition—moments when their world seemed a lot less strange than I had thought.

The world occupied by many young Indians was familiar because it reminded me of the country in which I had recently spent twelve years. This was a funny thing. I had left America, in many ways fled America, but in modern Indian culture (and particularly modern urban culture), I began to see traces of America.

It shouldn't really have come as a surprise. The types of companies that lined Rajiv Gandhi Salai, and where people like Hari and Selvi worked, were the most visible manifestations of a new closeness between India and the United States. In the years since India's economic reforms, commercial ties between the two nations had flourished: America was India's largest trading partner (it would be overtaken by China in 2008), its biggest export market, and its second most significant source of foreign investment.

The United States was also a role model of sorts, a source of inspiration for much of corporate India. Many of the country's leading entrepreneurs had been educated or worked in America. They returned animated by an American-style work ethic and faith in meritocracy. The businesses they built were like bridges between the two countries—infused with American habits and attitudes, and even with shifts that ran late into the night, and holidays for Thanksgiving and Martin Luther King Jr. Day, operating on American time.

I began to see that India's new economy was in many ways thoroughly Americanized. Inevitably, this Americanization rubbed off on the employees within that economy—on men and women like Hari and Selvi, who found themselves interacting every day with American clients, who attended orientation sessions where they learned about American culture, and training seminars where they were taught to make small talk about the weather in America.

At work, young Indians were given American aliases, presumably on the theory that Americans were more likely to buy something from a person called Harry or Sally than Hari or Selvi. Hari spent much of his time analyzing corporate reports and SEC filings from the United States. He knew a surprising amount about the options structures and bankruptcy filings of American companies.

Young Indians were learning to speak like Americans, too. They attended accent-training sessions at work. It was disorienting, and sometimes vaguely troubling, like hitting a nerve, to chance upon a sudden American twang under Hari's otherwise thick Indian accent. I had to laugh when young Indians called me "dude," or when they told me that a person—in this case, one of Hari's coworkers—was someone's "bitch."

Even television advertisements had changed. I noticed soon after returning that the old polished English accents had given way to angled American voices. The aspirations of Indian consumers had shifted; the old longing for the colonial metropolis had been replaced by the temptations of a new empire.

❧

There was much I welcomed about the Americanization of India. The estrangement between my two worlds had always disturbed me. I can still remember the family friends and distant relatives—they always lived in the cities, and they always had a monopoly on what it meant to be a true Indian—who belittled my American background. They made me feel like I could never fully belong. It was comforting, now, to know that India and America were no longer mutually exclusive.

But there were, inevitably, aspects of America's influence that I couldn't help feeling less enthusiastic about. I wondered if India's new drive and sense of purpose, its optimism and self-belief, had to manifest, also, as a kind of ruthless and self-centered ambition. I wondered if the new incomes and opportunities, the rousing sense of independence felt by so many young Indians, had to be accompanied by what I often felt was a shallow materialism and consumerism.

Coca-Cola ran a survey in India near the turn of the millennium. It found that the chief goal of Indians—in both cities and the countryside—was to "become rich."

There was a ubiquitous ad, a little jingle for an Indian financial services company that I couldn't get out of my mind. It ran: "It's all about the money, honey."

These were the kinds of things I had run away from in America. Now I started wondering if maybe it was all part of a package.

Maybe it wasn't possible to pick and choose what one took from America. Maybe the features I admired in the new India were inextricably bound with the features that I found increasingly dismaying.

Leo, the friend who had introduced me to Hari, said something interesting to me one day. He was almost forty, older than Hari. He had a little more perspective.

"Nobody knows where this is all going," he said once, after we had seen Hari. "These guys are just trying on roles, but they don't really know who they're becoming. Hari is doing great today—he's on top of the world. But sometimes I worry that the same things that make him happy today might make him miserable tomorrow."

Hari took me shopping one day. We went with Nikhil and Leo. We went to Spencer Plaza. It was a Saturday, shortly before the new year, and the shops and corridors of the mall were full. I felt a little daunted by the crowds, but Hari, ever exuberant, was undauntable.

A few days earlier, when he had invited me, he told me that if I went shopping with him, I would go "crazy." "Why is that?" I asked, and he laughed. "You don't know me," he said. "Everyone goes crazy when they shop with me. Once I start, I can't stop."

He told me, walking the noisy corridors of the mall, shouting a little above the din of thousands of equally avid shoppers, that he had spent 60,000 rupees that month—around four times his salary. He said he needed a new watch. He had already bought three that month, and he had fourteen—or maybe fifteen, he wasn't sure—at home. But he needed "one for every mood." "It depends on how I'm feeling that day," he said. "I need a different color for all my moods."

I asked him how he managed to pay for it all, and he nudged me. "That's my secret," he said. "I'll never tell anyone." I pressed him. "It's simple," he said. "I keep rotating."

He had five credit cards, and around 50,000 rupees of debt. It wasn't hard to get new credit cards; the banks were eager to lend to India's demographic dividend.

Hari's mother was worried about his debt. But he said he wasn't concerned. "See, when it comes to shopping, I never feel stressed," he told me. "I never feel poor. I just go be happy and buy whatever I want. Shopping is my natural stress-reliever. Whenever I buy something, a feeling of excitement comes automatically."

❦

We spent a long afternoon in Spencer Plaza. We started at a bookstore, where Hari bought a basketful of magazines (*Cosmopolitan, Filmfare, Men's Health*) and movies (including *The Little Mermaid* and a Barbie Doll dance video). We moved on to an underwear store, where Nikhil and Leo checked out a male mannequin in bikini underwear while Hari browsed through boxes of jockstraps. He said he had a "fetish" about underwear; he couldn't get enough. He bought several jockstraps.

He told me he had a policy: If he entered a store, he had to buy something. "You're a shopkeeper's dream," I said, and he said he thought it was only fair. He'd seen customers go into shops with long lists of questions. They took things down from shelves, they made a mess, and then they left without spending even fifty paisa. It wasn't correct.

We stopped in at a music store, where Hari bought four movies and flashed a frequent-buyer card. We had lunch at Subway, where the man sitting at the table next to us asked his friends: "At the end of the day, your ultimate aim is to make money, right?"

We ended up at a cosmetics store. Hari grilled the shopgirls about menthol face-wash and the difference between anti-greasing and anti-regreasing whitening cream. The girls seemed astonished by his questions; one, giggling, said that men never asked so much. Hari dismissed them with a wave of his hand. "How can you sell these products if you don't know anything about them?" he asked, and he picked a basket of cosmetics on his own.

Standing in line at the checkout, he told me that the reason he loved shopping so much was because he was a Gemini. He said that Geminis were very impulsive. "What Gemi wants Gemi has to get," he said. "Gemi can't control himself."

This was particularly true of love. Once a Gemini fell in love, he could never let go. That's why he would never fall in love—he wouldn't wish that fate on anyone. "Once we get in, we'll never leave," he said. "I don't want that to happen to anyone. I don't want to kill a person. Let him be free."

Outside the cosmetics store, Hari, Leo, and Nikhil rested against a metal parapet. Hari seemed kind of giddy. He was bouncing around, joking and playing with his friends. They were touching each other, friendly pats and a few caresses on their shoulders and backs.

Hari started talking about Geminis and love again. He said you didn't need love when you could shop; both were equally invigorating. He told me about everything he'd bought that month. He was especially happy with a new set-top box he'd installed at home.

He had spent more than 5,000 rupees that day, almost all on credit cards, and I asked him again if he wasn't worried about paying off his debt. He told me again he wasn't. "If you live in good times, then why should you worry about anything?" he asked.

"But what about the future? What about saving for tomorrow?" I asked.

Hari and Nikhil laughed. "Why save?" Hari said. "What's the use of saving?"

"Yeah, why should we save?" Nikhil asked. "I don't like the concept of saving."

They gave each other a high five, and Nikhil sang a film song I didn't recognize. They were swaying their hips.

"But what if you lose your job?" I asked.

"Then we'll get a new job," Nikhil said. "If we lose this job, we'll just get another."

"We work in technology," Hari said. "Don't you understand? There are thousands of jobs out there. Now's not the time for saving. Now's the time for enjoying."

"Yes, there's nothing to worry about—just be happy," Nikhil said.

They gave each other a high five again, and Hari told me to smile. "What's the matter, why so serious?" he asked. He slapped me on the back. He said I sounded like his mother.

Hari and Nikhil went to meet a friend, and I gave Leo a ride home. The roads outside Spencer Plaza were jammed. The city was alive; everyone had somewhere to go on a Saturday.

Leo and I talked while we were stuck in traffic. I said I noticed he hadn't bought anything. Maybe, I said, it was because he wasn't a Gemini. He laughed. He said maybe he just wasn't as confident as Hari. He couldn't be so sure it was all going to work out.

I asked if he thought Hari's confidence was justified.

"I guess so, if you're willing to work like him," he said. "If you're willing to take crazy hours, no holidays, and no control over your life, of course you'll always find a job in this economy. I'm sure if you put Europeans or Americans in Hari's job, they'd snap. They'd want ergonomic chairs, they'd want more holidays, they'd want health insurance, they'd complain a lot. But this generation is just willing to do it—they'll do anything to get ahead and make money. That's a huge advantage they have over mine.

"But then again," Leo said, "does Hari want to be doing this when he's forty?" He was quiet. Then he said: "Still, I guess when he's forty he'll probably be earning a lot more than I am."

We drove slowly, inching our way through the cars and vans and autorickshaws that were lined up, honking their horns. It was evening, a time between night and day, and the lights of the city were starting to come on.

We drove past the U.S. consulate, where security was tight, with guards behind sandbags and a blue riot control vehicle that looked like a mini-tank. The war in Iraq was raging.

We drove past a liquor store, where an old man with bowlegs and patchy skin on his face was swaying back and forth, leaning against a wall, while another man, maybe his friend, was spitting mucus so thick and copious onto the road that I thought he was vomiting.

We drove past a hotel that I knew had a nice bar. I asked Leo if he wanted to get a drink. He said he'd rather just get home. He seemed subdued. He started talking about what working in India had been like when he was Hari's age. There were no opportunities, there was no connection to the outside world. There was no real reason to be confident.

"Do you envy him?" I asked.

"Yes, I guess I do," Leo said. "I guess in a way I wish I could be Hari. It would be fun. They're having a good time, this new generation. They're definitely having a good time.

"Life just seems to work for them," he said. "They're coasting along. I guess it's a great country to be in right now."

THE SHANDY

It was Pongal, the Tamil harvest festival, and Sathy was having a feast at his house. He invited me to Molasur. "Come meet my family," he said. "Everyone's coming down, we're all going to be together."

I went to Molasur on a rainy day in January, the sky a sheet of metal, the ponds and irrigation channels along the road filled with muddy red water. Pongal is a joyful holiday, an occasion to celebrate the monsoons and the gifts they bring. The rains had been generous that year. The fields were green, alive, and tractors were decked out in flowers. Villages were crowded with made-up cows, their horns painted bright reds and blues and oranges, their necks garlanded with jasmine.

Sathy was outside his house, dressed in a purple *kurta* and white pants, deep in conversation with a man on a bicycle. The man left when he saw me; Sathy told me his story. He said the man was bereaved; he'd recently lost his brother. His brother had gone swimming in a well and suffered a seizure. He drowned. When his family found him, his eyes were missing; they'd been eaten by fish.

"Come, come inside," Sathy said, and he led me into his home, through a living room in the front, a space for official visitors and acquaintances, to another in the back, a more intimate living room for family and close friends. There were about thirty people spread around the more intimate room, on sofas and chairs, some on the floor. A group of children were playing carrom. A TV was turned to cartoons.

At the back of the house, in the kitchen, three men were grating coconuts and stirring a pot of *sambar*. One of the men was Sathy's cook; he'd been with the family for forty years. The second was the cook's helper, and the third was Sathy's masseur. Every self-respecting zamindar had to employ a masseur.

The men were cooking for more than two hundred people. Traditionally, Sathy told me, his family opened their house to the village on Pongal. It was a way to acknowledge the bounty from their fields, and to signal their wealth. Sathy conceded that the tradition had become a little expensive. There wasn't as much bounty, or wealth. Still, he said, citing a Tamil proverb: "No one has ever gone hungry by feeding too many people."

Sathy introduced me to his family. I met his brother, visiting from New Zealand, and I met Sathy's children. I met Banu, Sathy's wife. She was a short woman with a frank, inquisitive face. Her green silk sari caught the light, shone in the windowless living room. She wore red lipstick. She shook my hand and said she'd heard a lot about me. She laughed when she said this.

Darshan, Sathy's son, was shy; he had doe eyes. Sathy said he was going to be a scientist, and Darshan told me in a soft voice about atoms, about how they were the smallest elements. He told me, too, about reading *Who Moved My Cheese?* He said: "I learned from it that you should always look forward and don't stay in place and don't wait for things to happen. Make them happen."

Sathy stepped away, to help with preparations for the feast. I asked Banu if it was true that she wanted him to leave Molasur. She shook her head, furrowed her brow. She said: "It's too late for that. I keep trying, but I really don't think it's possible anymore. Sathy can't adapt to life in Bangalore. He'd be like a fish out of water there. He's still stuck in his zamindar mentality, stuck on the past and what his family means.

"I don't know how well you know Sathy, but when he sees someone in Bangalore that earns a lakh a month or more, he can't accept that they're above him socially. He can't face the fact that things have changed and that now it matters how much people earn. In the cities, people only care about money. They don't care about what his family used to be."

"Was it different when you first met him?" I asked her.

"Very different," she said. "That was before the outsourcing and IT companies and all of that had come to Bangalore. A person's background still mattered then. Now it only matters what you do, not who you are. There are so many people much younger than him, people who don't come from his type of family. Could he ever accept them being equal to him? I don't think so. I don't think he'll ever leave here."

I asked her: "What about you? Could you live here?"

"What would I do? Here, I just sit around reading books all day. It's nice for a holiday, but that's all. I'm not the kind of woman who sits in the kitchen all day. I need to do something. I can't even work in the fields because of his zamindar status. It would be looked down upon, it would be considered beneath me."

Banu told me about the period of time when she had tried to live in Molasur. It was after she and Sathy got married. They had lived in Chennai at first, but Sathy was unhappy, directionless, and she felt he wouldn't be satisfied unless he was living on his land. So she had given Molasur a try. She was a city girl; she'd never lived in the countryside. Nonetheless, she moved into the family home in Molasur and tried to bend herself to village life.

It wasn't easy. Sathy's family was very traditional, and they expected her to conform. The household was strictly vegetarian; Banu wasn't allowed to eat meat. She wasn't allowed to enter the kitchen when she was having her period. The family wanted her to place her jewelry and valuables in a cupboard to which they all had a key.

To keep occupied, Banu had started a small embroidery business. She employed women from the village; they would come to the house to stitch garments—shirts, dresses, aprons—that Banu would then sell to export companies. She discovered an entrepreneurial streak in herself. The business had done well; at one point, Banu said, she was making at least 50,000 rupees a month.

Soon, though, her business started causing tension in the family. Some of the women she employed were Dalits. Some members of the family weren't happy about that. They weren't comfortable with Dalits in the house.

Much of the tension was unspoken. Occasionally it would flare up. One time, a member of the family called Banu to the back of the house and asked her not to bring Dalits into the home anymore. Banu was astonished. "I wouldn't take it," she told me, years later. "For me, it was totally un-modern. I mean, I lived in the city, where caste is totally out—it's over. I said I couldn't accept that. It was really difficult for me."

Banu started talking about leaving the village, moving to Bangalore. Sathy resisted; he said maybe they could build a separate home, somewhere in the fields or outside the village, away from the family. Things were calm for a while, but then they blew up again over a dinner that Banu hosted for her workers.

Sathy's family was away for a few days, and Banu invited her employees into the house for a party. One of the women caught some fish in a well and cooked it for dinner. When they returned, Sathy's family was shocked: Dalits had been in the house, nonvegetarian food had been cooked. These were grave offenses. It was made clear to Banu that she had to shut the business down.

"How could I keep living here after that?" Banu asked me. "They think so differently from the way I do. I felt like I was losing myself to the family. All these rules and restrictions. I couldn't live like that anymore."

She took the kids with her to Bangalore. She told Sathy to come, but he asked what he would do there. She told him they'd figure it out. She said: "If you want to do something, if you have the willpower, you can do it anywhere." Sathy couldn't let go; maybe he didn't want to let go. Maybe, Banu told me at that Pongal feast, he didn't dare let go.

Now Banu lived in Bangalore, Sathy in Molasur, and the kids

saw their father only on holidays and weekends. It was difficult. Banu worried about her kids. At least, she said, the schools in Bangalore were better; the children would get a city education.

"I don't belong here," she told me that Pongal afternoon. "It's beautiful, no doubt. It's peaceful. But I can't have my own life here. In Bangalore, I feel like I am a person."

Pongal lunch was served on the floor, on banana leaves placed over a line of cane mats. Sathy's cook, shirtless, his chest glistening with sweat, served at least ten dishes from metal buckets carried by his assistants. It was, as Sathy had promised, a feast, and a delicious one. He beamed when I asked for seconds, and then for thirds.

"This is the way we have always eaten in this house," Sathy said. "As far back as I can remember, this is exactly the food we ate every Pongal." He told me that his grandfather's grandfather probably ate the same food. The only difference was that in the past, the food would have been made almost entirely out of produce from the family's farms. Now the farms weren't quite what they had been; only the rice was from their land. Who knew where everything else was from? Sathy muttered about industrial farming.

After the meal, Banu served me a cup of coffee, with milk from a cow at the back of the house. She asked about my family. She seemed curious to know how my wife was adjusting to life in India. "Why don't you all visit us sometime in Bangalore?" she asked, and I said I'd love to. I asked Sathy if he'd take me. They exchanged looks; they both laughed.

Sathy walked me to the front of the house, to my car. It was pouring now. The rain came down straight, at a right angle to the ground. I decided to wait it out on Sathy's veranda. The smell of the earth, of Molasur's fields and dusty streets, lifted to my nose.

I told Sathy about my conversation with Banu, about how she'd said he would never move to Bangalore. "It's true," he said. "I feel lost there. Here, I'm known. There, I have no power."

"Bangalore's really a useless place," he said. "You can't use anyone's name. You can't use any influence. Even with the traffic police—if he stops you and you tell him who you are, or who you know, he just doesn't care. He won't care at all. I have so many connections here. In the city, I feel useless."

He told me a story about going for a drive along the East Coast Road with his family recently. They had turned off the road at one point, to get closer to the ocean. The car got stuck in the sand. It was evening, getting dark, and the kids were worried. But Sathy wasn't worried; he was sure that everyone in the area knew who he was. If his car was seriously stuck, he could just summon a tractor to pull it out. Everyone would be eager to help; they wouldn't dare refuse him.

"They know me, they know my influence, Akash. They know that if they treat me badly I can easily come back with men from my village and teach them a lesson. I'm not saying I would do that, I'm not that type. But what would I do if that happened in Bangalore? I would feel so lost. No one would respond to me."

The rain came down harder; it was a real downpour. Sathy said rain on Pongal was auspicious. The coming year promised to be fertile. "Maybe it will be a lucky year for agriculture," he said, cupping a hand into the rain, as if trying to catch it. "We need a little luck around here. The farmers could use a little luck."

He talked about wells that had run dry, reservoirs that were silted up through years of neglect. A few decades ago, he said, you barely had to dig to reach water. You could scoop water out of wells with handheld buckets. Now you had to dig deeper and deeper, and in the summers, even the deepest wells ran dry.

He returned to his personal situation. He told me that Banu had been talking about moving to Dubai. She'd been offered a job there. It was a great opportunity. I could see he was proud, but he was also scared. "I could use a little luck, Akash," he said. "Tell me: What will I do if Banu leaves us and goes to Dubai? Who will take care of my family?"

Sathy and I were walking across his fields one day, not too long after that feast at his house. Pongal is a three-day festival. The feast marked the first day of the festival. Sathy was telling me, now, about the second day, known as Mattu Pongal, or Cow Pongal. The second day was dedicated to cows; it was an occasion to venerate them, to honor them for the service they'd provided in homes and on farms.

At the end of the second day, cows and their owners traditionally gathered in a clearing opposite Molasur's main temple. The village priests performed a *pooja*. They chanted over loudspeakers, they lit a fire, and they oversaw a ceremonial plowing with one of the biggest bulls in the village.

Sathy told me about the *pooja* that had taken place that year. It happened right by his house; he stood on his veranda and watched. He had been disappointed. He said that in the old days, Mattu Pongal had really been something. Sathy and his siblings would get dressed up; they'd cover their faces with powder. The village drummers would stop in at his house and lead his family in a procession to the temple. The whole village would be gathered; thousands of cows and bulls would be assembled. There was an air of solemnity, of seriousness.

This year, Sathy said, the crowds were thin, and unserious. There were just over a hundred cows, maybe not even a hundred. Kids ran around screaming, playing, popping balloons. Young men, some of them drunk, drove around on motorcycles, crashing into the crowd, honking their horns and making a nuisance of themselves. Sathy said he felt like "bashing them up."

It was disappointing, Sathy told me, but not really surprising. Agriculture was in decline, and Pongal was losing its meaning. This had been going on for years. He said that Pongal had become just another reason to go shopping—a holiday like Christmas or the New Year. People had forgotten what Pongal was all about; they no longer connected it to the earth, to the farms and the fields and the food they ate. "Who can blame them?" Sathy asked. "Young people don't care about farming anymore, so why should they even think about what Pongal means?"

He pointed to a large stretch of fallow land that ran by his fields. The property belonged to an agricultural family. Sathy remembered when the whole family—fathers and sons, and sometimes even the women—would gather on the land to farm it. Now the family had quit farming. Twenty years ago, Sathy said, it would have been impossible to imagine the land fallow.

It was the same story everywhere. Sathy told me about his cousin, a Reddiar from the neighboring village. His family had owned hundreds of acres of land. They had been big farmers, as powerful and wealthy as Sathy's family. But income from the farm dried up, the family mismanaged their affairs, and they lost everything. Now his cousin was selling tea and packaged snacks out of a small stall by a canal in Pondicherry.

His cousin's story was a tragedy. And it ate at Sathy to know that it was a tragedy being played out across the country—in villages throughout rural India, where farms were being sold, where indebted farmers were committing suicide, and where traditional agrarian communities were being hollowed out. People talked a lot about how India was changing, Sathy said; they got so excited about all the software and technology companies in the cities. But he had a question. He wanted to know: "If all the farms are gone, then who will feed all these fancy people?"

In the papers, I had been reading about inflation and food riots across the country. Despite all the economic growth since the nation's reforms, the number of undernourished Indians had actually risen in the first decade of the millennium (after falling during the nineties). The Peterson Institute, a Washington-based think tank, estimated that India's food production would decline by 30 percent over the first eighty years of the twenty-first century.

"Sometimes when I walk this land, I have a feeling of a village that's dying," Sathy said. "What's all this city, city, city rubbish?

Everyone is so happy that India is becoming modern. But I have a different feeling: I feel like all this modernity is killing people."

◟

As we walked through the fields, as Sathy bemoaned the challenges of agriculture and talked about dying villages, we came upon a man wrapped in a blue shawl. He was sitting on an embankment. His name was E. Krishnan. He was fifty-eight years old. Sathy greeted him and said to me: "This fellow will be a millionaire soon. I tell you: he's on his way up."

Krishnan's story was a familiar one. He had been a farmer. His family had cultivated two acres on the outskirts of Molasur. Then farming became tough; Krishnan struggled to earn a living; he quit the profession. He sold his land, and he started attending local markets where cows were traded and sold. Now he had a new profession: he worked as a cow broker, facilitating deals between buyers and sellers.

The cow markets were known as shandies. Krishnan had actually been attending them since he was a boy. He had dabbled in the profession before. But now the village economy was shifting, agriculture was becoming less important, and new jobs (like cow brokering) had become more lucrative. Sathy exaggerated—grossly—when he said Krishnan was on his way to becoming a millionaire, but Krishnan told me that it was true there was more money to be made in cow brokering than ever before.

The change at the shandies was part of a broader transformation; the same forces—of modernization, of urbanization—that were decimating agriculture were lifting the prospects of brokers like Krishnan. As Indians became more affluent, as they moved to the cities and became increasingly cosmopolitan, they were eating more beef. Between 1990 and the late 2000s, per capita consumption of beef in the country increased by around 60 percent. For many Indians, probably a majority, eating beef was still taboo. But for a growing number, social mores were changing.

The increasing acceptability of beef had lifted demand for cows. In recent years, cow prices at the shandies had more than quadrupled. This added to the woes of farmers. Small farmers, in particular, already unable to afford tractors, now had no way to plow their fields. But development is a process of trade-offs. One profession's loss was another's gain—the higher prices were a boon to men like Krishnan, who made an income off commissions.

"If you really want to see how the villages are changing, you should visit a shandy," Sathy said to me that day on his fields. He asked Krishnan if he'd show me around. Krishnan asked us to come any Wednesday to the nearby village of Brahmadesan, where one of the biggest shandies in the area was held.

When Krishnan left, Sathy shook his head. He said eating beef was a repulsive habit. He described it as a "sin." Every morning, he told me, his mother performed a *pooja* for the cows in their backyard. She recited prayers, she lit camphor; she fed the cows rice, and a jaggery sweet. No one in Sathy's family had ever eaten beef.

"Cows are something special for us, something holy," Sathy said. "We could never imagine slaughtering or eating them.

"Morality is changing, Akash," he went on. "People don't care as much about how to behave, they don't have values anymore. Boozing, womanizing, sex, beef—it's all okay now. Anything is acceptable."

He pointed across the fields, in the direction of a group of men at the edge of his land. He said they were bootleggers. They gathered every day outside the village and sold illicit home-brewed liquor. "See that? See that?" he asked. "That's exactly what I mean." He waved his bamboo stick at the bootleggers and yelled. "Get out, get out, you lousy dogs!" he shouted.

"It makes me sad sometimes," he said. "We were all brought up in a very nice way. We all had our drinks under hold, we knew how to control ourselves. But the whole thing is disturbed today. It's all . . . It's not like it was."

I visited a shandy in Brahmadesan the following week. It was my first time at a shandy, but not my first time in Brahmadesan. A few years earlier, during the Indian elections of 2004, I had reported a series of articles from the area. The elections were closely fought, and the outcome—a victory for the Congress-led opposition—a surprise. Most opinion polls suggested that the Bharatiya Janata Party (BJP)—led government would return to power. The government had campaigned on the uplifting slogan of "India Shining." The slogan was designed to appeal to nationalist sentiment, and to pride in the nation's economic progress.

In the aftermath of the elections, most analysts agreed that the slogan had backfired. While it worked with urban and middle-class populations—the largest beneficiaries of India's reforms—it spoke little to voters in rural areas, many of whom felt neglected, and even slighted by the slogan's presumption. In a farming village near Brahmadesan, I had spoken to a group of men outside a tea shop. One of them said to me: "The government says India's shining, but that's a lie. Do we look like we're shining here?"

A few years on, the area around Brahmadesan had moved up in the world. While it wasn't exactly shining, there was clear evidence of new prosperity. The main road in the village was freshly tarred. It was bordered by concrete houses that had only recently been thatch huts. The village had a new hospital, and two cellphone towers. Sathy told me about a power plant that was being planned in the area, and about an industrial zone that the government was talking about establishing up the road.

Like so much of rural India, Brahmadesan's economy was in transition. Between the early 1990s and the late 2000s, the share of India's GDP represented by agriculture fell from almost 32 percent to just under 17 percent. This pattern was evident around Brahmadesan, where land prices had risen rapidly, and where many farmers had sold their property and used the proceeds to set up shops or businesses. New jobs, and new types of jobs, were being created. People who had grown up as farmers, whose ancestors had always been farmers, were now working as construction workers, cooks, and drivers.

Sathy said: "These people are not the same way they used to be, Akash. I tell you, the same people who used to beg me for jobs, who were happy to work in my fields for ten rupees—now they refuse to join me even if I pay them ten times that."

It wasn't until we turned off the main road and followed a dirt track that led to the shandy that traces of the village's agricultural heritage were more evident. In a veterinary dispensary at the end of the track, a group of farmers stood around with their cows, and an ungloved doctor shoved his hand into the animals' vaginas to check if they were pregnant. If they weren't, he injected them with semen brought from Bangalore.

An old man, a wrinkled farmer, walked into the dispensary. He held a bleeding goat in his arms. The goat had been bitten on the neck by a dog. The farmer pleaded with the doctor for help. The doctor administered an injection, but he said the goat would die. I heard the old man tell someone that the goat was all he had—no land, no children, no other livestock.

The shandy was behind the dispensary. It was in a clearing set amid a grove of tamarind trees. It was a busy place, with at least a couple hundred people, and maybe three times as many cows and bulls. The cows were tied together with thick ropes. They were dragged around by their owners, their teats and mouths and vaginas examined by potential buyers. At the conclusion of a deal, they were loaded, protesting with loud moos, into trucks.

Sathy had described the shandies to me as agricultural fairs. I had expected something cheerful, maybe with dancing and music. But I saw quickly that there were no festivities at that shandy. The atmosphere was serious, even tense; it reminded me less of a fair than the floor of a stock market. Men hung around with intent looks, carrying or counting bundles of pink thousand-rupee notes. They shouted, and they shoved their way into deals, occasionally getting into heated arguments that hovered at the edge of violence.

Some of the men at the shandy were covered in earth and wore stained loincloths; these were sellers, poor farmers who had come to cash out their last possessions. Many were better dressed. They wore spotless white shirts and pants, and their eyes were hidden behind dark sunglasses. They were surrounded by a retinue of minions. These were buyers, owners or representatives of slaughterhouses.

Sathy said that when he used to attend the shandies as a young man, he never saw these kinds of people; he saw only farmers. He dismissed the well-dressed buyers as "businessmen."

We met Krishnan at the northern edge of the shandy. He was standing by a market where vendors in makeshift stalls sold ropes, whips, and fried snacks. He greeted us, but he seemed distracted. He had his eyes on a group of cows. He introduced me to a friend. The friend's name was R. Ramadas. Krishnan said: "This man can tell you whatever you need to know. He's a legend." He said that, and then he took off, practically ran into the scrum.

Ramadas was a short, stocky man, with a face darkened over the years by the sun. He was in his mid-fifties; he had a white beard, and restless eyes. He shook my hand, he asked what I was doing at the market—and then, before I could answer, he, too, took off.

The shandy was a place for business. There were deals to be made, money to be earned. There was no time for idle talk.

Sathy said: "I know that Ramadas. He used to hang around Molasur. He's famous here. Everybody knows Ramadas."

I followed Ramadas around the shandy that morning. I watched him strike a few deals. He wasn't easy to keep up with; Sathy joked that I should hook him up with a GPS device.

Ramadas prowled the northwest corner of the market, which he later told me was his territory. It was a tough area, dominated by businessmen from the slaughterhouses, people with little respect for brokers. But it was where the big money was made, and

Ramadas had been going to cow markets for forty-five years. He'd started as a boy with his father; he said he felt confident in any situation.

He had stubby, energetic legs, and a loud, screeching voice that he used to shout down rival brokers or hesitant buyers. He had a way of being smooth and aggressive, nonchalant and pushy, at the same time. He would keep an eye out for prospective sellers, farmers standing protectively by their cows, wary of being cheated, and when he spotted one, he'd swoop in and grab the cow and begin leading her toward a buyer. If the seller displayed any reluctance, Ramadas would take his hand, look him in the eye, and tell him: "You should trust me. I know what I'm doing. People buy cows just on my word. I'm known around here. You can trust me."

The first time I saw Ramadas in operation, he was trying to ingratiate himself with a tall man who had two bulls to sell. The man was a farmer; his face was lined, weather-beaten. Ramadas had almost closed a deal for him earlier that morning, but the farmer had backed out at the last minute, and now he was explaining to Ramadas that it wasn't about the money. He said he didn't like the buyer; he had something against him personally.

"Don't worry about all of that," Ramadas said, and he took the yellow rope that tied the man's two bulls together, pulled them toward another buyer. The new buyer was willing to pay 12,000 rupees for a bull, but the farmer wanted 12,500. Ramadas yelled at the buyer. "You'll get sixty kilos of meat off these bulls," he said. "Why don't you pay the right price?"

The buyer waved some money in front of Ramadas. "If you give up your commission, then the price will be all right," he said, and he looked at the seller meaningfully. The seller nodded in agreement.

Ramadas looked disgusted. "Why the hell should I do that?" he said, and he stomped away.

When I caught up with Ramadas, he was surrounded by a small crowd, his hand on another cow. He felt the cow's vagina and shook his head at the owner. "If she were pregnant, it would be wet," he said. "There's no liquid." The man, insisting his cow was pregnant, wanted more money, but Ramadas negotiated a lower price. The seller paid him a commission of fifty rupees, but the buyer gave him only twenty, and Ramadas shouted at him: "Why should I do all the work and not get paid for it?" He grabbed thirty rupees out of the buyer's hand and walked away. The buyer stared after him.

A man ran up to Ramadas and said that the weather-beaten farmer's two bulls were still available; the deal was open. Ramadas went back to the farmer, but he refused to look at Ramadas. "You had your chance, but you were too greedy for your commission," the farmer said.

"Why are you speaking to me like that?" Ramadas asked him. "Am I your enemy? Do I speak to you like that? Don't I speak to you like a friend?"

Ramadas hit one of the bulls on its haunches in a proprietorial manner, but it was too late: the sale went through with another broker. When the farmer paid the new broker less than he wanted, Ramadas took the part of his competitor. "What's your problem? Why won't you pay a proper commission?" he asked the farmer.

He raced into the crowd again, and when I found him, he had just sold three cows to a man in a flowing silk *kurta*. The man gave him a thirty-rupee commission. Ramadas complained, and the man, smiling, said: "You've made plenty of money off me. Why should I give you more?"

There was a moment of silence; Ramadas seemed tense. Then he smiled and slapped the man on the shoulder. "It's okay," Ramadas said to me. "We've done a lot of business together. If he wants, he gives me something. If he doesn't, that's also all right. It's as he wants."

"Hey," Ramadas called out to another man, leading five cows down a slope. "Where have you been? I've been trying to call you all morning. I thought we were friends."

"What nonsense," the man shouted back. "I tried to call you but you were too busy chasing other cows. Now I've sold mine without you." Ramadas laughed and patted one of the cows he'd just sold. He retreated to the side of the market, bought a cup of buttermilk from a woman working out of a thatch stall, and took a break.

I had a chance to catch up with Ramadas later, a little after noon. There were a few other people with us. Krishnan and Sathy were there, and also another cow broker, a big man with a pockmarked, bulbous nose. A couple farmers joined us; they were from Sathy's village.

We sat on the veranda of a government school, at the edge of the shandy. The veranda overlooked a playground. Kids in uniforms, the girls in blue-and-white *salwar kameez*, the boys in shorts and inexplicably pointed ties that aimed like daggers at their chests, ran around.

Ramadas had closed a few deals that morning; he was in a good mood. Krishnan praised his friend. He said again that Ramadas was a legend. One time, Krishnan said, Ramadas sold 1,500 cows in a single week. Ramadas corrected him: it was 1,500 in a month. Still, it was an accomplishment. He had sold the cows to a trader who shipped them to Kuwait, where they were slaughtered and eaten.

Now, Ramadas said, there was no need to ship cows to slaughterhouses in the Gulf; plenty of people in India ate beef. "Really?" I asked, and he held up his hands and said, "Of course, everyone eats beef now." He said that young people did, and so did people in the cities; even people in the villages had started eating beef.

Ramadas said that he ate beef himself. A lot of his friends did, too, but he wouldn't name them because they would be ashamed. "I eat beef," the big man with the bulbous nose said, in a surprisingly high-pitched voice. "I started eating it because my doctor told me to. I complained that I was always weak and sick, and he told me that if I ate more beef I would get fewer colds."

"Yes, lots of people eat beef now, and so the prices have gone up," Ramadas said. It started in the early nineties. Around that time, Ramadas began noticing a few changes in the shandies. He noticed, first, that more businessmen were showing up. They had lots of money; they bid up the price of cows, beyond what most farmers could pay. Then, inevitably, fewer farmers began attending the cow market. When a farmer did show up, it was almost always to sell a cow rather than to buy one.

The farmers sitting with us nodded. They talked about how hard it was to keep their farms running. "We have so many problems," one of them said, "and now we can't even afford cows." Sathy said that even a wealthy farmer like him had problems. He had been forced to sell the family's ten water buffaloes, because he couldn't afford to feed them anymore. "There's nothing like buffalo milk," Sathy said. "And buffalo manure is the best."

When he was a young man, Ramadas told me, the shandies had primarily been agricultural affairs. Every Wednesday, farmers from the area would pile into their bullock carts and gather in the clearing. Business was slow, low-key. On a good day, about twenty cows would trade in the market.

Over the last couple of decades, the shandies had become less about agriculture, and more about business. There were fewer bullock carts now, and more vans and trucks. Before, the shandies had also functioned as markets for local produce. Farmers would set up stalls at one end of the clearing and sell their tomatoes, onions, and spinach. Now few farmers in the area grew such produce. You couldn't buy vegetables or fruit at the shandies anymore.

The mood of the shandies had also changed. Ramadas said that striking a deal with a farmer was easy; the relationship between brokers and farmers was cordial, even social. People knew each other from around the village. But businessmen were impersonal, and hard-nosed. They weren't interested in socializing; they didn't ask about your family. They just pushed for the best deal they could get, and then they left.

Still, Ramadas said, he shouldn't complain too much. He did sometimes feel nostalgic for the old ways, but he made a lot more money these days. He emphasized to me that he was by no means a wealthy man; he struggled to make ends meet. But the influx of businessmen had made life a little easier. Now, he said, more than fifty cows traded in the market on a typical day. His take from commissions was much higher.

"A farmer could afford at most to pay eight thousand rupees for

a cow," he said. "They would buy just a few cows, and keep them
for years. They would only buy during the season. There was
hardly any money in it for me. But when a businessman would
show up, he'd buy ten, twenty, maybe even thirty cows. He'd offer
ten thousand or fifteen thousand rupees a cow. Businessmen have
a lot more money. They are shrewd, but they can spend more."

Ramadas told me about one businessman in particular, a
slaughterhouse owner he called Kottakuppam Kannan. (Kottakuppam was the name of a town in the area; Ramadas didn't know
his customer by another name.) Throughout the nineties, Kottakuppam Kannan was a regular customer. He'd call Ramadas, tell
him to keep a hundred cows ready, and then show up with trucks
or load carriers to ship them away.

Ramadas worked with Kottakuppam Kannan for more than
fifteen years. The money he earned during that time allowed him
to put his kids through school, and then college. He had three
children, two sons and a daughter. Each of them had, or was earning, an engineering degree.

I told Ramadas it was impressive that he'd managed to put his
three kids through college. He smiled widely. His pride was evident. He said his younger son was finishing college that year; he
wanted to work abroad. His daughter worked in an outsourcing
company in Chennai. And his other son? Ramadas pulled a picture out of a notebook he carried in his shirt pocket. His elder son
had died in a traffic accident a few years before. He'd been on a
motorcycle, he was hit by a bus early in the morning. Ramadas
said his son was a bright boy; he'd been offered a job in Canada.

Ramadas was particularly proud of his daughter. He said that
many of his acquaintances pulled their daughters out of school;

everyone expected him to do the same. But his daughter had always done so well, she had marks of 85 percent and above, how could he do that to her? He insisted that she focus on her studies.

"Congratulations," Sathy said. "That's really amazing. That's really something."

"Write about it in your book," Ramadas said to me. "I wanted to set a different example. I wanted people to see what a girl could do if she was educated."

Sathy turned to Krishnan. "You see, you dog," he said. "Why didn't you do the same with your own kids? They're useless, good for nothing."

"But sir, I tried," Krishnan protested. "I even tied them to a post and beat them, but they refused. I could never get them to study hard enough."

Ramadas laughed. He said: "What were you thinking, tying them up and beating them? Did you think they were cows?"

I met Ramadas several times after that first day at Brahmadesan. We met at the cow market, where he was friendly but often too busy to spend much time with me, and we met at a lodge in the nearby town of Tindivanam, where he stayed when he was visiting the shandy. In 2001, when Ramadas's son had died, his wife suffered a nervous breakdown. The family moved to Chennai, where she'd grown up, thinking it might help her recover. They'd stayed there, and now Ramadas commuted to work.

The lodge was a cheap, basic place, looking down on a flyover with noisy traffic. Rooms with a shared bathroom cost seventy rupees a night, about $1.50. Sometimes, Ramadas saved money by sleeping on the floor in a storeroom at the top of the lodge. The storeroom was like a cave—it had one dim light hanging from the ceiling, and a mosquito coil on the floor. The floor was hard, cold in the winter and hot in the summer, but Ramadas said he didn't mind. He didn't want to waste his money.

Ramadas told me that his children didn't like it when he came to Tindivanam. They said he was getting old; he should take it easy. They said he shouldn't waste the family's money on bus fares and hotel rooms. Actually, Ramadas said, the real reason they didn't want him in Tindivanam was that they didn't approve of his line of work. His children were deeply religious; they thought what their father did was against the gods.

In this, they took after their mother. She performed a *pooja* every day at four in the morning; she took the kids regularly to temples. Ramadas said the family complained when he spent money, but his wife was always buying gifts and making offerings to temple deities.

He laughed when he told me this—not derisively, but, I thought, indulgently, even affectionately. Ramadas was an atheist. He said he didn't mind that his family was religious, but he didn't share their beliefs. He had no intention of quitting his profession. Who could say what was against the gods? He said people always talked about gods and the miracles they'd supposedly performed. People believed the gods could heal a disease. But where was the proof? Ramadas believed only in what he could see. He believed in science. He believed in doctors and their injections.

Like Das, Ramadas was a Dalit. As I got to know him, I realized that his atheism had been shaped by his experiences as a Dalit—by the discrimination he'd suffered and seen all his life, by the taunts and insults he'd been forced to bear as a young man. He'd grown up at a time of great oppression, before the awakening that Das had spoken to me about. Ramadas could remember standing outside the homes of upper castes as a boy, being forced to drink water from his hands so he wouldn't contaminate the household vessels. He was restricted to the colony; he wasn't allowed in the *ur*, the part of the village where the upper castes lived.

"I suffered a lot when I was young," Ramadas told me once. "My community was always being stared at, hassled, being called names. I tried not to let it bother me, but it's true that we were often very mistreated."

When Ramadas was around sixteen years old, he discovered the teachings of E. V. Ramasamy Naicker, or Periyar, a twentieth-century social reformer and activist considered by many to be the father of modern Tamil culture. Periyar ("great man," in Tamil) fought against social inequality, and in particular against caste and gender discrimination. He was a committed rationalist and atheist; he believed that religion was often used as a tool to oppress minorities and women.

Ramadas was deeply influenced by Periyar's teachings. He was struck by Periyar's observations that the discrimination faced by Dalits—as well as the religious justifications provided for it—was really just a way for the upper castes to maintain their dominance.

One night, Periyar gave a public lecture outside Tindivanam. Ramadas attended the lecture, along with a crowd of thousands. They assembled in the open air, under the stars and a half-moon. It was a hot night, without a breeze, and the speech was long. But Ramadas was riveted by what Periyar said.

Periyar pointed out to the crowd that they spent thousands of rupees on religion and gods, things that they didn't even know for sure existed. He said that religion was just a creation of the mind. He told the crowd not to waste their money. They should spend their money on their families and friends instead—things they knew were real, things they could touch.

Everyone was silent when Periyar spoke. Some people were offended. But, Ramadas told me decades later, he had been inspired.

Until then, he said, he had blindly followed what he was taught. "I was just a child," he told me. "What did I really know? I bowed down, I went to churches and temples, I sang songs, I said prayers. I was sixteen when I realized it was all wrong. I went to a temple one day with my parents, and I saw people untie their hair, shouting that they were possessed, that they had a god in them. I realized something was off, it just didn't make sense."

He started walking around the villages, going to barbershops and tea shops, preaching what he had learned from Periyar. In a loud voice, often in what he described as a "vulgar manner," he would proclaim his atheism. Sometimes people would get upset. They would beat their heads in despair. A few friends told him that it was fine if he wanted to believe in Periyar, but he should respect their belief in God.

"Why?" Ramadas would ask. "What proof do you have?" He would ask them how they knew that God existed. Had they ever seen anything, had any of their prayers ever worked? He laughed about one friend whose wife was unable to conceive and who was spending a fortune in offerings to the gods. Ramadas told him: "Why are you wasting your money? Just take her for a nice walk, go to the beach, feed her some fish or mutton, and make love to her nicely. Just sleep with her properly and you'll get children."

Ramadas said again it didn't bother him that his children and wife were religious. He respected their beliefs, and they respected his. Of one thing, though, he was certain. No matter how much they pleaded, he would never stop working as a cow broker.

"I'm a businessman," Ramadas said. "As long as my blood flows, I'll be in this business. Why should I do what anyone tells me? If I was a watchman or a mason, then I would have to answer to someone." He folded his hands as he said this, and looked up at the sky, like a supplicant. "But I'm independent, I'm my own king. If I have ten rupees in my pocket, it's my money. I earned it, I can spend it how I want."

Ramadas was unabashed about his atheism; he proclaimed it to anyone who would listen, and to many who would rather not. It wasn't unheard-of for a person to be an atheist, especially in the state of Tamil Nadu, where Periyar's rationalist movement had considerable influence. But it was rare, and it was even rarer for someone to advertise his atheism as loudly as Ramadas did.

The area around Molasur was profoundly religious, steeped in rites and rituals, dotted with temples and ancient shrines. Even most cow brokers, whose trade involved the slaughter of an ostensibly holy animal, were devout. For many modern Indians, there was no contradiction between eating beef and their religious beliefs. Social mores were changing, adherence to some specific religious precepts were perhaps easing; but religion, and in particular the Hindu religion, continued to play a central role in the public and private lives of the vast majority of Indians.

Krishnan told me once that he was scared to discuss religion with Ramadas. He said Ramadas would attack him, question him aggressively about the basis for his faith. Krishnan said Ramadas was so compelling that he worried Ramadas would manage to convert him to atheism. He was joking, of course, but I did wonder about how Ramadas navigated the religious world in which he lived. I wondered, especially, about his relations with his own family.

I visited Ramadas and his family in Chennai one time. He and his wife and their two grown children lived in a small one-bedroom apartment in the suburb of Ramavaram. Ramadas said that Ramavaram had once been posh, a country retreat for the city's elite. There were a few coconut trees left, reminders of an earlier, pastoral moment. But the ugly city had pretty much invaded. Like much of Chennai, Ramavaram was now a gritty collection of tightly hemmed-in apartments, uncovered gutters, and sandpiles for construction projects.

I visited the family on a Sunday afternoon. I sat with Ramadas and his son, R. Varunprasad, or Varun, in the living room. His wife, R. Malligeswari, a small, self-effacing woman, was in the kitchen, cooking eggplant pakoras. She walked in and out of the living room, batter dripping from her hands. Ramadas apologized for his daughter's absence. She had been called to her job at the last minute. Companies were like that these days; they expected people to work on weekends.

The family talked about their financial difficulties. They had monthly expenses of 15,000 to 20,000 rupees. Ramadas made only a couple thousand as a cow broker. Malligeswari, who worked in a leather company, made about the same amount. They were living off the daughter's 15,000-rupee salary. They barely managed to keep the household running.

They had two hopes for the future. The first was that Varun would get a good job. He was due to get his degree in a few months; he was hoping to go to Australia. The second hope was that their daughter would marry well. They had been searching for "a good alliance." They wanted someone from the city, someone cultured and educated, not too modern, but with good character.

Malligeswari stood at the entrance to the living room, one eye on her frying pakoras, and said: "If our son had lived, everything would be different. Life would be much easier for us—we wouldn't have to worry so much about money."

She told me how her son had died. It happened at five-forty in the morning. The bus driver who crashed into him had been driving all night; maybe he'd fallen asleep. Ramadas got a call from a traffic policeman, a relative, saying his son was in the hospital. When Ramadas got to the hospital, his son was already dead. He didn't have a single wound; he must have died from internal bleeding.

"If he had lived just three more months, he would have been working in Canada," Malligeswari said. "He had a job all arranged there."

"I would have gone to Canada with him," Ramadas said. "I would have moved there."

Malligeswari and Varun laughed. Malligeswari said Ramadas would never leave this area. He was a man of habit. She and the kids had been trying for years to get him to quit the cow business, but he was too stubborn. He wouldn't change his ways.

Varun was sitting on a low stool, just above the floor. I asked him if it was true that he disapproved of his father's profession.

"It's not like that," he said. He said he respected his father. He knew all the sacrifices his father had made; he'd lived a tough life. When his father was a young man, Varun said, he'd been offered a good job in the railways, but he'd been pressured to work in cows with his own father, and he'd never lived up to his potential.

Varun hadn't really answered my question, so I asked him again if he disapproved of his father's job. He said: "I am not a vegetarian, but for me it's a sin. What my father does is a kind of sin."

Malligeswari said: "See, I was brought up in Chennai, I was taught manners and culture. My family was very religious, and I want my children brought up the same way. I don't want them to eat beef, and I don't like it that my husband's business is beef."

Ramadas sat impassively through all of this; he'd heard it before. He smiled at his wife and told me: "I eat what I want to eat, she can eat what she wants. I told you already, I don't believe in all those things. What difference does it make if I eat beef or chicken? Who can say what's a sin?"

Malligeswari pointed to some shelves at the back of the kitchen. "You can see how religious I am," she said. The kitchen doubled as the family's *pooja* room. The shelves were stacked with about a dozen images of deities, many garlanded in flowers and rubbed with red powder. Above the deities was a framed picture of their dead son. It looked like a blown-up passport photo, with a blue background, wrapped in a garland of yellow marigold. The dead son resembled his brother; they had the same long face, inherited from their mother.

Malligeswari said that sometimes it was hard to live with a husband who didn't believe in any of these things. When their daughter had her first period, he refused to do the traditional puberty ceremony. When they went to temples, he stayed outside. Even after his own father died, he refused to participate in the one-year death anniversary ceremony. She had to take it upon herself to honor her father-in-law.

She told me about a time the family had gone on a pilgrimage to a temple, one of the holiest in South India. Ramadas went with his wife and children, but he refused to go into the temple. He rented a room in a lodge outside, and hung around watching TV while they waited to get in. The lines at the temple were long; they waited for three days and two nights before they could see the deity.

Malligeswari said she had a revelation in front of the deity. She remembered shivering, being covered in goose bumps. She prayed hard. She asked for things to work out for her family. She prayed for Varun to do well in school. She felt her prayers had been answered; despite some hardships, they had survived, her children had done well.

Ramadas laughed. "We gave him clothes, didn't we?" he asked. "We gave him books. He has a brain. He studied. That's why it worked out. It was our effort. Everyone goes and prays and asks the gods to help with their children—do they all do well? Do all the kids in this country get a good education?"

He turned to me. "These are all dogmatic thoughts," he said. "Look, it's very simple: I had to drop out of school because of my family. They didn't support my education. But this family supports education, and that's what made the difference in his life."

Malligeswari served us the pakoras. She opened a bottle of orange cola and insisted that I take a sip. I asked if she and her husband fought over their religious differences. She said that maybe in the early days they had, but never any longer. He didn't try to control her; she didn't control him.

"He lets me pray to whomever I want, so I also don't force him," she said. "He never says, 'Don't pray.' He never stopped me from teaching the kids about religion. You know, he may look rough, and he speaks harshly sometimes, but he's never tried to force me into anything. He has a soft heart, he's a good person."

"Still," Varun said from his stool on the floor, "I wish he would quit his work."

"Why?" I asked, and he told me that his father was getting old. He said his father hardly made any money anyway. It was too much work, and it just wasn't worth it.

"Is that the only reason?" I asked.

Varun hesitated. I could see he was trying to decide whether to say something. Then he said it: "When my brother had his accident, some relatives said it was because of my father's job. They said he died because of the work my father did."

"How did that make you feel?"

"I felt very bad. I felt very bad that people were talking that way."

"But did you believe it?"

Varun turned to his father; he looked like he was asking his father a question. "Maybe," he said, and he nodded. "Maybe something in me believed that that was why it happened."

I asked Malligeswari if she felt the same way. "I did wonder," she said. "I had to wonder, and sometimes I still wonder if that's why my son died."

Everyone was very calm; I didn't sense any animosity or conflict in the room. Ramadas's chin was up, like he was looking over his family's heads, at nothing in particular, maybe at the blue-green walls of his living room. I asked him how he felt when he heard that kind of thing. "I don't care," he said. "People might say that, but I don't believe it. It's nonsense. I told my son not to go out that early morning, I told him not to go driving in the dark. Had he listened to me, nothing would have happened to him. I don't think it had anything to do with my job. I don't care what people say. They can believe what they want."

"You don't care?" Varun asked. "What do you mean, you don't care?"

"You want to know the truth?" Ramadas said, and he looked at me. "The truth is it makes my heart feel hard. It makes me feel heavy.

"What can I say?" he said. "How do you think it makes me feel that my family believes my work killed my son?"

He said that when his son died, he participated in all the religious ceremonies. He was there at the traditional eleventh-day ceremony, where a priest came to their house and performed a *pooja*, and he sat with his relatives a year later, when another *pooja* took place. After the eleventh-day ceremony, he spread his son's ashes in the ocean. He tried to throw himself in the water; he wanted to die. His family members held him back.

He felt that all the *pooja*s and religiosity were wrong, meaningless. He didn't believe in any of the things he did at those ceremonies. But he did them because of what people might say. "I didn't want people to think I didn't care about my son," he said. "I didn't want them to say I didn't love him.

"So now, when you ask me how I feel, when you ask me to talk about my son and how he died, how do you think I feel?" He put his hand on his chest, flattened his palm against his heart. "It pains me here," he said. "It hurts. That's how I feel."

*Sathy, Krishnan, and I went to another shandy in Brah-*madesan. Sathy had told me that Krishnan was becoming one of the biggest cow brokers in the region, bigger even than Ramadas, and I wanted to see him in operation.

We went too late. It was almost noon by the time we got to Brahmadesan, and the show was over. There were still a few traces of the morning's business—piles of dung, some straw—but, apart from a small group of vendors packing up in the corner, pretty much everyone had moved on.

I thought I'd sit in the shade of a tree and catch up with Sathy and Krishnan. But there were no trees remaining, and no shade. A real estate developer had recently bought eighty acres of land in the area, including the clearing where the shandy was held. He'd cut down all the trees around the clearing. He'd flattened the surrounding fields, and reduced a nearby forest to a graveyard of stumps.

Standing under the sun, sweat streaming down his face, Krishnan said: "I have been coming to this market since I was a boy. Those trees have always been here. The first time that I saw they were cut, my heart felt heavy. Then I saw how the fields were also going. I felt very bad.

"Before, a man could at least plant his land with peanuts or tomatoes or rice and keep his stomach full," he said. "Even a small farm can feed a family for months. Now there's no land for agriculture anymore."

Krishnan said that whenever he visited vegetable and fruit markets in the area, when he saw how prices were rising, he felt anxious. He knew that farmers everywhere were being forced by financial hardship to sell their land. It had happened to him; he could understand the pressures. Throughout India, farms were turning into real estate. Some people were getting rich off the deals, but Krishnan felt many more would go hungry.

We stood on that denuded land, under a harsh midday sun, and we talked a little about my visit to Ramadas's apartment. I told Krishnan that I had been taken aback by Ramadas's atheism. He laughed. He said that as far back as he could remember, Ramadas had always been that way. He didn't even talk to Ramadas about religion anymore. Sathy laughed, too, but his laugh was less mirthful, more guarded. I felt Sathy couldn't quite believe some of the things Ramadas had said, how he had been reluctant even to perform religious ceremonies for his dead father and son.

I asked Sathy if he was offended by Ramadas's atheism. "No, not offended," Sathy said. "After all, I have to respect his beliefs the same way he respects his family's. Maybe a few years ago I might have been more upset. But these days, Akash, anything is okay in this country. People do whatever they want. Even people who proclaim their religion, who shout it so loud, often it's just for show. So who am I to judge? It's very difficult to know what's right and wrong anymore."

"The only thing I can say," Sathy went on, "is that Ramadas is lucky he lives today. He has lots of ways to make a living, which is a good thing for him. Before, he would have had no choice but to be a farmer. And one thing I know: A farmer can't be an atheist. We see God everywhere—in the seasons, in the crops, in the harvest. We have to believe in God. So in a way, Ramadas is a modern man. It's good for him that he lives at a time when no one cares about farming. These days you don't need to believe in God to survive."

I walked around the market by myself for a while. I went to the edge of the clearing, to a pile of stumps from ancient tamarind trees, and I stepped out of the clearing, to a field that had been green the last time I was there, but was now barren.

At one corner of the shandy, in the meager shade of a shrub, I found an old man, a farmer, hunched over. He was a tall, skinny man, with thinning hair and a white beard. He had a brown cow with him. Her eyes were gentle, sweet, but she, too, looked old, and not very healthy.

I sat on the ground with the man, and he told me his story. His name was Kathirvel. He was sixty-seven years old. He'd been coming to this market for forty years. He had come to the shandy today because he needed a new cow for his farm, but he'd been forced to confront the fact that he could no longer afford cows. The prices were too high.

Kathirvel's story was a variation on a story I'd heard many times—from small farmers like him, from big farmers like Sathy, and from former farmers like Krishnan. It was a story I had heard, too, from people like Ramadas, men who recognized the crisis of agriculture in the region, who worried about it and bemoaned it, yet who were also in a sense beneficiaries of it. As Kathirvel told me about his troubles, I found myself thinking of just how complicated the concept of progress was, how uneven the process of development transforming the countryside.

Kathirvel listed the woes confronting agriculture: declining water tables and soil fertility, rising input prices, a lack of support from the government, a general lack of interest among the population, especially the young. He said he had five children, three daughters and two sons. None of them made much money, but they weren't interested in the family farm. He had asked them many times to come back and take over, but they said anything was better than agriculture.

"My children all say farming has no future," Kathirvel said, and he stood up, pulled his cow by her rope. She hobbled to her feet. Kathirvel told me again he'd come to the market to buy a cow. Now, when he saw how expensive they had become, he thought maybe he'd be selling his cow instead. She was his only livestock. They'd been together for more than twelve years. The thought that she might be slaughtered, and then eaten, was a hard one to bear. But what choice did he have? At least, he said, if he sold her he'd have food on his family's plate for a few months.

"And after that?" I asked him.

"After that," he said. He seemed to hesitate. "After that, what else can I do? I will have to hope that there is still a God who watches over farmers."

GARDEN CITY

Banu, Sathy's wife, wanted to live in the city. She wanted to be somewhere modern—somewhere where there was life, where she could have a career, where her kids could go to good schools. She wanted to live unfettered by the constraints of village tradition.

She had invited me, at that Pongal lunch, to visit her in Bangalore, and I stopped by her family home one time, on a trip to the city. She lived with her mother, and her two brothers and their families, in the neighborhood of Kamanhalli. They lived in a big house, with thick walls and stone floors, set in a compounded garden dominated by a shady peepal tree. The house had been built by Banu's father in the eighties. It was grand; it had ten bedrooms.

A couple of decades ago, when the house was being built, Kamanhalli was a village at the edge of a city. In the pockets of alleyways and low, plastered houses that had survived the Bangalore real estate onslaught, parts of the neighborhood still had a rural feel. Kids played naked in the mud. Housewives beat their laundry against stones on unpaved streets. Stray dogs, their ears upright, burrowed in piles of garbage.

But Kamanhalli wasn't a village anymore. Bangalore was at the epicenter of India's technology boom, and the city had exploded in recent years. It had extended into the surrounding countryside, subsuming villages and farms and forests. First Kamanhalli had become a suburb, and then the suburb was absorbed into the city. Now Kamanhalli was a thriving, prosperous neighborhood in one of India's most thriving, prosperous towns.

Banu walked me around Kamanhalli one morning. She showed me the houses and stores that had come up since she was a girl. She showed me the fields that had been turned into motorcycle repair shops, the mango orchard that had given way to an orange mansion that belonged to a government official.

Many of the buildings Banu showed me had been built on plots of land that used to belong to her family. Her father was a shrewd investor; he bought when land was cheap, and now the family was wealthy. Banu showed me a white building with an asbestos roof. It was the office of an electronics vendor now, but it was where she had lived when she was a girl. It was decidedly more humble than the current family home.

"It used to be all farmland around here," Banu said, waving her hand over the city landscape. "This was a rural area, it was wild. We used to be scared."

Back at her house, she showed me a freshly painted shed in the garden, under the peepal tree. The shed had a sign on it that said "Anvikshaki Research, Training and Counselling Center." Anvikshaki refers to a branch of traditional learning in ancient Indian philosophy. Banu ran her consulting business out of the shed.

She had started the business soon after returning from Molasur. She taught what she called "soft skills" to employees at some of Bangalore's leading companies. She taught them to handle international customer queries, and she helped them improve their language skills. Oddly, because Banu's accent was distinctly local, she taught them how to talk in American and English accents.

Banu's business was doing well. She told me she was making good money. But she also said she worked hard for her money. She got up at six-thirty in the morning, spent hours driving around the city, stuck in Bangalore's interminable traffic jams. Often, she didn't get back home till seven-thirty in the evening, after which she had to cook dinner, feed and bathe the kids, and then put them to sleep. She didn't usually get to bed until past eleven.

She was proud of what she was achieving. She liked being financially independent. She told me: "I used to try to play the role of the typical old housewife, holding Sathy's hand and giving up my life. I thought that was how I had to be. But now I know that I can stand up for myself. I'm very bold. Sometimes, in the past, when I had no money, I used to depend on my family, and they had a hold over me. People would try to control me. But today I stand up and tell my family, 'I don't care what you say. It's my life, and I run my life.'"

Banu attributed her independent streak to her father. He had always encouraged her to be her own woman. He had pushed her to get an education. She had gone to college in Bangalore, getting first an engineering degree, and then an MBA. Now, she said, she could live life on her own terms. She enjoyed the freedom.

Still, as she showed me around the neighborhood, and then as she invited me back to her house and served me lunch under the green walls of her living room, I felt Banu was perhaps a little less clear about her freedom than she let on. She said a couple times that she was "bold," and she said it proudly, unapologetically. But she told me, too, that she was worried about the long hours she spent away from her children. She said she was determined to seize her career, make something of herself. But she said, also, that for her, family came first.

"I prefer to be at home, a *pakka* wife," she told me. "There's so much I'd like to give the kids. I'd like to be with the family. If Sathy had a business he could travel around and I could stay at home with Darshan and Thaniya. Consulting is going well, but it's tough for the kids. They need me."

"But I thought you were worried you would lose your identity if you were just a housewife," I said to her.

"So what?" she said. "If I want my identity, then why get married in the first place? If I want my own identity, then there's no need to be married. A woman needs to give herself to her family and not be obsessed with her identity. We ape the West. People read the papers and they're full of women's equality. But what is equality? Is equality just about making the same amount of money as in the West?"

I told her she sounded unsure of what she wanted. She said she wasn't. She knew exactly what she wanted. She was just forced to play the career woman because of Sathy's shortcomings. She said Sathy poured everything he had into his land, into farming, and it was a waste of time and money. He needed to get out of agriculture; he needed to get a job, a career.

"I believe in families. I was brought up that way. I believe kids should be with two parents," she said. "I really do. But what can I do if I have a husband who can't get it together, who runs around without settling down?

"Sathy's so attached to his fields. I've told him a hundred times to forget his land. I've told him there's no future in farming. He won't listen. The truth is, I don't need any of this city stuff—all the Mercedes, the ten cars, the big houses. I don't need any of it. I could even move back to the village."

"You'd walk away from your business?" I asked.

She said: "Maybe I could live in Molasur and travel to Bangalore for work. You know, I already gave up the embroidery business. Things are just starting to go well now; it's really the right time to be building a business in Bangalore. I think I have a long way to go. I would regret it if I quit again."

We were standing outside the shed from which she ran her business. Once, she and Sathy had talked about tearing down the shed and building a home there. That was when it seemed Sathy might move to Bangalore. That was before the family was divided.

"No, I'm not ready to walk away," Banu said. "But I believe there has to be a way to combine the two. Why do I have to choose—can't I have my family and still build a career?"

Speaking about his marriage one time, Sathy said to me: "Banu and I care about each other, we try so hard to make it work, but at the end of the day maybe I'm too old-fashioned for her. I'm a farmer. She's modern. Career will always matter to her. I don't know if she could ever live in the village."

I asked Banu if she agreed with Sathy's assessment of her. She hesitated, she demurred. She said she was committed to her family. She said maybe Sathy was correct. But then she said she wasn't sure.

I thought things were a little bit more complicated than Sathy made them out to be. He was right that Banu cared about her career. But it was clear, too, that she cared deeply about her family, and that she was determined to be a mother to her children. Banu was indeed a modern woman—but her modernity lay precisely in her confusion, in the tug she felt between career and family, between the city and the village.

It wasn't easy being a woman in the new India. Banu's generation was the first to be told it was all right, desirable even, to work outside the home. They were the first to have the option of a career. That option was a form of liberation; it came as emancipation. But it was also a burden, or at any rate a challenge. Banu—and millions of women like her—were following an untrodden path. They didn't always know where they wanted to go.

When Banu talked about her clients and her business and the way it was growing, I sensed pride. I saw ambition. But when she talked about her family, when she complained about the long hours she worked and the way the kids needed her, I sensed ambivalence and even anxiety. Sometimes I could see the anxiety on her face. Her eyes—she had big, round eyes—would narrow; her brow would fold up into a little ridge.

I felt that cities like Bangalore exacerbated the ambivalence. They nurtured the ambition, but they also fed the anxiety. A city—a nation, a moment—so full of possibility could not be denied. India was alight with opportunity. No matter how much a woman wanted to stay home and raise her children, no matter how attached she felt to her family, it was hard to turn away from all the excitement outside the home.

So many women I talked to—successful, accomplished women, women who loved their jobs and felt proud of their achievements—told me that in a way, things had been simpler for their mothers and aunts and grandmothers. They never had to choose. They never had the option of a career. And although this lack of choice was a kind of imprisonment—"slavery," as one woman put it—it was also enviable, like a balm for the anxiety felt by so many women today.

I spoke to Banu once in Molasur. She was taking a break from Bangalore and her business, bringing the family together for a few weeks. When we met, I thought at first she seemed a little bored, maybe restless. She talked about jobs in the cities, about flights she would normally be catching to Hyderabad and Chennai. But when I asked her how she felt being so far away from it all, her answer surprised me.

She said she felt calm. In Bangalore, she said, she was always tense, perpetually trying to balance her personal and professional lives. Now, although she knew that she was missing out on business, losing clients and money while she sat in a sleepy village, she felt at ease.

"I feel peaceful," she told me. "It's strange, but I feel settled."

India was booming; its options and possibilities were seductive, almost irresistible. I felt this myself whenever I visited Bangalore, when I considered the life I might lead if I lived somewhere like there. Amid the plenitude and dynamism of India's metropolises, it was easy to wonder if living in the countryside (or, indeed, staying at home with the family) was a mistake. Sometimes I felt like I was sitting outside history, missing out on a once-in-a-lifetime chance to participate in the remaking of a nation.

It was hard to believe now, but I could remember a time when Bangalore was little more than a sleepy town. It had always been a cosmopolitan place, but when I was a boy, it felt like an overgrown hill station, a holiday destination where the air was cool, the girls wore jeans, and the draft beer ran plentiful. My friends and I would take a bus from Auroville for the weekend. We'd visit the city's ubiquitous pubs, we'd sit around one of the many parks. Bangalore was a green town. It was known as the Garden City.

Already back then, though, in the seventies and the eighties, Bangalore was emerging as a hub of India's technology industry. It was home to the government's aerospace company, and to the country's main space research lab. In the 1970s, the state set up one of India's leading technology parks, in Bangalore. All of this laid the foundations for the stunning growth of the city's software and technology businesses after India's economic reforms.

By the time I returned to India, shortly after the turn of the millennium, Bangalore was known as India's Silicon Valley. It was one of the fastest growing cities in the world. But it was also so much more than a city. It was a verb (to be "Bangalored" was to lose your Western job to outsourcing), and it was a metaphor—an emblem of the new, shining India, a totem to global capitalism.

It was, too, a magnet: for the millions of young Indians who migrated to the city, who were drawn by the abundance of jobs and careers, Bangalore was an opportunity to reinvent themselves. Between the early nineties and the mid-2000s, Bangalore's population grew 150 percent, from around four to six million. More than a third of the city's population were first-generation migrants.

These migrants came from across India, and from around the world. Bangalore had one of India's largest expatriate populations. Every time I saw these men and women, crowding into the city's pubs and restaurants, filling the air with their chatter of dialects and languages and accents, the thought came to me that Bangalore was India's America: a chance at a new life, a beacon on a hill that attracted the young and the ambitious and the talented from across the globe.

In Bangalore, I got to know one migrant to the city, a young woman named Veena Sharma. She was in her mid-thirties, a marketing professional with wavy black hair and a small mouth that puckered up, like a bird's, when she smiled. She had grown up in Jaipur, in the northern state of Rajasthan. She moved to Bangalore in the winter of 2006.

Before moving to Bangalore, Veena had lived for a time in a small town near Chennai. She had lived with her boyfriend, a man named Arvind, in a two-bedroom apartment by the ocean. They had good jobs; they had comfortable lives. But after a while, they decided they wanted more than comfortable lives.

I knew Veena a little bit before she moved to Bangalore. We hadn't spent much time together. We'd see each other at a restaurant or a shop sometimes, nod in mutual recognition, maybe say hi. But we had a lot of friends in common, and after she moved I kept hearing from them about how well she and Arvind were doing—how they'd gotten jobs right away, how they'd already been promoted, how they were earning so much money.

I looked Veena up on one of my trips to the city. We met, on a smoggy April evening, in a coffee shop near the center of town.

The coffee shop was in an old Victorian building with stone walls. It was a noisy, smoky place, and when Veena showed up, late, dressed in blue jeans and white sneakers, I could hardly hear her over the din of college students and radio music. I suggested we go to a quieter place. But where, in a city like Bangalore, do you find a corner of silence? Outside, the roar of traffic was overpowering, and every restaurant or coffee shop we looked into was equally smoky, loud, and crowded.

We ended up in Cariappa Park, a twenty-two-acre expanse of green in the heart of the city. There weren't too many people around, just a few middle-aged couples, men in shorts and women in pants, on evening walks. The sounds of traffic and commerce felt far away, softened by the trees.

"I love the parks in Bangalore," Veena said, and I agreed. But the truth was that the trees didn't seem to be in very good shape. They were droopy and pallid. Many were denuded, their dead leaves scattered around. I thought the gardens in the Garden City were dying.

We sat on the ground, Veena on the brick ledge of a flower bed, and I on a newspaper. "I've never been in here before," I said, and Veena said she hadn't, either. She'd been in Bangalore only a few months; she was still getting to know the city.

She said that she and Arvind spent the weekends exploring; it was one of the best things about living in a new place. They went to shopping malls, to movie theaters, and they tried new restaurants. Arvind, who had never lived in a big city before, had tasted Japanese and Thai food for the first time. The variety, the diversity of people and experiences, was exhilarating.

Things were going well for them; I could tell they'd landed on their feet. They'd found an apartment they liked, and jobs that were satisfying. She worked at a technology start-up. He worked with a retail franchise, helping to set up new stores. She said they were learning a lot. The pay was good, too; combined, they were earning twice as much as they had been before moving to Bangalore.

She was, in fact, about to switch jobs. She would soon be starting at an advertising company. She hadn't gone looking for the job; they'd found her. Now, she said, they were going to pay her "obscene amounts of money." At the interview, they asked how much she wanted, and when she named her price, they just threw on an extra 70,000 rupees to her package.

She never really imagined she could make so much. She had moved to Bangalore hoping she could improve her prospects, but she didn't think it would happen so quickly. She knew it was only money, but still, she said, it gave her a real sense of accomplishment.

"The money is important," she told me. She put her hand gently on my forehead, pressed it down. The park was full of mosquitoes.

"The money is important because you need it, but also because, in the end, it's a measure of achievement. That's the way it is. In a place like Bangalore, the kind of money you're earning tells you where you are and where you've reached. It gives you a kind of value."

Even more important than the money, she said, was "the power." She would be managing fourteen men in her new job. That would be an experience.

"Power is good," she said, laughing. "I grew up with this very Indian concept that a woman doesn't do a lot of things. I grew up thinking that a woman was essentially less than her husband. So of course the power gives me a kind of high—knowing that I'm doing equally well or better than all these men, and knowing that they have to listen to me."

She laughed again. She said: "I know I probably sound power hungry, like one of those Western women in pantsuits you see on TV or whatever. Well, you can see I'm not like that. But still, sometimes when I watch them, I think they're on to something."

It wasn't strictly true that the current generation of Indian women was the first to work outside the home. As far back as I can remember, I have always seen and known Indian women working in shops, offices, hospitals, farms, and markets. My aunt, now in her late sixties, has worked as a doctor all her professional life. My grandmother worked in an embroidery workshop even during the 1950s.

Women have always worked in agriculture. When I was a boy, it was mainly women, their saris stained red with mud, sometimes a wet cloth covering their heads to protect them from the sun, that I saw bent over in the fields around Auroville.

Of course the number of working women has increased as the economy has changed. (Between 1981 and 2001, the percentage of women in the workforce grew from 19.7 percent to 25.7 percent.) Although a formidable glass ceiling remains—and although India continues to perform abysmally on global rankings of gender equality—pay for women employees has also increased over the last few decades. But the real change is in the way women approach their jobs, and in the significance those jobs have for their lives.

Veena told me one time that when she was younger, in her twenties, she had a job as a customer agent in Jaipur. She said that virtually all the customer agents in her office were women. It was seen as female work—placating customers, calming them down. She said she did the work primarily as a "time-pass kind of thing." It didn't mean much to her. She did it for a little pocket money, to get out of the house, for a small sense of independence.

This, in Veena's opinion, was the big difference between the way women worked now and the way they had worked before. In the past, women took jobs primarily to supplement the household income, or maybe to get away from the house or a bad marriage. Now women took jobs because they were ambitious—because they wanted to build careers, because they wanted independence, or quite simply because they wanted power.

From a "time-pass" thing, work had become a vehicle for self-expression, and even self-creation. "You get defined when your career does well," Veena told me. "If you do well at what you're good at, then you become a better person. It defines you in your own eyes, and also the eyes of others."

Veena was certainly ambitious. It was one of the first things that struck me as I got to know her. She complained that some people saw her as "aggressive," and it's true that she had a gentle side, a caring personality that seemed always to be worried about or supporting friends in need. But I could see why people might think she was aggressive; when it came to work, to getting ahead, she exuded a kind of clarity, a single-mindedness and sense of purpose that I thought was in many ways characteristic of the new Indian generation.

She was ambitious for herself, and she was ambitious for Arvind. She told me that the first time she met him, he was working as a salesman in the town where she was living with her husband. She felt right away that he was a man with potential, that he could really make something of himself—if only he could escape the narrow horizons of the small town where he had grown up.

Arvind and his college friends would go out late on weekends, and often on weekdays. They'd get drunk, get into brawls with strangers. He didn't take his job seriously. It was frustrating to Veena. She felt he was bogged down, restricted by the pettiness of his world.

When they moved to Bangalore, Veena was determined to help Arvind grow beyond that pettiness. She helped him adjust to city life. She taught him how to dress formally, how to talk to colleagues at work, and how to conduct himself in interviews. She felt he was sometimes a little too easygoing; it was her role to make him more disciplined.

Now, she said, Arvind was flourishing. He, too, was about to start a new job, and it was a big job. He'd been hired as the head of retail at one of Bangalore's largest shopping malls. He would be managing tens of thousands of square feet of shops, and hundreds of people. It was a major step up for him.

Arvind told me one time about how he got that job. He said that Veena had encouraged him to try for it. So he applied, he went through a few rounds of interviews, and then one night a woman called him and asked if he'd come out to the company's headquarters for a final round. It was about eight p.m. The headquarters were far out of town. Arvind told the woman he could come only the next morning.

When he called Veena, who was at work, and told her what he'd said to the woman, Veena asked him if he was crazy. She told him it was a test; they were gauging his level of commitment. She told him to head straight home, get dressed, and wait for her. She left work early and met him at their apartment, and they took a taxi together to the interview.

After the interview, the woman who had called, the head of human resources for the company, confirmed that the call was a test. Arvind said he passed his test because of Veena.

He told me this one afternoon at the mall, as he gave me a tour of the area he managed. The mall was impressive, new and airy, filled with natural light. We were standing outside a row of fashion stores, with sparrows circling and chirping at our feet. Arvind said they lived in the mall.

I asked him if he thought Veena was more ambitious than he was. "Yes, definitely," he said. "Much more. She's much more confident than I am to go for things." He smiled when he told me that. He had a pleasant, relaxed smile. He was, as Veena said, easygoing.

Once, I asked Veena where she got her confidence. We were sitting in the garden of a hotel, having a coffee. She put her cup down, wiped her lips, and smiled. She said she'd been asked a very similar question recently, in a job interview. The interviewer had looked at her résumé and pointed out that she lacked an MBA, the typical qualification at the position for which she'd applied.

"Why should we hire you?" the interviewer asked.

"It's very simple," Veena told him. "People like me don't know anything about anything, so we end up being very fast learners all the time. You can throw us into anything and we'll manage very well."

The interviewer asked Veena where she got her confidence. She told me she gave him a generic answer, something about her parents and hard work and determination. Now, sitting with me in that hotel, she said that the truth was that she didn't really know; she wasn't sure how she had ended up believing in herself.

But one thing she did know: She hadn't always been that way.

Before getting together with Arvind, Veena had been married to another man for six years. She'd never believed in herself during that time; she was neither confident nor ambitious. She said her mother had always been a housewife. She figured she'd be the same.

In Jaipur, her husband was the breadwinner. She cooked his meals, organized his laundry, supported his career. When his company, an engineering firm, posted him to Chennai, she followed despite her misgivings about moving so far from friends and family.

She became what she called a "full-time housewife." She stayed at home and did the chores. She supervised the servants, she cleaned up. One day her father visited from Jaipur. He surprised her in the middle of the afternoon. He found her mopping the floor. He asked what was happening to her. "Why are you sitting around doing this with your life?" he asked. "Is this why you got an education?"

His questions got Veena thinking; she decided maybe she should get a job. She interviewed for a position at a store. She started as a personal assistant, but she was quickly promoted. She got a lot of praise at work; she started making decent money. "It was the first time I started thinking I was smart," she told me. "I mean, I'd thought I was smart in other ways—I was a good dancer or a good sister or good at relationships—but I never thought I was smart in that way. I never imagined I could have a career. It was just not something I had considered."

As Veena's self-confidence went up, her marriage went down. Things had already been tough in Jaipur. She'd married a childhood friend; she had her doubts from the start, but she didn't have the confidence to resist her family's pressure. She hoped for the best. Soon, though, she found out that she and her husband were incompatible in many ways. The "physical side" of the marriage wasn't working, she said, and, perhaps as a consequence, they bickered a lot.

Things got worse when Veena started working. Her success seemed to threaten her husband. She said that if she stayed out late, he'd get upset. When, at a subsequent job, she was sent to Europe, he seemed unhappy with the way she was building her own life. Veena said her husband was a good man, but they just seemed to have different ideas of their roles in the marriage.

One night there was a big scene at home. Veena was on the

sofa, sick with a fever. Her husband got angry about something she said. He kicked a table. The table broke and a piece grazed Veena's shoulder. She felt she had to get out. It was raining outside.

She started walking, getting drenched in the rain, still burning from her fever. She searched for a phone booth. A man on a cycle crashed into her and groped her breast. She felt violated—violated at home, violated in the street. She said she never cried, but on this occasion she was in tears. She found a phone booth and called her parents. She told them her marriage was over. She asked them never to press her again to try to make it work. She said it was irretrievable.

Soon after that, she asked her husband for a divorce. He refused, but they moved into separate bedrooms. Her parents were also opposed to the idea of a divorce. Her father told her she needed psychiatric help. Her mother came down south to convince her daughter that these things didn't happen in families like theirs.

By then, Veena was already living with Arvind. Their relationship started as a casual affair, but, to her surprise, had grown into something more serious. When Veena's husband found a job in another city, Arvind moved in. Her mother was scandalized. At some point during her trip, she took her daughter aside and asked her: "Why are you doing this?"

Veena said: "What's wrong with what I'm doing? Do you realize that I can sleep with any man I want, and I don't have to stay with any of them? I want to check things out this time. If I ever marry again, and I'm not at all sure I'm going to marry Arvind, I want to stay with the man this time. You should know that my generation can choose to sleep with a man and not marry him; it's our choice."

Her mother wasn't happy. "I mean, I think she's only been with one man in her life," Veena told me. "She gets upset when she thinks I've slept with more than one person. We don't talk about it too much, but she knows in the back of her mind what I've been doing. Her feelings are always written on her face."

"What does she look like?" I asked.

"It's hard to describe the look. I guess it's a little bit of disgust and a lot of disbelief."

It took three years for Veena to get a divorce. At the court hearing, she was accompanied by her brother. She hugged her husband when he arrived. She hadn't seen him in almost two years. He had shaved his mustache. She told him he looked good.

The judge told Veena to think carefully about what she was doing. He reminded her that in India, divorce still carried a social stigma. He asked if she was sure she wanted to go through with it, and she said yes. She and her husband signed the papers, and he broke down in tears. She patted him on the back. She felt empty.

Veena told me later that she went through a difficult period around the time she was getting divorced. People thought she was crazy; they thought she didn't know what she was doing. Her family and friends wondered how she would support herself. People questioned her decision to live with Arvind, and then, when they moved to Bangalore, they thought she was making another mistake. They didn't think she'd be able to make it in the city.

But now, she said, everyone could see she'd come out all right. "I took some risks, and they paid off," she said. Maybe it was this—this experience of being doubted, of taking chances, of trusting her instincts and seeing them vindicated—that had made her confident. "If you take some risky decisions and you end up okay, then people realize you're smart," she said. "They don't doubt you anymore. You don't doubt yourself."

Recently, her father had called. He said he and his wife had been talking about her. They were discussing the fact that their daughter had been through some difficult times. But they had to acknowledge that she had persevered; she hadn't just succumbed to the circumstances of her life.

He told her: "You know, we are so proud of all that you've achieved. We feel we have something to learn from you."

Banu and Veena were in Bangalore for similar reasons: they were drawn by the city's opportunities, by the jobs and the chance to find a little freedom. But they were different in so many ways. They dressed differently—Veena in jeans and T-shirts, Banu always in a sari—and they talked differently. Veena swore liberally. Banu was much more discreet. It would have been unthinkable for her to speak about sex as freely as Veena did. It would have been unimaginable for her to live openly with a boyfriend.

Veena's life seemed simpler to me—less burdened by tradition, less encumbered by family and society. She was a little bit younger than Banu, and I thought that maybe she had been born just on the easier—or at any rate more modern—side of a generational divide. She didn't seem bothered by the same ambivalence and self-doubt that sometimes seemed to haunt Banu. In many ways, she was like a lot of women I had known in New York: just a girl in the city, navigating the shoals of love and career.

Then one day Veena and I took a trip together to the suburb of

Whitefield, an emerging hub of Bangalore's software industry, and on the way, stuck in traffic, with diesel fumes curling outside our air-conditioned taxi, she told me: "You know, sometimes I feel that it was actually simpler for our parents. I think of my mother. There was no question of her ever working outside the house. In a way, it was all clearer for her. For us, everything's so mixed up. We have so many options, so many things we can do. Choice is supposed to be good, but sometimes I wonder."

We had been talking about her relationship with Arvind. One of the wonderful things about living in Bangalore, she said, was the way they were thriving as a couple. Before, she'd always felt they were just sharing an apartment. Now, when they went shopping together, when they cooked meals or did the household chores together, she felt like they were sharing a home.

Recently, inevitably, their families had started putting pressure on them to get married. Arvind's parents, in particular, were unhappy about the fact that their son was living with a girlfriend. They wanted grandchildren.

I asked Veena if she wanted children. "It's complicated," she said. "I'm actually very confused. You see, I have this little problem: I'm not a man, and if I have a kid, I have to have it inside me. I can't outsource it. So I really don't know what to do.

"I like my job, I'm still learning, and I still have place to move up. You know, the way the market works is, you get a price if you are in something pricey. I feel like I'm only getting going. If I quit now, before I'm at my full earning potential, then I won't earn as much when I come back."

Veena had recently started yet another job, this one at a software company. It was her third job in just over a year and a half;

her salary and level of responsibility kept going up. She said she had so much further to go; she couldn't really imagine having kids now. But if not now, then when? She wondered when the right moment would come along.

She said various aunts and uncles had been calling, asking when she was going to have a child. Veena didn't know what to say to them. "See, my whole point of view about motherhood is inspired by my own mother, who I think is the best mother one could ever hope for," she told me. "She gave up most of her life for us, and I feel we turned out to be decent kids. She worked really hard. I know that being a mother isn't just a time-pass kind of thing. I've seen some time-pass parents, and I've found that the kids go very wrong. My mother wasn't like that—she slogged her butt off.

"But you know, when I was old enough to understand about jobs and careers and so on, I looked at my mother and I saw that there were probably moments in her life where she felt she didn't do enough with herself. I realized that she actually had a streak of dissatisfaction, which as kids we never understood. I don't think she ever saw having a job as an option. Maybe that made it simpler for her. But now when I think about her, I think, 'What a waste, a woman like her just sitting at home.'"

"And so how does that make you feel?" I asked. "Does that make you less likely to have kids?"

"I guess so," she said. "I can't think of a situation where I wouldn't work. My mother sits around in her fifties, with all the elements of a successful working professional, and thinks, 'Why didn't I do it? Why didn't I make it?' She doesn't have a very happy existence. But you know, I guess there's a chance I might get old and have the opposite problem: 'Why didn't I have kids? Why didn't I do it?' I guess I'll have my own not-so-happy existence."

She said sometimes she just felt resigned to the fact that she wasn't going to lead the "typical woman's life"—whatever that meant. She'd always been a bit strange anyway, a bit different. After all, she'd gotten divorced, she'd slept with men while unmarried. For some reason, she hadn't lived the way a woman in India was expected to.

"Why do you think that is?" I asked her.

"I have no clue," she said, and she started giggling. "It all came very naturally to me. I mean, sex is the most natural stepping-stone to liking a person. I never got what the big deal was about it. How can I explain this to you? Maybe let me crystallize it into a very simple example. If I'm hungry, I'll eat, right? I grew up in a traditional family. I never ate pork or beef. The first time I had pork was when I was in Europe and I was dying for something non-vegetarian. I was so sick of cheese and bread. So I said, 'Just let me put a piece of ham into this bread and see how it tastes.' It tasted fine. My point is this: If you're hungry, you will eat. If you want a man, you will sleep. That's how it works in my mind."

"So simple?" I asked.

"Yeah, it's a very basic instinct. Look, this is how my life works. I've found that I go in cycles—sometimes I feel very carnal and have spells of maybe what we might call debauchery. And then there are periods of time when I just feel more spiritual, and I live a much more basic life. That's just the way it is with me. It's who I am. It may sound weird to others, I know it shocks some people. But to me, it's very natural."

In Whitefield, at a restaurant in the basement of the International Tech Park, Veena and I had a snack. The International Tech Park was a massive building. It was a self-contained world, with laundromats and banks and an attached hotel. It had more than 2 million square feet of built-up space. It dwarfed anything I had seen in Chennai. It was testament to Bangalore's status as the center of India's technology industry.

We complained about the ride over. What should have been a half-hour trip from the city had turned into almost an hour and a half. Traffic had been impossible. At the edge of Bangalore, before the roads opened up a bit, gave way to the relative ease of the suburbs, the cars and vans and autorickshaws were packed so tight that even motorcyclists were stuck, unable to squeeze through.

Veena said it was the worst part about living in Bangalore. Sometimes, she said, it took her forty minutes to make the five-kilometer trip from her house to her office. It was maddening. It was impossible to plan anything.

Whitefield was more pleasant. It was still a suburb, green and relatively uncongested. In Whitefield, you felt like you could breathe. Veena said she and Arvind talked occasionally about moving there. It would be a good place to bring up kids, I said, and she sighed. "Kids again," she said. "Why is it that every conversation I have these days seems to come back to kids?"

I asked her what Arvind felt about having kids. She said he wasn't putting any pressure on her. He was very relaxed; she was lucky to have found a modern guy. In fact, now that she'd started her new job, they had agreed to put everything on hold. They tried not to talk about kids anymore.

She told me about the day she found out she had gotten the new job. When she came home and told Arvind, he said he was happy for her. He was proud of her. They talked about how the job would change their lives. They thought maybe they'd get a new apartment, move into a bigger place. Then Arvind, who had had a couple drinks, asked: "What about that other thing? You want to get into it now, or you want to wait, or what?"

She wasn't sure what he meant at first. Then, when she realized he was talking about kids, she told him she wasn't sure. She hadn't expected to get this job, and now she didn't know what to do. He changed the topic. They didn't talk about it anymore that night.

A few days later, Arvind brought it up again. He told Veena: "If you don't want to have kids, it's fine with me. I'll just adopt one."

Veena said she found his attitude refreshing. She appreciated how understanding he was about the whole thing. I said it sounded like he was maybe more concerned than he was letting on. He didn't sound that relaxed about it to me.

She thought for a moment. "Maybe," she said. "Maybe you're right. But he's got a point, you know. I guess I can't go on like this. I guess I better start figuring out what I want. I'm acting like a horse with blinkers on. I don't want to see the dilemma, I don't want to face the problem. I know it will just confuse me and I'll get all riled up. But I guess I can't avoid it. I need to look at the issue more closely.

"At some point, I'm really going to have to make a decision, or at least put a time frame on things. I can't just go on like this, drifting, forever."

Banu had pulled her children out of their school in the city. She'd put them in a Montessori school outside town. The new school was set on the grounds of a five-acre farm. It was green, the air was breathable, and there wasn't a car or bus in sight.

Like Veena—like pretty much everybody I knew in Bangalore—Banu complained about the pollution and congestion of the city. Bangalore was a victim of its own success. It had grown too fast, and the government hadn't managed to keep up. The air quality was abominable; families with young children worried about an epidemic of respiratory illnesses. The infrastructure was creaking, in some cases virtually nonexistent. It was always astounding—and more than a little depressing—to get stuck in one of Bangalore's blackouts or on its potholed back roads. Bangalore was the showcase for India's new economy; its woes kind of made you question the solidity of that economy.

Banu said Bangalore's overdevelopment was enough to make her occasionally miss Molasur. Whenever she went to the village, she felt like her lungs were expanding. She loved watching her children play in the fields. They'd pick mangoes, they'd ride around on Sathy's tractor. The children were marked by the time they had spent in Molasur. They loved nature; they had a hard time dealing with the harshness of the city.

Banu took me with her to pick the kids up from their new school one afternoon. She said I lived in the country; she thought I'd appreciate the school. We made our way—slowly, painfully—through the crowded streets of Kamanhalli, and then we emerged onto a new highway that was being built to connect the city to the airport. We passed by apartment blocks, hospitals, and small shops and then, gradually, as we drove farther out, the land opened up. There was less concrete and steel, more green. There were fewer motorized vehicles, more bicycles, and even the occasional bullock cart.

I hadn't seen Banu in a while, but Sathy had kept me updated on their marriage. He was gloomy; he complained that Banu kept changing her mind, asking him for new things. Now, as Banu and I spoke on the drive to their children's school, she seemed more sanguine. "Things have become much clearer for me," she said. "I guess it's true I was confused, but I don't feel like I'm confused anymore. I know what I want now. I know what's good for me, and I know what's good for the kids."

She said she had decided that she would stay in Bangalore and build her business. But she didn't want Sathy coming up on weekends anymore. It was pointless: he was always thinking about work, taking calls from people in the village, and he never had enough time for the kids anyway. She had decided that the best way was for the kids to alternate between her and Sathy. They would spend a month with her, and then a month with Sathy.

I said it sounded like a difficult arrangement to work out. I asked what she planned to do about their school. She said she'd thought it through and this plan made the most sense. The kids were getting to an age when they needed to see more of their father. On the other hand, the family also needed an income. This way, they could go to Molasur and be with their father, and she could stay in Bangalore and earn money.

She said that this latest decision—and the clarity that had led to it—had made things better between her and Sathy. Before, they used to "pick on each other, shout and say all kinds of nasty things in front of the kids."

"Now I'm calmer," she said. "I've learned to appreciate Sathy's good traits. You know, I've realized that he's a very egotistic person, but basically, inwardly, he is very soft-natured and affectionate. He's very smart, too. I used to get so irritated with him, I used to feel resentful. I've sacrificed a lot. I've given up things that no city girl would ever give up. But now I speak more softly with him, and he also speaks more softly with me. I think we see each other's qualities better now."

We turned off the airport highway, down a dirt path that led by farmhouses, a country club, and a few fields where cows and goats were grazing. We passed by several schools; they all had green campuses, with big lawns and old trees. Banu wasn't the only one who wanted to get her kids out of the city.

Darshan and Thaniya's school was lush and expansive; it reminded me of the landscape around Molasur, except that it was cooler, less humid. The buildings were made of natural materials—thatch, stone, terra-cotta, bricks. Darshan was on a lawn, kicking a ball with some friends, and when he came over, greeted me as "Akash uncle," Banu left to talk to a group of teachers.

I told Darshan he was lucky to have such a beautiful school, and he agreed. He said the teachers were good, too; they gave students individual attention. I asked him if he missed the village. "Of course," he said. "That's like my home. This is a new place—I'm just a visitor here."

"What do you miss most about the village?" I asked. "The fields," he said. "Riding around the farm on a tractor."

"What about your father?" I asked. He nodded, but he didn't

say anything. He looked away. I thought maybe it wasn't a good question to ask.

Banu came over, told Darshan one of his teachers wanted to see him. When he was gone, I told Banu about our conversation. I said I thought Darshan missed his father.

"I know he does," she said. "I think it's especially difficult for him. He's really at the stage when he needs a father's influence. You know, fathers are more analytical than mothers. They're more practical and organized.

"I know my plan won't be easy. Sathy is opposed—he thinks it's just a ploy to have him do more work. But I really think it will be better for the children. I care about families too much to not have them around their father."

I must have looked skeptical. Banu turned to me with eyes that seemed almost beseeching, maybe a little sad, and said: "Akash, I've learned to accept that our situation isn't ideal. One reason I'm calmer now is because I accept that I can't have an ideal family setup. It's too much pressure for me to have to take care of the kids on my own. It's too exhausting. I want a career, and I want my children to have a father. I used to think I couldn't have both. Now I hope I can."

Darshan and Thaniya came over, waved good-bye to some of their friends. "See you," the friends said. "Bye, dude," one said. It started raining, thin, hazy drops that were more like dew, and we got into our car and drove back to the city.

❦

The pressure on Veena and Arvind to get married was growing. One evening, Arvind's father telephoned him and said: "Look, you have to set a date, don't delay anymore. If you delay any further, your mother says she won't visit you in Bangalore."

They'd been lying in bed on a Sunday afternoon. Arvind got off the phone, turned to Veena, who was still in bed, and, with a shrug, said: "I guess we better figure out a date, man."

They both acted nonchalant about the whole thing. Veena said she didn't care about the institution of marriage; she was just doing it to make the families happy. She had resisted marrying Arvind for a while because she wanted to make sure she didn't repeat her last mistake. But now, after living together in Bangalore, she felt more sure about him. She realized she could relax with him. "I felt like maybe I could build a life with this man," she told me. "I was enjoying our time together. I could talk to him. Even our silences were comfortable."

They had wanted a low-key, nontraditional marriage. But by the time Veena invited me to the wedding, in a text message she sent to let me know it would happen at six on a Sunday morning, their parents had managed to convince them to have a more elaborate ceremony.

The ceremony took place in a wood-paneled hall in a hotel outside Chennai. Veena and Arvind sat on the stage, with musicians and two shirtless priests with holy ash across their chests. The priests recited *shloka*s at a frenetic pace, struggling to be heard over the tabla and horn players. They spent a lot of time giving directions to Veena and Arvind, guiding them through the ceremony.

Arvind was dressed in a white *kurta*; Veena was in a red sari with a gold border. Her neck and arms were covered with gold jewelry. Arvind looked relaxed, and he smiled out at the crowd a lot. Veena looked less relaxed; she kept her eyes mostly on the ground.

The music was loud; it reverberated off the low ceiling. I'd been up late the night before and had a little too much to drink. My mouth was sour. There was a trigger-happy cameraman in front of the stage and he kept letting off flashes of light. The room felt stuffy, hot. The music was in my head.

The horns reached a painful crescendo. One of the priests held his arm up in the air, as if he'd just won a boxing match. Veena and Arvind garlanded each other; they were officially married.

Family members flooded the stage, trading gifts and congratulations. Veena and Arvind stayed on the ground, sitting, exchanging more garlands, smiling and laughing intimately, as if at a private joke.

I stepped out of the marriage hall, away from the horns and flashing lights, into the corridor outside, where European tourists in shorts were milling around, trying to peek into the wedding. Soon the crowd started spilling out. Veena and Arvind followed. They were tied to each other with a string. Arvind pulled Veena down the corridor, to a hotel room.

When I next saw them, Arvind had changed into a three-piece beige-and-white suit. Veena was in a new red sari. "Congratulations," I said, and shook Arvind's hand. He smiled broadly.

"Congratulations," I said to Veena, and she gave me a cynical look, although I thought she looked happier than she had on the stage.

"You seemed less relaxed than Arvind up there," I said.

"That's because he didn't have two hundred kilos of gold

weighing him down!" she said, and they walked back to the stage, where the cameraman with his hot flash awaited eagerly.

A few months after the wedding, I met Veena in Bangalore. She looked tired; she had circles under her eyes. She said work was stressful, the hours were long. "Sometimes I wonder what I'm doing," she said. "I feel like a cabbage. I come home in the evenings and I can't even read a single page of a book. I just conk out."

"Are you getting tired of life in Bangalore?" I asked.

"No, not really," she said. "I still have a long way to go in this city. But I was thinking that maybe one day—who knows? Maybe one day when I've made a lot of money I'll retire and live somewhere peaceful and green like you do."

She said she wondered sometimes why she and Arvind worked so hard. She tried not to, but she couldn't help thinking about the sacrifices they were making in their personal lives. Kids, family, just a sense of personal peace and well-being: all these were on hold while they pursued their careers. Was it worth it? She figured time would tell.

I asked her how married life was going, and her face lit up. She said it was great. She said that given her history, she had been a little worried. She'd felt tense at the wedding, and a little sad; the memory of her last marriage had been like a scar. But since then, she'd felt calm, secure, and happy. She was really enjoying being married again.

"Were you worried that your relationship with Arvind would change after getting married?" I asked.

"Not really," she said. "This time felt completely different. It just felt like a natural extension of our relationship. Last time, I felt like marriage would change everything for me. I was sort of resigned to giving up my identity and becoming a housewife. I can't say I felt great about it, but I felt accepting; if it happened, it happened."

"And this time you don't feel like you'll have to give up a part of your life for marriage?" I asked.

"Hell no," she said, laughing. "I mean, I might be slightly more obliged to attend family functions or something, but nothing's going to stop in the way I dress, or the way I socialize, or anything like that."

"What about work?" I asked.

"No way," she said. "Nothing messes with the work. Working is so the first thing I do in my life. That's just the bottom line. There's no way that marriage, or anything really, can change that."

Banu had a new plan. She'd stopped working, and moved with the kids to Pondicherry. She said she'd put her business on hold. She needed to give the family priority.

Sathy rented the first floor of a house on the outskirts of town. It was part of an effort to reunite the family on middle ground, between the village where Banu couldn't live and the busy metropolis that Sathy couldn't abide. He missed the village; he kept a room there, and he sneaked away to his fields as often as he could. But he was also happy: for the first time in years, the family was together.

I visited Banu in that house one afternoon. She was home alone. I sat with her in her new living room, under stained-glass windows, on wooden furniture she'd shipped from Bangalore. The room was dominated by a large dining table; the rented house felt homely.

I asked Banu how she felt about giving up her consulting business, and she said she hadn't given it up; she was just taking a break. She said she kept thinking she'd go back to it. But she acknowledged that starting again could be tough: once you were out of the game, it was hard to get back in.

"Obviously, if I want one thing, I have to give up another thing," she said. "There's always an opportunity cost. My kids are happy here, my family is happy. It's so nice to see the kids getting closer to their father. It gives me a very different kind of satisfaction than what I had when I was working in Bangalore."

She said there were aspects of her old life she missed—interacting with interesting people, for example, or the financial independence she had when she was earning her own money. She found herself holding back on certain purchases, spending less on jewelry, clothes, and household decorations. It wasn't that Sathy restricted her purchases; it was just instinctual, a feeling that it wasn't her money.

"Do you get bored sitting at home?" I asked her.

She said she managed to keep busy. She was thinking of taking a job as a teacher at Darshan and Thaniya's new school in Pondicherry. It was a bit of a step down for her; from making 10,000 rupees a day, she would be making the same amount in a month. Sathy had laughed at her for considering the job, but she didn't mind. She was just happy that things were more relaxed on the home front.

"But what about your ambition?" I asked. She had seemed so determined to grow her consulting business. She had worked so hard to get it off the ground.

"You have to trade with your ambition," she said. "Of course it's always there. If I wasn't married, if I didn't have kids, I would have gone behind my ambition and made something of myself. Who knows what I would have done by now? But you have to accept trade-offs."

She offered me a cup of tea. She talked about the challenges of maintaining a large home. As I was leaving, she instructed the maidservant about the night's dinner.

Later, she would dust the living room, clean the house, and make the evening beds. She would cook dinner for Sathy. He would come home late. She'd wait for him. They'd eat together at ten-thirty. He would tell her about his day at work.

"I'm still learning," she told me that afternoon, sitting in her living room. "Every day is an adjustment to my new role."

A DROWNING

Meanwhile, back in Chennai, Selvi was still resisting the tempta-
tions of city life, and Hari was getting ready to go to England.

He'd been chosen by his company for a three-month posting in
London. It hadn't been easy getting selected. Twenty-one people
had applied. As part of the application process, they were asked to
research the top ten companies in the Atlanta, Georgia, area. A
short-listed group of candidates was interviewed by videoconfer-
ence from London.

A few days after the interview, Hari and his colleagues were
sitting around their computers. Some of them started getting
rejection e-mails in their inboxes. Hari didn't get an e-mail, so
everyone crowded around him in anticipation. People cheered and
clapped when he got his acceptance message. They sang "I'm a
London Boy" to the tune of Aqua's "Barbie Girl." They danced
around the office.

Things were hectic for Hari in the weeks leading up to his departure. He had to buy warm clothes, he had to apply for a passport and a visa. I didn't see him much. I called him once and he was standing outside the British consulate in Chennai, waiting in line. He said he was exhausted; his mother had been dragging him around to temples, offering *pooja*s and praying for his safety.

A couple weeks before he left, he invited me to his hometown of Tindivanam. He was going to see his parents for the weekend. He suggested I join him. It was a long way from Tindivanam to London; I think he wanted me to see just how long.

We met, on a hot Sunday afternoon, at a crossroads near a crowded marketplace in the center of Tindivanam. Hari was, as ever, fashionably dressed. He wore a tight-fitting white T-shirt and torn blue jeans. He looked fresh, colorful, and clean. He stood out against the drab, small-town landscape of his former home.

Tindivanam wasn't a very charming place. The sidewalks were piled with heaps of garbage, and the roads lined with discarded plastic bags and rotting vegetables and fruit. There were stray cats and dogs everywhere, and a few pigs, blackened from sewage.

Still, I was struck by the town's transformation. Streets that had once been filled with pedestrians and cyclists were now jammed with cars. There wasn't a thatch hut to be seen. Many of the new houses and shops were decked out in glass panels and elaborate masonry.

Hari was eager to show me these changes; he wanted me to know how Tindivanam had developed. As we walked around, he talked about colleges that had come up at the outskirts of town, and about the restaurants, many serving modern dishes like pizza and veggie burgers, that had taken the place of tea shacks he used to frequent as a boy. He pointed to a new department store, a pink three-story building that he said represented a "revolution in shopping." Before, he and his mother used to shop at the provisions store, where you wrote what you wanted on a piece of paper, and the clerk selected your purchases at the back. Now, Hari said, you could choose your own brands.

He took me to his house. It was behind the new bus station. When Hari was a boy, the bus station had been marshland; during the rainy season, he would go fishing and hunting for frogs in it. Now it was the biggest station in the region, and farmers from surrounding villages congregated there, balancing gunnysacks of produce on their shoulders, arguing with conductors who refused to seat their cows and goats.

Hari's house was painted white and pink. It had wooden nameplates on the ground floor, bearing the names and work positions of his parents. Upstairs, in a narrow living room with a television at one end and a kitchen at the other, Hari introduced me to his parents. All they wanted to talk about was his trip to London. His father pointed to an announcement on television: a British Airways flight from Delhi to London had been delayed for fourteen hours. Hari told him not to worry; he didn't know what airline he would be flying. He had never been in a plane.

Hari's father showed me the computer that the family had recently bought. It was silver, and it was in a room that had been outfitted, also recently, with an air conditioner. The computer had a webcam; Hari's mother said she would use it to communicate with her son when he went to London. She would check that he was eating properly; she would make sure he dressed warmly, and that he didn't spend too much.

Hari wanted me to see his old school. He asked his mother for directions. "What, have you forgotten?" I asked, and he said, "No, it's just that when I was a kid there were no roads or paths here. I get confused sometimes. There were hardly any buildings."

We walked around, looking for Hari's school, and he talked about some of the houses we passed. He showed me one place, a gaudy imitation of a Mediterranean villa, with sculpted columns and archways, a car in the driveway. He said it was the house of a local electronics merchant; it hadn't been there when he was a boy.

Few of the houses had. Hari pointed to another new building that was painted in a shocking neon green. "Look at all these colors," he said. "Before, you used to get these kinds of colors only in Chennai. But now everything has come to Tindivanam!"

He showed me a tall house with red concrete beams running along its exterior façade. It was the house of an engineer who worked in the government telecoms department. It was an imposing structure, and one of the few houses that had been there when Hari was a boy. He remembered when it was built. Everyone talked about it; he used to walk past it on his way to school.

He remembered that the engineer's children had been showoffs. They would play loud music from their bedrooms, and stand outside their house with their toys and gadgets. They had remote-controlled cars and dart guns. Hari said he would think about them, wonder why they had so much more than he did. Now he realized it was because their father was educated: he had a post-graduate degree in engineering.

We got to Hari's school, but the guard wouldn't let us in. From what I could see, the grounds were impressive, the garbage and smell of urine by the entrance less so. Hari said: "Everything I am today is because of this place. It is because my parents sacrificed for me and pushed me. I owe them so much."

On our way back, we stopped outside the engineer's house again. We stood in its shade and I drank from a bottle of mineral water. A pig ran across the road.

In a way, Hari said, he would be happier if he were going to America. When he thought of a "cool place," he didn't think of England. England was the past; it was common. "When I was a kid I dreamed about America," he said. "The U.S. is number one. It's the most powerful ever. Who doesn't want to go there?"

He worried that his sense of fashion wouldn't fit well in England; he thought that he dressed more like an American. "I like to mix and match," he said. "I'm very casual." In the United States, he had heard, even a CEO could go to work in a polo shirt. But someone told him that the English were more conservative, and not just when it came to fashion. "They have more dos and don'ts. In America, they have only dos," he said.

"You don't sound very excited," I said.

He said I was wrong; he knew his time in London was a big break. It would enhance his résumé. It would make him more desirable on the job market. When he got back, he planned to start looking for a new job right away.

"To tell the truth, you feel like you've achieved something," he said. "You feel you're moving somewhere. When I think of some of my friends, I know that I overtook them. I won the competition."

Hari said again it was all because of his education; he pointed in the direction of his school and said it all started there. And yet, he knew it was also because of the times he lived in. "He was also educated," he said, of the engineer, outside whose house we were standing. "But he just came back to Tindivanam and did nothing. There weren't so many opportunities in those days. I know that if I had been educated in the sixties I would have probably just returned to Tindivanam and gotten old and lazy, playing with my grandchildren.

"Still, life is like that: we are lucky to get whatever opportunities we can. We should grab them when they come."

Hari said he hadn't waited around; he'd gone after life. He'd left home, moved to the city. He'd hunted for a job and worked hard when he found one. Yes, there had been times when he felt tired or scared, when he thought it would be easier for him just to move back to Tindivanam and have a safe life. But he had always been determined; he always knew he wanted to do something with himself.

He'd been thinking about some of his friends from Tindivanam recently. At school, he had been poorer than many of the boys in his class, and sometimes, that made him feel bad. There was one classmate in particular, a wealthy boy who used to bully him and mock him for always trying to speak English. He was one of the boys who used to make fun of Hari's accent; he used to accuse him of putting on airs.

Hari didn't know what had happened to that boy. The last he heard, he'd tried to get into college but flunked his exams. "Do you know what I would say to that boy if I saw him now?" Hari asked me. "I would tell him: 'You are going nowhere, you stand nowhere. But I am going somewhere. I am going to London.'"

Selvi was also looking ahead, thinking of higher salaries and bet-ter jobs. She, too, was planning for the future. But she wasn't as ambitious as Hari. She wasn't planning to quit her company or start a new job. She said she felt loyal to her company.

At her job interview, the recruiter had asked her where she saw herself five years down the road. Selvi replied that she hoped to be in the same position as the recruiter. I thought it was a good stra-tegic answer. But Selvi meant it sincerely. She was kind of old-fashioned; she wanted to move up the rungs at a single company.

We'd been meeting, now, for over a year. I thought we knew each other pretty well. She seemed more comfortable with me. When we talked, she looked me in the eye. She sometimes asked about my personal life. She didn't dress up for me anymore; in the mornings, she'd occasionally meet me in her nightgown.

Selvi still wouldn't see me outside the apartment, though, and our meetings had a furtive, shady quality that made me feel vaguely guilty, like I was transgressing some boundary. The guard would sign me in, follow me through a courtyard that led to her building, and then wait outside, as if to make sure I really was taking the stairs to her apartment.

There was a woman in Selvi's building, a neighbor I assumed, whom I met a couple times on the stairs. Her hair was pulled back in a tight bun, and she had a severe, unwelcoming face. She stared at me the first time she saw me. The second time we walked past each other, I smiled and she looked away. She seemed angry.

I met Selvi one Republic Day, January 26, a date that marks

the formal adoption of the Indian Constitution. The road from Auroville to Chennai was decorated with flags and portraits of freedom fighters. All over the countryside, children in blue and khaki uniforms were standing at attention in schoolyards as the national flag was raised and the anthem played.

Selvi had the day off; she seemed relaxed. She told me about eating at a restaurant the night before with her friends. She emphasized that they didn't eat at any "fancy, hi-fi places," but it was nonetheless an indulgence, something she did rarely, and that she wouldn't have done at home. It was one of the privileges of living in a city; it made her feel special.

"Maybe one time I could come with you?" I asked.

To my surprise, she said she would be fine with that, if her roommates agreed. She went into the bathroom, where two of them were brushing their teeth. I heard a discussion, vague behind the sound of running water, and then one of Selvi's roommates came out to meet me.

Her name was Sudha. She had a round face, and she was dressed in an orange *salwar kameez*. I introduced myself, I told her that I was writing a book and would love to know a little bit about her life. She seemed to know who I was and why I was there. She said she'd be happy to talk to me, but today she was rushing out because her father was in town.

Her father was a priest. He worked at a temple in the north of the state. He was often in Chennai to officiate at weddings and religious functions, and she was on her way to a *pooja* right now. She was running late; she seemed to be in a hurry.

She gave me her phone number; she told me to call. She stood around for a while, eager to get going, but too polite just to take off. "Okay, I'll be leaving now," she said, finally, and she did something unusual: she stuck out her hand and shook mine.

Selvi started talking about life in Chennai again. She told me about how some of her roommates were going to clubs and bars. They were staying out late, especially on weekends. The city was doing something to them, she said. She leaned a little closer, conspiratorially, and, in a low voice, told me that some of her friends even had boyfriends.

She laughed, a little nervously I thought, and drew back. I asked if she had a boyfriend and she shook her head. "No, I will never go that way. Some people in the office flirt with boys during their break, or at dinnertime. But not me. I always mind my own business. I'm very focused on my work."

"What about Sudha?" I asked. "Does she have a boyfriend?"

Selvi laughed again; it was a girlish giggle, coy, almost flirtatious. I had never heard her laugh like that before. She ran her hand down the side of her hair, feeling for knots. "You'll have to ask her," she said, and she arched her eyebrows. "That's not a question to ask me."

I was eager to get to know Sudha. The temple her father worked at was one of the holiest in South India. It attracted hundreds of thousands of pilgrims a year. He would have been an important man. He would have been a pious man. She would have grown up in a religious household. I was curious to know how she was adapting to the city.

I called Sudha a few weeks after our first meeting. The phone rang, but she didn't pick up. I tried again a couple hours later; still no answer. I sent a text message. She hadn't answered by late in the afternoon, so I called Selvi and said I was trying to get in touch with Sudha. Was she by any chance around the apartment?

There was a pause. "I'm very sorry to tell you," Selvi said. "Sudha died."

"What?"

Sudha had skipped work two days before and gone to the coastal town of Mahabalipuram with a friend. A lifeguard had seen them standing on the beach, not far from Mahabalipuram's famous shore temples. He warned them not to go swimming; he said it was a bad season, the current was strong. Apparently, they didn't listen. Their bodies were found washed up on the beach half an hour later.

"We're not keeping very well," Selvi said. "Sorry, I can't talk now."

I got more details about Sudha's death later that day. Murugan, their landlord, and the person who had introduced me to Selvi, told me that in fact, Sudha had been at the beach with a boyfriend. They had gone together the day before they drowned, a Sunday, and spent the night at a resort. They checked in under false names. The hotel should have asked if they were married, he said, but no one cared about those kinds of things anymore.

Murugan was upset. He was getting angry phone calls from Sudha's parents, blaming him for not keeping a closer eye on their daughter. "What am I supposed to do about something like this?" he asked. "I'm just their landlord. To me, this is a total problem of adjustment getting failed. They had too much freedom in the city, and the girls didn't know what to do with it. Just running around—now look what has happened."

Murugan said all the girls were in trouble. Everyone was sure they knew Sudha had a boyfriend; they were supposed to look after each other, prevent these types of things from happening. The girls denied that they knew anything, but Murugan didn't believe them: he said they were just scared.

They were scared of what their families would say, and they were scared that Murugan was going to evict them (he had no intention of doing that). Most of all, they were scared for their reputations. Murugan said that if word leaked that they were associated with "something like this," their names would be ruined.

"They don't know what's going on, they don't know what to do," Murugan said. "They're just village girls in the city. They thought they could handle everything. They acted like they were on top of the world, without any problems, like they could just ride this wave. They thought they'd keep going, get bigger and bigger. But they totally lack street smarts and the wherewithal to survive in Chennai. City-bred girls are a different lot—they're much smarter."

Murugan said he should have seen this coming. He knew they weren't adapting well. They didn't know how to live on their own. Their financial situation was a mess; they didn't know how to keep accounts, how to share costs. Their rent was often late.

Now everything was a mess, and everyone was in trouble. Selvi's "uncle," the distant relative who lived in Chennai, had vis-

ited the flat and screamed at the girls. Their neighbors were talking about them. People blamed Murugan and his wife.

"Look how it is," Murugan said. "Village girls move to the city
and ruin their lives. I wish I hadn't been caught up in this thing."

Murugan advised me not to call Selvi for a while, and I agreed. She
needed a little space. I waited about a month. When I finally called
her, from a car on the highway, the cell-phone connection fading in
and out, she sounded composed. She said things had been hard, but
that she was feeling a bit better now. She told me, unprompted, that
she hadn't known anything about Sudha's affair. She said Sudha
kept to herself; she was on another project at work. "She didn't share
these things with us," she said. "We didn't know her so well. Really,
we didn't."

I asked when we could meet again, and she said there were two
new roommates in the apartment. She would have to check with
them. She said that since Sudha's death, her uncle and a few elders
in the building had stepped in and imposed some rules. "They are
very strict with us, especially with boys," she said. "They don't want
to allow boys in the apartment at all. We've changed a lot."

I said that if she was uncomfortable with seeing me alone, I
could come with my wife. "That might be okay," she said. "I'll
inform you tomorrow."

I waited a couple days for her call, and then I sent her a text
message saying I was coming to Chennai; I asked if I could stop
in. She called right away; she told me to come alone. "Are you

sure?" I asked. "Yes, come," she said, in that direct manner that always made me feel slightly reprimanded.

I took the East Coast Road to Chennai. Almost every time I took that road, following the jagged shoreline, the ocean outside my window, I thought of that day after Christmas in 2004, when the tsunami had devastated the coast. More than seven thousand people had been killed in my state of Tamil Nadu; tens of thousands lost their homes.

I was at home on that Sunday morning. By the time I got to the ocean, the waters had receded somewhat, but they were still gurgling at the edge of the road, tossing debris—slabs of concrete, shards from motorboats, uprooted coconut trees, thatch paneling from huts—and eating into the sand.

I made my way up the beach. I was excited; I had never seen anything like it before. It was only when I saw the body of a dead boy on the sand, a crowd standing in a circle above him, a coast guard helicopter hovering overhead, that I understood I was witness to a tragedy.

Now when I drove along the East Coast Road, I had two more bodies to think of. It was hard to imagine, really; the waters looked so calm. But people were saying that there was a terrible current these days, like a river running under the ocean. An African tourist had washed up dead in Pondicherry a few days before. A friend told me he had rescued two drowning people at the beach recently. The monsoon had been heavy; the ocean was swollen. I guess

Sudha and her boyfriend picked the wrong time of year to go swimming.

Selvi was friendly when I got to her apartment. She asked if I wanted a cup of tea. We chatted for a while. She asked how my family was, she said she'd like to meet them sometime. I said she looked tired, and she said there had been some complications with the keys the night before. Sudha had drowned with one of the keys to the apartment; it was harder than ever for Selvi to coordinate with her roommates. She said she'd been waiting outside, late into the night. Then, when she finally got in, she stayed up talking to her roommates.

They talked a lot these days, after work. She couldn't explain it, but she hated to be alone. She was scared of the dark; she was scared of silence. She told me again—again unprompted—that she hadn't known anything about Sudha's affair. She said Sudha was a very private person. She'd taken a look at her diary after she died, and she was shocked by some of the things she found. She asked me if I could promise to keep some of the things she had learned about Sudha secret. I said I could. She told me something and I repeated it out loud, in surprise. "Don't talk so loud," she said. "My roommates will get upset with me for telling you."

I started taking notes as she spoke. She got a scared look on her face. "To tell you frankly, my friends told me I shouldn't do this anymore," she said.

I said that if she wanted to stop, that would be fine. It was important that she feel comfortable. I knew she'd been through a tough time. Did she want me to leave?

"No, not like that. Not like that at all," she said. "I told them I don't mind, I told them you don't ask anything funny. For me, it's fine, but it's so difficult, Akash. They are my friends, they know me well. They know what's right for me. And they are all asking me, 'Selvi, why are you doing this? You've just been in so much trouble—why are you doing something like this?'"

She told me that she felt everyone was watching her, judging her. When she walked around her apartment complex, she could feel eyes peering from behind windows, looking at her through metal grilles. She heard them whispering about her and her roommates. She knew people were gossiping about "those call center girls."

The security guard asked her all kinds of questions. He wanted details about what had happened to Sudha. He wanted to know about Sudha's life. He asked if any of the other girls had boyfriends, and he asked Selvi about her social life. His questions made her sick.

She had cut all the men out of her life. All her school friends, all her friends from home—they used to chat online, or sometimes on the phone. She had asked them not to call anymore. She missed talking to them; they were old friends. But now she knew: "If you are very free with guys, they take advantage of you."

She said: "You know, Akash, with all my friends and family, I was always the strong one, I was always the bossy one. At school, I always told everyone what to do. But now everyone is bossing me, and they're asking me why I'm doing this with you. They say it's unnecessary. They say, 'Selvi, you're always so naughty. You skipped so many classes, you bunked school. Now after you've been through such a horrible thing, why do you want to get yourself in a ditch again?'"

"Do you feel that speaking with me is a ditch?" I asked.

"I don't know," she said. "I thought maybe this should be the last time we speak. I don't feel it's a ditch, but that's what they said. I don't know what to think. I feel fine with you, but my friends and my family are looking after me, and that's what they say. My parents brought me up. They know what's right for me. When they say I shouldn't do something, I have to listen to them.

"My friends have changed—we've all changed. We used to be so young and freaky, we didn't care about anything. But now all my friends are settled down, some have children. Maybe that's why they're giving me this advice. They're telling me to stop behaving like a child. You know, we're not so young anymore. We have to be more careful."

One of Selvi's roommates walked into the living room. I had met her before. I said hello. I said, "How are you?" She mumbled a reply. She averted her eyes. She left quickly.

*Selvi and I talked for more than two hours. It was like an uncom-*fortable dance. She wanted to stop talking to me, she had been told she had to stop talking to me. And yet it was clear that she wanted to talk; she needed to talk.

She wanted this to be the last time, she didn't want it to be the last time. I told her many times I would go home, let her think over things. I said I'd wait for her call. But then, just as I would start packing up, getting ready to go, she'd start talking again. She was agitated; she seemed conflicted.

She told me she'd been home recently. For the first time, her parents started talking about marriage. They had been scouting for boys, but they were having a tough time. It wasn't easy finding families in their village who would be comfortable with a girl like her, so independent-minded, who lived in the city and worked at a call center. She could tell her parents were worried.

She'd never really thought much about marriage before; it had always seemed a distant possibility. But now, when she realized the difficulties her parents were having in finding a match, and when she thought about what she had been through, she started wondering: "What if the man they choose comes to know about what happened here? Who knows what kind of man will be my fate? I might get a man who is the jealous and possessive type. Even small things can lead to big things after marriage. I don't want to ruin my future. If he finds out what happened, he might wonder about me, also. He might think I'm the wrong kind of girl.

"None of this would have bothered me before. I always thought: 'I am young, I will come to the city, I will have a job, a good career.' I always thought about my future that way. But now I think: 'Selvi, what are you doing? You know where you come from. Just finish your work here in the city and get married and go back home. Get married and go back to where you belong. The city isn't for people like you.'"

She said she realized that the city changed people; it "spoiled" them. Sudha wasn't "that way" when she first moved to the city. She had been a good girl.

"Do you think Sudha was a bad person?" I asked.

"No, no," she said. She said a lot of people were saying that now, and it broke her heart. People at work, Sudha's supervisors and colleagues, people who used to talk in such glowing terms about her—now they said they always knew she was trouble, that she was too free, too wild. "How can they say that? Now I wonder also what they might say about me. What do they say when I'm not there? What if they come to know about the way you and I talk so freely—maybe they would say the same type of things about me."

Selvi started to cry; tears ran down her bony face. She said—her voice weak, breaking—that there was one thing she had learned from this whole experience: she knew now that you can never trust anyone.

She'd read some things in Sudha's diary, and they had shocked her. Sudha had written about a man who betrayed her. She had trusted him, and he had broken that trust. The man had really hurt Sudha.

Selvi said: "When I read that, I thought: 'This is the world. This is how things are.' It's a very important experience for us. I've learned so much. You can't trust anyone, you never know that anyone is telling you the truth. In the future, I'll know much better about life."

Selvi finally stopped talking. We sat around for a while, not really looking at each other, and then I stood up. I said I was sorry if I made her uncomfortable. She said she didn't feel uncomfortable. She said she was fine with talking to me; she enjoyed it.

But then she said—as she had said so many times that day—that she had to listen to people around her. They knew what was good for her. They knew better than she did. What we had done together so far was fine, but she couldn't see me again.

At the door, she asked: "You're not feeling upset with me, are you?"

"No, not at all," I said. "Are you upset with me?"

"I hope I didn't ruin your life," I said, and we both laughed, and she put her hand on my arm. She had never touched me before.

"Good-bye," she said, and she started closing the door.

"Well, I don't know if I'll see you again," I said, and she smiled and nodded.

"I hope things go well in your life," I said. "Good luck."

I called Murugan after leaving Selvi's apartment. I told him what had happened. I said Selvi sounded confused. She seemed to want to speak with me; at the same time, she said she couldn't. I said I was confused, too; I wasn't sure what to do.

Murugan said he'd talk to her, and he called me back about a week later. He said Selvi was "acting very strange." He said: "It looks like she wants to talk to you, but someone has gotten to her. It's probably her parents. They've given her a gag order or something. She says what's happened until now is okay, but she can't go on. She says things like, 'Everything I am is because of them, they have given me everything, they have made me. Even if they're wrong, I have to follow what they instruct me to do.'"

He described Selvi's way of talking as "quaint." He said: "You know how it is, Akash, they are from the village. They live in the past. A girl can't do what she wants. That's how they think."

A few weeks later, on a visit to Bangalore, I found myself talking to Veena about Selvi. I told her the story about Sudha's drowning, and I told her about my conversation with Selvi. I said I was having a hard time figuring things out. Maybe it was because I was a man; I felt like I was missing part of the picture.

Veena tightened her lips. She brought her hands together, as if in prayer; she looked irritated. She said Selvi's argument that her parents had brought her up and that she had to listen to them was "bullshit." There was no "intrinsic power in titles like parents and husband and blah blah blah—people who tell you to do things, who tell you what's right for you." Children had no inherent responsibility to agree to the wishes of unreasonable parents.

She told me about her grandmother, who was widowed at the age of thirty-three, but never allowed to remarry. She had to spend the rest of her life eating only vegetarian food. It had been hard for her; Veena heard that before she became a widow, her grandmother would never eat a meal without chicken or fish. It was only because of an oppressive and nonsensical tradition that her grandmother had to spend the next sixty years of her life eating vegetarian food.

"Oppression has been so much the way of life for women in India, and now she's just succumbing to it," Veena said, of Selvi. "She's accepting it."

"So do you feel bad for her?" I asked.

"No, not at all. How can I feel pity when she's in a situation that she could clearly work out?"

"What do you feel then?"

"A little bit of anger. Why can't she just go and tell her parents and friends that this is what she wants to do, that it's her life and that she thinks it's good for her? Tell me: if a woman is hit by a man, can't she hit back? I think women allow this kind of harassment."

She told me that a friend who worked for a tabloid newspaper had called her recently and asked if she'd ever suffered sexual harassment at work. "I said, 'Hell no! If I slept with any of my bosses, I did it because I had the choice.' I was very clear that it was my choice. I think that all these women who keep on whining about sexual harassment indulge in it and then don't know how to get out of it. And so that's their way out: 'What could I do when I was so innocent?'"

Veena kept shaking her head; she had strong feelings about these issues. "You know, a lot of people are not able to stand up and tell their parents or so-called well-wishers that it's their life and it's only their life. I don't know many people who would say that. But I will choose to live my life the best way that I know. I would be miserable living on anyone else's terms."

She started talking about her grandmother again. She said it was very hard for people in her family to stick to a pure vegetarian diet. She said everyone in her ancestral village, no matter what caste, had to eat meat. She said: "I mean, if someone asked me to give up chicken and fish, I would just tell them to fuck off."

The night after I said good-bye to Selvi, I paid a visit to the Marina Beach in Chennai. I had never been before, but Chennaites talked about it a lot. They were proud of their beach. They liked to say it was the longest city beach in the world. This was incorrect: San Francisco's is longer, but it was part of Chennai's urban mythology, and I rarely contradicted people when they said it.

I went to the beach at around six p.m. It was crowded. Hundreds of kids and parents and lovers and friends were relaxing at the end of a day, strolling on the yellow sand, chasing each other and holding hands. There were peanut vendors and trinket sellers and, at the front of the beach, closer to the water, merry-go-rounds and puppet shows and cotton candy stands.

I had been thinking about Selvi all day, ever since I left her apartment. I left feeling uneasy. I wasn't sure what, exactly, but something about our conversation had made me uncomfortable.

I sat on the beach and tried to clear my head. The air was cool, the sound of waves soothing. The sand was clean.

When Selvi had first moved to the city, she assured her father that she would never fall in love. Love was for bad girls. Now Sudha, with her tragic affair, had further tarnished love's name. But what, really, was so wrong with love?

All around me on the beach, there were lovers, walking together, holding hands, touching each other, looking into each other's eyes. They looked happy enough. They didn't look like they were ruining their lives.

A middle-aged couple walked by me, sharing a packet of roasted peanuts wrapped in a newspaper. The man said something that made the woman laugh. He put a peanut in her mouth. I thought they looked like each other; they must have been married for a long time.

In front of me a young man in a black shirt and a girl in a blue *salwar kameez* were sitting on a cloth laid over the sand. He pulled her toward him, and she leaned into him, cautiously, her head and neck moving toward his shoulder but her body pointing resolutely away, toward the ocean where I could just see the outlines of fishing boats bringing in the day's catch.

Behind me, another woman had her head in her lover's lap.

They were less shy. He was leaning over her, one hand on her shoulder. He cracked the fingers on his other hand, and then he brought it down, onto her hips.

A couple young men came over, one of them holding a parrot. They stopped at the shy lovers in front of me and started taunting them. I couldn't hear what they were saying, but I could see that they were being unpleasant, harassing the girl. The boyfriend kept his face down, looking at the sand. He was meek; he didn't rise to the occasion.

The men finally left them alone, but the girl had moved away now, and she sat upright, her face looking straight ahead, her hands clutching a bag. The boy kept putting his arm on her shoulder, trying to pull her toward him, but she was unyielding. He had a hungry look on his face, and I thought his moment had passed. But then, suddenly, she loosened her grip on her bag, put an arm around his shoulder, slid it down to his waist, and leaned into him, melting her body into his.

A group of schoolkids ran by, laughing in their blue uniforms. Their teachers followed, trying to control the kids, slow them down, but they were also laughing. The teachers gave up and the whole group—about seventy kids and ten teachers—went running and laughing down to the water, toward the merry-go-rounds.

I thought of what Veena had said about Selvi. Veena was a tough woman; she had come through some difficult times. I thought maybe she was being a bit hard on Selvi. Still, I understood her point. I, too, felt a little exasperated by Selvi's ambivalence. I shared Veena's frustration at living in a country where a girl couldn't talk to a man if she wanted, where gossiping neighbors could make a woman retreat into herself and away from the city, give up her independence, and where a roommate's failed love affair could doom a future marriage.

I knew what it was about my conversation with Selvi that was disturbing me. For all India's modernity, the weight of tradition was still formidable. For all the enthusiasm of my homecoming, there was still so much in my home I couldn't relate to.

Once, I would have felt estranged, like an outsider to my country. Now I just felt angry. I found myself questioning the new India. What good was all the money, all the big houses and cars, the fancy jobs, if men like Hari still had to deny who they were, if women like Selvi just went running back to their villages when their families ordered them to? What good was all this development if all it did was allow people to buy more? That wasn't real freedom; that didn't strike me as progress.

I had been in India for almost five years. The sheen was coming off the country's new prosperity. I had started to see things differently. My vision had broadened, and in the process grown darker.

The thin light of evening was giving way to the thick light of night. The darkness was like a sheet, pulled over the ocean by the waves. There was a hazy, almost milky, quality to the advancing night. I knew it was the pollution of the city, but still, I thought it was beautiful.

A trio of floodlights turned on behind me. The beach was lit up. The light was harsh. I decided it was time to leave.

On my way out, I came across a soothsayer woman, dressed in a red sari and wearing heavy red lipstick. She was holding what looked like a flute. She was calling out, offering her services to anyone who wanted to know their future. A sad-looking middle-aged man walked up to her and they sat in the sand and she waved the flute around and she told him that she could see that something good was going to happen this month.

"Does it involve love? Does it involve marriage?" the man asked, and he told her there was someone he knew who needed to find a wife.

The soothsayer grew impatient; the man had interrupted her speech. She said that yes, she could see a marriage, but when the man asked who, she said that she couldn't say. He pressed her a little and she stood up abruptly and asked the man for her payment. They haggled over the price, like a whore and a client, and then the man walked away, without his answer, toward the lovers on the beach.

part II

BLINDNESS

There was so much I loved about living in rural India. I loved the clean air, loved the starry nights, the open fields, and the sense of space. I loved the stillness. Sometimes, in the evenings, after the village temples had turned off their music, I would sit on my terrace and hear nothing—nothing at all—but the rustle of leaves in the wind.

I would go for walks in the forest behind my house. I would go at the end of the day, when the afternoon heat had lifted, along a path that led between acacia and palmyra trees to a small earth dam. I sat on the dam. I stared at the muddy water. I knew there were snakes in that water. I knew the forest was full of scorpions and centipedes. But I felt very safe in Auroville. I was far away from the chaos—the noise, the frenzied pace, the cultural dislocations and moral dilemmas—of a nation in the midst of tumultuous change.

My life in Auroville was peaceful, and for that I was grateful.

There were times, though, when the smallness of my world could grow oppressive. I lived three hours from the nearest airport, in Chennai. Sometimes I felt cut off. I didn't have much of a social life. I found myself longing for simple pleasures—going to a bar, making eye contact with a girl I didn't know, just hanging out at a party in a room full of strangers—that I had taken for granted when I lived in New York.

The villages around me were parochial. For all their superficial modernity, they were in many ways stuck in the past. I was surrounded by the same social and cultural conservatism that had made me feel so uncomfortable, so frustrated and angry, after my last meeting with Selvi.

Sathy told me a story about his driver. He was by all accounts a modern man. He drove a car, he was studying for a law degree. But when his sister—an adult woman, in her twenties—insisted on marrying a man from a different caste, Sathy's driver and his parents threw her out of the house. They refused to have anything to do with her. She now had two children; they would grow up not knowing their grandparents.

In a village not far from Rajiv Gandhi Salai, outside Chennai, I heard about a man who killed himself. He swallowed fertilizer and drowned in his vomit. He was a shopkeeper; he'd lost everything to his debts. He left his wife and children behind.

In Kuilapalayam, outside Auroville, I knew a woman whose husband had been run over by a bus. She had a daughter, and a younger son. The daughter was approaching puberty, and the woman told me of her plans to pull her out of school. The son would stay in.

"Why?" I asked the mother. "What's the use of keeping her in?"

she asked me. She said school was expensive; she'd have to pay a big dowry when her daughter got married. She couldn't afford her daughter.

I lived in a place where girls were liabilities, where impoverished fathers took their lives in the shadow of glossy software complexes, and where, for all the talk of Dalit upliftment, the ancient manacles of caste were still fastened tight. Sometimes it felt positively medieval. It was stifling. It was like living at the edge of the world, and there were days when I just felt I had to get out.

Mumbai was where I went when it all became too much for me. Mumbai was my escape. An hour and a half by plane from Chennai, Mumbai, with its millions of dreamers and strivers from around the country and the world, was cosmopolitan, modern, and bathed in the neon signs and billboards of a city that never stopped. Mumbai was far, far removed from the countryside.

Mumbai was a global city; and it was a triumphal city, the capital of Indian finance, the engine of the country's surging economy. It was home to the nation's two leading stock exchanges. A third of the country's taxes were collected there; the city's per capita income was almost three times the national average. In sparkly car dealerships, in photo galleries filled with men and women in deceptively simple designer *kurta*s and saris, in jewelry stores with fist-size pendants that could feed a village for months, Indian capitalism, its exaltation and veneration, reached new heights.

All the prosperity could be seductive. I loved visiting Mumbai's bars and restaurants, sitting on a sofa drinking imported wine, watching the city's bankers and lawyers and actors flirt with each other after a day's work. I frequented art auctions where the cocktail snacks were plentiful and the businessmen spent millions on paintings that looked like scribbles to me. It's true it was a little vacuous, but something about that vacuousness felt soothing. I felt as if I could be anywhere in the world—and that sense of normalcy, of being immersed once more in the frivolity of global capitalism, was comforting, reassurance that India was progressing beyond the poverty and austerity that had so long set it apart.

All these feelings were particularly true when I first moved back to India—when I still missed my life in New York, and when, I suppose, I was looking for validation of my decision to return. After a few years, my feelings changed. It became harder to overlook the vacuousness. The consumerism and prosperity started feeling false, even a little offensive.

I attended an art show in Mumbai one evening. It was held in the ballroom of a five-star hotel, under chandeliers and an ornate ceiling. It was a high-class event, with women in low-cut dresses and men in expensive tailored suits. Waiters in white gloves served Moët & Chandon champagne.

I skirted the edges of the show, getting a little tipsy, marveling— almost choking—over some of the price tags on the paintings. I listened in on some of the conversations. I heard financiers express awe (and satisfaction) at the way demand for Indian art had risen, I heard collectors talk about auctions they'd attended in New York and Hong Kong and London. It was a wealthy crowd. One woman, dressed in a green silk sari, a shimmering wonder that reflected the glow of the chandeliers, walked around with a man who I guessed was some kind of financial adviser.

They discussed the merits of art as an investment. The man thought art represented a good "asset class." The woman was skeptical. She curled her lips and said she preferred to put her money in equities.

Once, I might have taken satisfaction from that scene. I might have seen it as evidence of India's globalization and new, prosperous modernity. But I left the show feeling a little depressed, increasingly disillusioned by the ostentation and commercialism on display. I felt a kind of blindness in the room, a willful and self-indulgent denial of all that lay outside.

That blindness, I had increasingly come to believe, lay at the heart of large segments of modern India. The nation was enthralled—and, in the process, had become entranced—by its recent economic success. Politicians promised that India would soon ascend to global economic leadership; pundits peddled visions of Mumbai (and other metropolises) as global centers of business and finance. These promises were attractive. I felt their allure myself. But they also seemed out of touch with reality.

I had to wonder: Was the India of millionaire art collectors the same nation in which almost one half of rural children were underweight? Was the India of aspiring global financial centers the same India in which more people had cell phones than access to a toilet? Did the bankers I saw in Mumbai, so confident and smooth, live in the same country as the more than 300 million who, after almost two decades of economic reforms, still lived on less than one dollar a day?

India had shed the straitjacket of state-led socialism and embraced capitalism. The new economy had delivered a lot. Sometimes, though, when I left the thatch huts and country roads around my home for the glitter of Mumbai, I felt as if I was travers-ing worlds. Even within Mumbai, where millions of people lived in dismal slums, and a tiny slice of the population towered over those slums in luxury apartments with swimming pools and roof gar-dens, India could often feel like two nations.

I didn't know which one to believe in. I didn't know which India was the real one.

When in Mumbai, I often stayed with my friend Naresh Fer-nandes. Naresh was a journalist and editor. He was in his late thirties. He'd grown up in Mumbai, in the northern suburb of Bandra, a neighborhood of winding streets and whitewashed churches. He'd attended a Catholic parish school there, and then a Jesuit college in the south of the city.

In 1996, Naresh moved to New York, where he graduated from Columbia Journalism School and later got a job at *The Wall Street Journal*. He was in the *Journal*'s offices, looking out onto the Twin Towers, when the two planes hit on September 11. He returned to Mumbai shortly after that and worked as an editor, first at one of India's leading newspapers, and then at a lifestyle magazine.

Naresh enjoyed his time in New York. We shared a common nostalgia for the city. He talked about going to jazz clubs, sampling ethnic food in the outer boroughs, and riding his bicycle through the parks. For all his love of the city, though, Naresh had never doubted that he would return to India. His roots were in Mumbai, and, he felt, something tremendous was happening in the country, that it was changing in new and exciting ways. Like so many

Indians living abroad—like me—he wanted to return and see where the nation was going.

Naresh returned to India full of idealism and enthusiasm. He launched himself into his work as a journalist, he attended documentary screenings, and he started a book on Mumbai's jazz musicians. He was excited about what he felt was an impending cultural and intellectual revival in the nation. By the time I met him, though, about two years after he'd come back, some of that idealism had curdled. India's cultural life hadn't quite developed in the way Naresh had envisioned. From his vantage point as a journalist, he saw instead a commodification of public discourse, and the general commercialism of daily life. He saw a city—and a country—that he believed was increasingly under the spell of money.

This trend, Naresh felt, was part of a general movement that had started with the economic reforms of the early nineties. Naresh wasn't a big fan of India's recent model of development. Although he recognized the new wealth that was being generated, he felt that the fruits of India's economic growth were being distributed unequally. He railed against the inequities of the nation. He complained about a "neoliberal" economy that condemned millions to poverty even while it created a tiny class of billionaires.

Naresh seemed especially dismayed—angry, even—at the way the city of his youth had developed (if indeed that was the right word). Mumbai was an urban nightmare. Almost 20 million people were crammed into some of the most densely packed real estate in the world. More than 60 percent of that population lived in slums. Various studies had concluded that Mumbai was one of the loudest cities in the world. Of course, Mumbai had always been an intense place, but Naresh felt that it had really started deteriorating with the unchecked growth and development that followed India's economic reforms.

Naresh's frustration with Mumbai could manifest in odd—sometimes comical—ways. Walking around the city, he would gesticulate animatedly, and complain in a loud voice about buildings he said had come up illegally. Mumbai's anarchic traffic was a particular source of consternation. Naresh would stand in front of vehicles driving too fast, or the wrong way up one-way roads, and block their paths. Often, too, he would tap taxi and autorickshaw drivers on the shoulder and ask them not to use their horns. The drivers would turn and look at Naresh in bewilderment, incredulous that anyone expected them to navigate the chaos—and cacophony—of Mumbai's roads in silence.

Naresh told me once about a recent (and typical) confrontation he'd had with a man driving the wrong way up the street that ran below his apartment. The man, as Naresh described him, was an exemplar of the newly wealthy and privileged class that had emerged in recent decades. He was driving an air-conditioned SUV. Naresh stood in the middle of the road and stopped him. The man rolled down his window, leaned out, and stared at Naresh in astonishment.

"What goes of yours?" the driver asked, in a piece of Mumbai idiom whose syntax was borrowed from Hindi.

"Any sense of respect I have for you, motherfucker," Naresh responded.

"You don't know how to talk, or what?" the infuriated driver asked.

"You don't know how to drive?" Naresh asked.

Naresh broke into something like a laugh when he told me that story. He had an oval face, with a prominent, jutting mouth; he

could open that mouth in an expression that simultaneously con-
veyed amusement and horror. Now I saw more horror than amusement. He told me about all the people he knew who had been hit,
many fatally, on Mumbai's roads. Often, the drivers just took off;
they were never brought to justice.

Naresh felt that his city, and indeed the whole country, had been
infected by a kind of "social Darwinism"—a me-centered capitalist
culture that was replacing the more collective-minded socialism of
another generation. Mumbai, he liked to say, had become "the
physical manifestation of neoliberalism": an uncontrolled, unequal,
and unpleasant cityscape where private greed encroached on the
commons.

"Everyone's out for themselves in India now days," he told me
once. "It's the worst manifestation of Reaganism and Thatcherism.
There's no value given to the larger public good. There's an ideo-
logical climate in this country that encourages a kind of selfish
attitude."

Naresh walked me around the neighborhood of Bandra one after-
noon. He wanted me to see how the landscape of his youth had
changed. His concern over the deterioration of Mumbai had
spurred an interest in urban planning. He was engaged, alongside
his work as a journalist, on an urban geography project that was
part of a fellowship attached to New York University. In many
ways, Bandra was the laboratory for that project—it was there, in
the streets where he'd grown up, that Naresh first started noticing
the havoc that India's new economy was wreaking on his city.

Bandra was Naresh's world. Save for the five years he had spent in America, he had lived there his whole life. He remembered a laid-back, genteel place—a collection of fishing villages, spinach fields, and coconut plantations. The streets were lined by tile-roofed villas, the homes of a close-knit population that paid regular visits to each other and interacted at church every Sunday. Much of Bandra's population was Roman Catholic, converted by Portuguese colonizers in the sixteenth century.

Some thirty years later, the roads in Bandra still had names like St. Cyril, St. Alexius, St. Paul, and St. Leo. On leafy side streets, co-lonial villas with high, arched windows and wooden verandas bore nameplates announcing the homes of Carvalho, de Souza, Pereira, and de Silva. But Bandra was no longer a laid-back place. Now it was a happening—and crowded, and noisy, and dirty—suburb of Mum-bai. The city's movie stars, attracted by the sea views and the relative proximity to film studios, had moved in. The masses had followed, and today Naresh lived in one of Mumbai's most desirable areas.

Development had been unkind to Bandra. The growl of autorick-shaws, the horns of irate motorists, and the grind of construction congealed over the neighborhood like an awful urban symphony. As Naresh walked me around that afternoon, he spoke nostalgically about a quieter, more peaceful, and certainly more livable time. He complained about commercial establishments that he said were built on streets zoned to be residential, and about apartment towers that had encroached on sidewalks, effectively privatizing public space. The newspapers were full of stories about illegal construc-tions in Mumbai (and, indeed, throughout the country). Naresh said that certain well-connected developers had become experts at exploiting loopholes in the city's building codes.

Naresh offered to take me to Bandra's waterfront, to the remnants of a former fishing village. We walked along the playing fields of St. Andrew's School, his alma mater, and past a construction site that he said had once been a "wonder marshland" that drew herons and kingfishers. We passed through a cluster of high-rises, and then we entered a winding alley of tightly packed huts, many with metal roofs.

The streets were unpaved; men and women hung around, apparently liberated from the busyness of the city. The feeling was sort of sleepy. It was true that the low buildings and swaying coconut trees bore traces of a village past, except that now they were towered over by expensive apartment complexes.

Naresh and I stood at the edge of the village, near the waterfront, on an open stretch of land piled with construction rubble and garbage festooned over sagging mangroves. The water was black; it stank of sewage. Fishing boats bobbed on the water, and underneath the smell of sewage it was just possible to discern a whiff of drying fish. Naresh remembered fishing around there when he was a boy. Now, he said, you'd probably get a "dermatological condition" if you ate anything caught in those waters.

He laughed, but then he turned serious. He talked about the way Bandra's villages were being destroyed, the way the neighborhood he knew had simply been wiped away, pulverized and replaced in a frenzy of misdirected reinvention. He could still remember the enthusiasm advocates of India's reforms felt in the early nineties—all the promises they made that India would be rid of poverty, that Mumbai would become a world-class city with world-class infrastructure.

"And what did deregulation really lead to?" Naresh asked me

now, standing by those black waters, under the afternoon sun, looking out at the smog-enshrouded towers that lined Bandra's waterfront. "It opened the economy, but it didn't put into place checks and balances. There were no checks and balances to make sure this great wave of entrepreneurial energy that everyone was so excited about didn't just flatten everything in its path.

"Looking at Bombay physically, it's exactly the way we imagined it would turn out when the reforms started," Naresh said, using the old name for his city, in a gesture that I felt was as much out of habit as an act of resistance against the new order. "Sometimes I'm bewildered by how quickly it came to pass. We could have built parks, we could have built affordable housing, we could have widened the roads. But we just left it to the free market. The idea was that the market would find a solution, but the market didn't find a solution. You had to be foolish not to see this coming. Of course it was all going to result in urban chaos."

We ended our tour of Bandra in another former village, a warren of sloping roads and old villas where Naresh's grandfather had once lived. Naresh bumped into a few people he knew, family friends from an earlier era. They lapsed into a kind of Bandra brogue when they spoke, a lilt that Naresh later told me he believed was descended from Irish priests who had settled the area. They caught up on relatives and acquaintances, complained about some of the new buildings that were coming up, and took guesses about which villa was likely to be torn down next.

Naresh showed me a spot where he'd recently had an argument with a woman. She was parking her car on the sidewalk, and he asked her why she was doing that. The woman replied that if she didn't, someone else would.

"She didn't bat an eyelid," Naresh said, and he added that her response pretty much embodied the attitude of the city's upper and middle classes. He shook his head and tightened his jaw. I could see he was angry. I asked him about that. I said I understood that he missed the old city, I agreed that Mumbai was a mess. But where did all the anger come from?

"The anger is that people are not mindful of the rights of others," he said. "That they won't wait for my mother to cross the street, that they'll chuck plastic out of a moving car. All this wealth has led to a real sense of entitlement. People just don't care anymore. There's no such thing as society or social good."

He told me that he was reading an anthology of collected writings and speeches by some of India's founding political figures. What really struck him about the book was that every time the word "reform" was used, it was used to describe an act or moment of personal reinvention or improvement. That was the old way. Now, he said, "reform is what happens to the environment. Reform is what happens around you. Reform is something that demands no responsibilities. It's something that I personally benefit from.

"This really sums up the change in modern India," he said. "Everyone has a great sense of what the world owes them, not what they owe the world."

***

Naresh had strong opinions. He could be forceful, even a little aggressive, when airing them. I admired his passion and conviction, but I didn't always entirely agree with him. I didn't disagree, exactly, when he talked about India's inequalities or when he complained about the nation's lack of civic consciousness, but I did think he could be a little strident.

Naresh's views harked back to an earlier moment in India's history—before the dismantling of the nation's socialist economy, before its tryst with capitalism. Like many on the left, he seemed not entirely to have accommodated himself to the passing of that moment. I often felt that he exaggerated the negative aspects of India's new economy, and tended to give too little credit to the benefits of economic reforms. Sometimes, I would jokingly call him a "commie."

Naresh told me one day that if I wanted to better understand the injustices of the new India, I should meet his friend Vinod Shetty. Vinod was a labor lawyer and activist. He fought for the rights of workers, many of whom were displaced or ill-treated by companies looking to increase profits in a newly competitive economy. In addition to his work as a lawyer, Vinod was also the founder of a nonprofit organization that helped workers in India's huge informal sector. Among other things, Vinod's organization helped small shopkeepers whose livelihoods were being threatened by the arrival of large multinationals, and provided various forms of support to the thousands of scavengers who lived in Mumbai's slums and collected waste from across the city.

Vinod lived just a few streets away from Naresh. We met in Bandra one Saturday afternoon, in a coffee shop overlooking the waterfront. We sat outside, under umbrellas, in the path of heavy, loud fans that blew at the napkins and cardboard cups on our table. It was a hot day. The breeze lifting off the ocean stank a little, but it was cool, and, even with the stench, a welcome respite from the grit of the city.

Vinod was forty-nine years old, a broad, heavy man with a prominent mustache. He was in pain the afternoon we met. He'd just returned from a holiday in the hills, where he'd pulled his shoulder while playing volleyball. He had circles under his eyes. His flight had been delayed by more than seven hours the night before. He got home at five in the morning.

He'd been flying Indian, the national air carrier. He said he always flew it, out of loyalty to the public sector and its employees. Like many Indian leftists, Vinod was against the privatization of the nation's state industries. Now, when he told me about the delay, he grimaced, and said, wryly: "One is romantic about such things, but one gets screwed as a result. One must pay for one's beliefs."

Vinod was tired and in pain, but he came to life as he started telling me about his work. He had strong feelings about what he saw as the failings of India's new economy. He said that the reforms were a form of "violence against the poor." He told me that in opening its markets to foreign capital and corporations, India was killing traditional livelihoods. "When you take away livelihoods, it's the worst form of oppression," he said.

As a student, Vinod had been influenced by workers' movements and struggles for social justice around the world. He read Karl Marx and Gandhi; he followed the struggle for civil rights in America, and the 1968 student protests in Paris. His worldview was informed by a broad, progressive tradition that grew out of India's anti-colonial movement, and that had guided public discourse for the first three or four decades of independence. That tradition was leftist, even socialist, but not doctrinaire communist. Mostly, Vinod told me once, explaining his own attitude, it was motivated by what he called "humanism"—a concern for the poor and marginalized, a determination to dismantle oppressive structures of power.

For Vinod, the promise of Indian capitalism was something of a chimera. He, too, remembered all the assurances advocates of economic reforms had given, all the starry-eyed predictions that the nation was entering a new period of prosperity. Looking at the state of Mumbai today, considering the millions across the country who remained in deprivation, it was clear to him that those assurances had been hollow.

He gave me the example of India's technology industry. That industry was often upheld as a shining success story. But it employed only a little over two million people. Its success was good for India's self-esteem, maybe, but it was foolhardy to imagine software or outsourcing could provide real succor to a nation of more than one billion people.

It was a curious thing, really. As I talked to Vinod that afternoon, it struck me that one man's freedom was another man's prison. The same economic path that in so many minds had unleashed India, set it on a trajectory to self-sufficiency, to Vinod marked a kind of national enslavement. The nation's reforms, he told me, had started "the mortgaging of India." He said he'd seen what happened to other countries that followed the diktats of the International Monetary Fund and the World Bank. They became, in his view, "neo colonies."

"It's like with the East India Company," he said, referring to the English trading business that had served as a beachhead for the British Empire. "It's the same thing that happened hundreds of years ago, when the British came and various people were too relaxed and let their markets open. The East India Company first broke traditional systems, took over Indian markets, and the result was hundreds of years of slavery."

As an illustration of this process, Vinod told me about his work with the small shopkeepers of Mumbai. These were mostly vegetable vendors who bought from farmers and sold out of stalls in traditional bazaars. People called them middlemen, and argued that cutting them out of the supply chain would introduce greater efficiency into India's vegetable markets. This argument was being used to justify a push to further open India's retail sector to large multinational companies.

Vinod had launched a campaign to resist this push. If India's traditional markets were opened, he said, the inevitable result would be unemployment for small traders across the nation. What was the use of efficiency, he asked, if it put millions of people out of work? Shouldn't the main objective of economic reforms—of any economic policy—be to provide employment and livelihoods to its people?

"It's so easy just to call crores of people middlemen and dump them into the sea," he said. "But it's very dangerous to effectively disenfranchise a large part of the population in the name of globalization or economic growth. What does it do to your society?"

He looked out toward the waterfront when he said that, to where men and women in colorful weekend clothes were milling along Bandra's promenade. Some of them were holding hands. Others were flying kites. It was a cheerful, carefree scene.

"This society could do so much more for the poor," Vinod said. "I mean, the poor have given the rich so much. For centuries, they bowed and tilled the land and built factories, and for hundreds of years they built wealth. No one is asking for that money to be returned. We're not asking for accounts. We're just asking them to change things now, to change the way wealth is distributed in this country. But even that is being opposed.

"We're not asking for accounts," he repeated, and he trailed off, still looking at the waterfront, pensive in a way that made me wonder if he wasn't, in fact, waiting for amends to be paid.

*I spent some time with Vinod in the months after that first meet-*ing on Bandra's waterfront. I got to know him a little. Once, voices like his—drawing attention to the poor, to the downtrodden and the forgotten—would have dominated public discourse. For all its self-righteousness and at times grating piety, the rhetoric, at least, of socialist India was deeply inclusive and egalitarian.

By the time I met Vinod, though, an era had passed, and the old discourse had been replaced by one that emphasized self-creation, self-sufficiency, and the fabulous riches that flowed from entrepreneurship. Voices like Vinod's hadn't exactly disappeared from the landscape of modern India, but they were being muffled—and often muzzled—by all the celebratory fervor, the din of a nation intent on enjoying its economic renaissance.

Some of Vinod's views, it is true, struck me as a little anachronistic. But as I learned more about his work, I came to see that they were shaped by genuine, on-the-ground experience. His language might have seemed a holdover from a different moment, but it was in fact informed by a reality that was very current. In his work, Vinod came into daily contact with those being left behind by the nation's economic growth; he was exposed to the seamier side of India's development.

He was involved in an impressive range of projects. I met him, once, at his legal office, a small, cramped space on the second floor of a walk-up overlooking a noisy construction site. He'd been in court earlier that day. He was still dressed in his courtroom outfit: black pants, polished leather shoes, and a white shirt. He talked a little about the workers he represented. He said that, having advocated for globalization, Indian companies were now being forced to cut costs in order to survive. The easiest way to do that was to squeeze their employees.

One Sunday morning, I went with Vinod to Dadar, a congested neighborhood in the center of the city, where he walked me around a traditional market. The market was crowded with vegetable vendors, spice traders, and sugarcane juice stalls. Vinod said it had existed on the same spot for some seventy-five years. It was the type of place, he told me, that would be destroyed if India let in foreign retail firms.

In a cobwebbed warehouse at one end of the market, with the smell of spices strong in the air, rising in a tickle up my nose, he talked about the East India Company again. He said that economic liberalization didn't just threaten the livelihoods of the types of traders we were seeing. It threatened, also, the social fabric of the city, and ultimately the country. Markets like these, Vinod said, held together different religions and castes in a tenuous web of commercial relationships. Destroy the market, and you destroy the web. That's why capitalism was a form of cultural as well as commercial imperialism.

Vinod took me with him to Dharavi one afternoon. Dharavi was Mumbai's largest slum. Vinod's nonprofit organization ran a number of environmental programs there. It organized educational events for children, and it defended the rights of Dharavi's scavengers (or ragpickers, as they are known in India), who fanned out every day across the city and collected much of Mumbai's waste. I wanted to see Vinod's work in Dharavi; and I wanted, also, to see the slum through his eyes.

I had been to Dharavi before. I found it a profoundly depressing place. It was a nearly five-hundred-acre panorama of ramshackle huts, festering piles of garbage, and small workshops out of which toxic black fumes billowed into the sky. Around a million people were crammed into its narrow alleys. They lived amid pigs and rats and open sewers. The poverty, the filth, the environmental depredation were to me like giant blots on the sheen of India's new economy.

Dharavi was the kind of place that made me question the system. It gave the lie to all the rhetoric about a new, shining India. In Dharavi, I found myself inching toward the kinds of views held by people like Naresh and Vinod.

Vinod and I went to Dharavi by autorickshaw. It was a wild ride. On a four-lane flyover, an elevated highway above the slum, the autorickshaw's engine suddenly gave out. We were forced to scamper across the road, dodging cars and vans and motorcycles whose drivers seemed oblivious to our presence. I felt like a target.

We walked the rest of the way. When we got to Dharavi, I followed Vinod along a road lined with discarded refrigerators, washing machines, and piles of plastic and metal waste. Much of Dharavi's informal economy revolved around the recycling of waste collected by the slum's ragpickers. The waste was disassembled, segregated, repackaged, and recast and remade. The industriousness of

Dharavi's population was legendary; for all its poverty, it had acquired a reputation as a dynamic and entrepreneurial place.

Vinod and I walked along a narrow lane bordered by recycling units and other commercial establishments. We passed a bakery, a snacks packaging unit, and a plastics recycling center. These places operated out of holes in the wall, many partially subterranean, their ceilings blackened by years of dirt and smoke. The ground was a confetti of plastic and paper and rubber waste. It was splotched with fetid pools of water that glistened with a chemical tint. Children, many shirtless, some without pants, all without footwear, played in the puddles.

Dickensian was the thought that came to mind whenever I walked through Dharavi. Dickensian—and cruel, and gruesome, and ghastly, and no matter how many times I had previously been there, a profound sense of shock. Dharavi seemed like an act of betrayal to me, a treacherous stab at the heart of all the promises that had accompanied the nation's reforms.

Up the road from Dharavi, to the east, was the massive Bandra Kurla Complex, a glass-fronted office building that housed India's leading stock exchange and some of its biggest companies. To the west was the soaring Sealink, a nearly five-kilometer bridge that cut across the Arabian Sea, and that was upheld as a marvel of modern engineering. Standing in Dharavi, squeezed between these two paragons of the new nation, I found it hard not to believe that the economic course being followed by India was profoundly misguided.

I was horrified by Dharavi. But as Vinod and I walked around that afternoon, I came to see that he had a somewhat more nuanced take. He agreed that conditions in Dharavi were abysmal.

He agreed that the slum's residents had been betrayed by the system; he said they had been "forgotten" by the nation. But in Dharavi's workshops and factories, in its recycling units that processed an estimated 4,000 metric tons of waste a day, Vinod saw a triumph of the human spirit. He extolled the ingenuity of a people who had managed to build a life for themselves despite being left outside the formal economy. He celebrated the resilience of a population that refused to be crushed.

Dharavi's existence, Vinod told me, could be seen as "a kind of success." Standing outside a factory, talking above the whine of machinery, he said: "The question is whether you want to focus on the living conditions, which are terrible, or whether you want to focus on the dynamism and energy of this place. I see it as lakhs of people doing an honest day's work. Yes, it's unhygienic and it's underpaid. But they're doing it, and they're contributing to the economy. The efforts of these people are subsidizing the economy."

We made our way to the office of Vinod's nonprofit organization. It was in a small wooden shack on a bridge overlooking Dharavi. It was piled with paper and plastic and electronic waste, and decorated with posters explaining how to recycle and fight climate change. Vinod sat with two artists visiting from New York. Dharavi had been featured in the Oscar-winning film *Slumdog Millionaire*, and it had given the slum a certain international cachet. People spoke (grotesquely, in my view) about a "Dharavi chic." The artists were there to decorate the slum with murals and installation pieces.

I waited on the bridge outside Vinod's office. I stood in a swarm of mosquitoes, overlooking a vista of corrugated iron roofs and plastic sheeting that barely held Dharavi's factories and homes together. The bridge shook every time a heavy vehicle passed over it. I imagined the bridge crumbling; I had visions of myself falling through the air, landing on the huge pile of garbage below me.

A group of children were playing on that pile. Rats ran around. Two goats tore at rotting fruit and bits of paper and plastic. The goats were stained a bright shade of indigo from pigment dumped by a nearby dye factory. The kids were playing in the same pigment.

In front of me, on the bridge, a father and son were sifting through a pile of glass and plastic cups. These would have been collected from tea shops across the city; many still had the grainy residues of tea or coffee. When they were done, the father and son cleaned up the sidewalk where they had been working, picking up bits of leftover plastic and a few shards of broken glass. They piled the cups into plastic bags, and then the father put his arm around the son, and they sat for a moment against a parapet on the bridge, catching a respite at the end of the day.

I thought of what Vinod had said to me earlier. Yes, I thought, these people have just finished an honest day's work. In the way the father held his son, wrapped his arm around his shoulders, I caught a glimpse of the humanity—and human spirit—that Vinod told me about and seemed to celebrate. But still, I couldn't get beyond the scene below me: the spectacle of those children playing in garbage, surrounded by rats and goats being poisoned by toxic dyes.

Vinod came out and I told him what I was thinking. I told him I had a hard time seeing Dharavi as a "success." He took a deep breath. He seemed tired. He, too, was at the end of a day's work. "Akash, no one is saying that the conditions here are ideal," he said. "To see Dharavi as a way of life is a misnomer. Dharavi is a way of survival, a way of sustenance and a way to earn a livelihood against all odds.

"Of course this isn't a shining story, or a success story. The only success story here is the people—it's their spirit, the fact that they work, the fact that they don't get angry and try to burn everything down. It's not a success story for the country as a whole or its society or its system. When I talk about India, I try to focus on the people. These people get up every day and work and survive. That's a success story."

As we made our way out of Dharavi, negotiating the end-of-day traffic, the Bandra Kurla Complex golden now under the evening sun, he went on: "The anger you feel is justified. I understand it. But if you want to make a change, you have to swallow anger. Feeling angry doesn't help—it's just a flame that could burn through these people. These people can't afford that anger. It could drag down their lives and families. They can't express anger, they can't feel it, or it would burn out of control."

Vinod, Naresh, and I went to a bar in Bandra. It was a modern place, the kind of establishment that drew a trendy, upscale crowd. It was, as Naresh might have said, "a physical embodiment" of India's economic transformation.

We sat in low, reclining chairs, and we watched as women in impossibly short skirts walked in, leading their boyfriends by the hand. We drank foreign beer. We ordered a serving of french fries with wasabi sauce.

"See, not everything about the new India is depressing," I said to Naresh, and he laughed and said that it was good we could afford to come to places like this so we knew what to criticize. Naresh wasn't above a little self-deprecation.

The talk turned to the financial crash that had swept through the West and lapped up on the shores of India. Around the world, capitalism was in crisis. There was no doubt that the economic system Vinod and Naresh so reviled was reeling. But it was hard to figure out just how this crisis was playing out in India.

In the papers, there were reports of pink slips and hiring freezes. The stock market was down dramatically—more than 50 percent, at one point. But corporate earnings seemed relatively healthy, Indian banks didn't face the existential crises of their counterparts in the West, and, most of all, the country's spirit seemed unabated. I saw little sign that India's exuberance was in any way shaken.

"Is the recession for real?" asked a headline in one of India's leading newspapers, over an article about the persistence of conspicuous consumption in the country.

A number of papers reported on a business confidence survey that found—in the somewhat impenetrable language of the reports—that India was the "third best country that will tide over the global economic crisis."

Naresh and Vinod had a slightly different take on things. For them, the crisis validated their skepticism about capitalism. Vinod talked about watching America bail out its banks and car companies. He said these were "socialist measures." It was exactly what people like him had been saying India should do for decades. So why was the country so eager to sell off and shut down its ailing public sector industries? Why did so many thousands of workers have to lose their jobs in the name of efficiency?

Vinod said: "India's greatest strength was its public sector—its banks, its railways. But when the public sector was going down, we were always told we had to dump the whole system. Does the West do that when it has problems in capitalism? They don't dump the whole system.

"What we always suspected about those financial firms was shown to be true. Before, we were always criticized as doomsday people. People would mock me. They'd say I didn't get that India was going places. They would call me a commie. They would bash us just because we said that the country should take it a little easy. Now that this whole thing has gone down, they have nowhere to hide."

The irony was delightful; it was hard to avoid the feeling that people got what they had coming. Vinod said that watching the system implode was a bit like watching a glutton who eats himself to death. He spoke of "poetic justice."

Still, Vinod and Naresh both agreed, they couldn't take too much satisfaction from the situation. Naresh pointed to the nation's resilient cheeriness. In fact, people were saying that India's relatively controlled brand of capitalism—its more tightly regulated capital markets, its remaining controls on foreign capital and investment—would allow the nation to ride things out and even position it to emerge at the top of an Asian Century. In some ways, Naresh said, India's comparative economic health had strengthened its faith in a model that he continued to believe was unjust and inegalitarian.

"India's the one place in the world where there hasn't been a real debate over capitalism," Naresh said. "The country's growing at six percent instead of eight percent, so everyone thinks everything is okay."

"They still don't admit that it's a failure of the system," Vinod said. "Corporate greed in this country has reached a point of no return. Its appetite is insatiable. But if we keep following these kinds of policies, I believe they will blow up in our faces one day."

We finished our beers, we ate the last french fries. The bartender turned the music up, and it became hard to hold a conversation. The evening was just beginning in that bar; it promised to be a fun night. For us, it was time to leave.

Vinod got into a car, went home. I was staying at Naresh's. On our way back to his place, walking through the buzz of Bandra's busy nightlife, stumbling a little on the cracked pavement, we came across a family living on the street. There was a father, a mother, and three children. They had set up a tent of sorts, fabric strung over a pole. A couple cardboard boxes, containing what I assumed were their worldly possessions, were piled under the tent.

One of the children sat with his father by the boxes; two were sleeping on the sidewalk with their mother. The children slept on tattered fabrics; the mother slept on concrete. A stray dog hung around. I wasn't sure if he was domesticated, waiting for a scrap of food, or maybe just searching for solace in the shared company of the dispossessed.

"Look at that," I said to Naresh, as we walked past the homeless family. "That's quite a contrast with the place we were just at. I should write about that."

"It would be a bit of a cliché, wouldn't it?" Naresh asked, and he laughed. "I think there's been plenty written about Indian misery."

Naresh was right. It was a cliché to write about poverty in India, a cliché to point out the contrasts and inequalities within the nation. These stories have been told for decades. India is tired of hearing them, as is much of the world. And so, over the last decade or two, the narrative has changed: now people write stories about Indian upliftment, about a nation on the move, emerging from the shadows of poverty into the glitter of twenty-first-century prosperity.

This more cheerful India is real. But as Naresh and I continued on our way that night, it struck me that its reality didn't in any way negate the existence of another, far less cheerful, India. I could understand why people were tired of hearing about misery. I could understand why they wanted happy stories. Still, I couldn't help feeling that we were replacing the old cliché with a new one—that the new, happy narrative was just as simplistic as the old, depressing one.

In that simplification lay the blindness of the nation. I felt a kind of turning away, a refusal (or inability) to stare in the face of all that remained undone. And I couldn't help feeling, too, that the blindness was a form of complicity—that it was a way of consigning the poor to an immutable state of poverty, and that it was, ultimately, part of the oppression and injustice of modern India.

GOONDAGIRI

It was a Friday afternoon, the start of a weekend, and I was in a car coming back home from Bangalore. It had been a long week. I was tired; I was looking forward to seeing my children.

My driver might have been in a hurry. Earlier that morning in Bangalore, we had been held up by roadwork. We were diverted onto side streets. They were too narrow for the traffic. Buses couldn't take the turns; cars, vans, and autorickshaws were stuck behind the buses. Everyone used horns liberally. It was pointless, it was maddening, and it lasted for two hours.

It was good to get out of the city, into the open country and onto the uncrowded highways. I suppose we were driving too fast.

At around two-thirty, just about fifteen kilometers from home, we hit two boys on a moped. It happened in slow motion. I saw the moped pull away from under a tamarind tree. It cut across the road at an angle, heading into our path. I saw it, I wanted to scream at the driver to stop, but it was too late. I was blocked, as in a dream, and I couldn't say anything.

We hit the moped from behind. The boys were lifted onto our hood, and then dropped to the road. They were carrying lunch in a tiffin. The tiffin flew open; the cover was stuck behind one of our wipers. The windshield was covered in yellow *sambar* and rice. It looked like vomit.

I had rehearsed this moment in my mind a hundred times. Traffic on the roads around Auroville was chaotic. Accidents were common, and they were often followed by an enraged mob. I had heard about drivers—and passengers—who were dragged from their vehicles, beaten and even murdered by the mobs. The driver of my car looked at me, terrified. We escaped to the nearest police station. We left to report the accident before the mob.

As we drove away, I looked behind. I wanted to know that everything was all right. One of the boys, in a blue shirt, was standing. But his friend was on the ground. He was lying in a pool of blood. His right arm was twitching. The boy in blue dragged his friend off the road, back to the shade of the tamarind tree from which they had come.

The police station was in a red brick building, with the wrecks of vehicles—a crushed car, a burned-out van—scattered in its courtyard. It was a rural outpost on a hot afternoon. Four or five policemen were sitting around, their shirts off, their bellies protruding through white undershirts. The inspector was in his office, slouched over his desk. His shirt was off, too. His pistol was on his desk; it was out of its holster.

The policemen got up, slowly, and led us into the station. They sat me on a bench. Two of them took the driver into a space at the back. They asked him what happened. They started to hit him. He said: "It wasn't my fault, they came in front of me." One of the policemen said: "Why did you turn to the right, you fool?" I heard the crack of his hand against my driver's face.

A man ran to the station, called from outside. The inspector stood up, put his shirt on, tightened his belt, and walked out. The man said something to him, and the inspector came back in and told his men to get dressed. "Is it all right?" I asked, and the inspector didn't say anything.

There was a moment of silence, a stillness. The police had stopped hitting the driver. We were waiting for whatever would happen next.

I watched through a window as a boy ran to a house outside the station. He called a name, a woman came out, he told her something, she screamed and fell to the ground, howling, rolling in the sand.

A man pulled her to her feet. A crowd of mostly men gathered in front of the house. They made their way in a procession, about thirty of them, to the station.

The policemen shut the windows. They double-bolted the front door. One of them told me to move farther back, away from the windows and the door. "Family, riot," he said. He shoved me behind a wall. We crouched together. He was very young; he looked scared.

The men from the village gathered outside the station. They started pushing my car, rocking it, as if they were trying to topple it. Some of them came up to the station. They were carrying sticks.

A policeman opened the door, told them to leave. They pushed back, started surging toward the station; the policeman closed the door and retreated inside. The men were now banging on the shuttered windows. A few were throwing stones. They were shouting; they were saying a name; they were demanding to be let in.

The policemen seemed confused, unsure how to handle the situation. One of them started hitting the driver again. He needed to show the mob he was doing something.

The inspector was back in his office, at his desk. He put his pistol in a drawer. He played with his cell phone. I didn't get the feeling he would help me.

I thought of Sathy. I was in his neighborhood. I called him; his phone was busy. I sent him a message: "Call. Urgent." He called and I told him what had happened. "Don't do anything," he said. "I'm on my way. This is my area."

"Hurry," I said. "There's a crowd outside. I think a boy has died."

Sathy arrived about twenty minutes later. He pushed through the crowd. One of the men said something and approached him, a little too close I thought. Sathy stood his ground. The man pulled back, and Sathy got into the station.

A policeman tried to stop him, but Sathy just patted him on the shoulder and kept going. "He's my man," he said, pointing at me, and went into the inspector's room. The policeman asked: "Who is that?"

Sathy came back out and said: "I'm the Reddiar from Molasur. This is my place. My uncle is the president of this village. Everyone knows me."

He went into the inspector's room again; he shut the door. They came out together a little while later. The inspector had a hat on now, and his pistol was holstered on his belt. He opened the door to the station and in a loud voice told everyone to disperse. The crowd pushed forward; a young man started shouting at the inspector. The inspector raised his hand, as if he was going to hit the man. Another man, older, pulled the young man away. The crowd receded.

The inspector turned to me. "You can go now," he said. "Take everything from the car—CD players, cassette players, anything valuable. Take it and go."

The boy was in a coma for three days. I was told he had perma-nent brain damage. I was told he wouldn't make it. For three days—and many after—I was afflicted by a searing sense of guilt. I wanted to visit the boy in the hospital, I wanted to visit his fam-ily. Sathy advised against it; he said the situation was volatile. Then, one day, Sathy told me that the boy had come out of his coma and that he was discharged from the hospital. He had some trouble walking, but otherwise he would be all right. The driver went to court three months later. The judge let him off with a warning and a fine.

So everything turned out all right; the mob dispersed, the boy didn't die; the case was closed. But what I remember most when I think of that day is the face of one of the men in the crowd outside the station. It was a round face, puffy, like a drinker's, and it was pressed up against the metal bars of a window. He had black circles under narrow eyes. He was looking at me as he shook the bars. He didn't seem angry; he seemed deliberate. I felt that if he got in, anything could happen.

It was clear the police weren't going to do much to protect me. I found out later they knew the boys and their families. The police were part of the local community. I was an outsider. I had killed (or so we thought) someone they knew. I wasn't worth saving. It was only when Sathy showed up and, as he told me later, convinced them I was someone important, someone with political connections, that I seemed worth protecting.

What scared me that afternoon was the sense of utter lawlessness. Things felt out of control. I was at the mercy of an angry mob. And all of this was happening in a police station.

๑

I had started seeing a Hindi expression with increasing frequency in the papers: *goondagiri*. A *goonda* is a thug. *Goondagiri* is something like a state of thuggery; it refers to a situation in which mobs have run rampant, taken the law into their hands.

The first time I saw the term was after a series of riots in Mumbai. A mob had attacked out-of-state migrants to the city. They'd beaten up a group of workers; at least one man was killed. The police stood by, helpless, or unwilling to help. A couple days later—and too late—the state chief minister announced that the government would "not tolerate *goondagiri*."

But *goondagiri* wasn't restricted to Mumbai. All over India, there was a sense that the law-and-order machinery was weakening, even breaking down. The papers were full of lurid stories about kidnappings and rapes and mob violence. Parts of the country had become virtually ungovernable.

In the so-called Cow Belt, a stretch of land that extended over the Hindi heartland of north and central India, corrupt politicians and landed elite (modern-day zamindars) conspired to run what the press called a Mafia Raj. In parts of the northeast, an indecipherable mix of tribes and separatist groups terrorized the local population and profited from the drug trade.

Large swathes of central India—territory referred to as the "Red Corridor"—was virtually under the control of a hardline group of Maoist rebels known as the Naxalites. The Naxal movement was fueled in part by economic and social resentment, a sense of exclusion from the fruits of development. Its goal was to overthrow the state. Every month seemed to bring new stories of Naxal attacks, of bombings and land mines and shootings that the government was unable to control.

India was in upheaval. A few decades ago, in the late eighties, V. S. Naipaul had traveled through the country and noticed an incipient "liberation of spirit." He wrote of a nation awakening from decades of postcolonial inertia. He wrote about stockbrokers and businessmen seizing new economic opportunities, about politicians and revolutionaries, and ordinary citizens, trying on new identities.

Naipaul was prescient. The social and economic emancipation that I was living now was just beginning to manifest when he traveled through the country; it would intensify in the nineties. This process was invigorating, and often inspiring. But Naipaul was prescient, too, about the flip side of the emancipation: the violence and even a sense of anarchy that would accompany India's redefinition.

India's liberation, Naipaul wrote, "could not come as release alone. In India, with its layer below layer of distress and cruelty, it had to come as disturbance. It had to come as rage and revolt. India was now a country of a million little mutinies."

The nation was on the move. It was all very exciting. But it also felt dangerous. The process of liberation was messy; the old order was crumbling, and sometimes it seemed like all that was stepping into the vacuum was chaos.

The mutinies—the rage, the revolt, the messy sense of freedom, tantalizing yet threatening—were all around me. In the villages near my home, gang violence had metastasized into something more random, more unpredictable. What began as organized crime—targeted assassinations, political hits—had degenerated into a culture of violence. It felt like it could erupt at any moment.

A casual comment could quickly be misinterpreted and end in a fight. A minor traffic accident led to extortionate demands for payment. Workers who were fired in the morning returned that evening with friends to attack their employers.

People had seen their peers get away with murder. They knew the police were often pliable, the courts bogged down by caseloads that could take years to work through. Local politicians were supportive. Some politicians nurtured their own army of *goonda*s. For many young men, crime had become a way of life.

All along the East Coast Road, I heard stories about men and women who had suffered brutal attacks, and who were often murdered. Sometimes the attacks took place near or in the victims' homes. Sometimes they happened on a highway, on the beach, or maybe at a movie theater, on a Sunday, while the victim was out relaxing with his family.

Most of the attacks involved knives and axes. Victims were cut up, dismembered, occasionally after being disabled by a throw of red chili powder to the eyes. Increasingly, incredibly, I heard stories about attacks involving bombs—crude country versions of Molotov cocktails, made with petrol or kerosene.

That was something new: bomb attacks in my country home, on a landscape I had always thought of as a rural idyll. "It's like living in Baghdad," a friend said one day, after we'd heard about the latest victim killed by a bomb. "Sometimes I feel like I should just get the hell out of here." My friend was French. He'd spent all his life in India, but now he was talking about moving to France.

He was being a little dramatic. But I could relate to what he was feeling. A few of the victims were people I knew. The sense of danger—to myself, to my family—was palpable. It was frightening, and more than a little hard to believe. I found myself astonished, and often agonized. What had happened to the villages I knew as a boy? How did those fields and forest and beaches that seemed so sedate, so peaceable, turn into places I was often scared to visit at night?

✺

According to Sathy, one thing was at the root of the violence: money. He said that too much money was flooding into the villages. It changed people's sense of themselves, and their relations with others. People no longer knew how they fit into society. They were losing their bearings.

The escalating value of land, in particular, had a major role to play. The wealth being generated in cities was trickling down to the real estate market in villages. Young software professionals who a generation ago might have lived with their parents were now looking for second homes in the country. They were buying up farmland and properties that had been neglected for decades. Often, they bought without even intending to build: they bought village land as an investment, as a place to park their surplus funds.

The new money was stirring things up. It led to friction within families, and between neighbors. Sons who had migrated to cities, who had abandoned farms to their siblings or cousins, came back now and demanded their share of the family fortune. Merchants and civil servants who had always looked down on farmers—as impoverished, illiterate manual laborers—woke up one day to find that the farmers were incalculably richer than they were.

The resulting resentments—the sense of enmity and conflict— were powerful, like a riptide running below the surface of long-established village hierarchies. Sathy said some people were greedy, some had a lot to prove, and some were just too proud: they couldn't accept their changed status. He reflected on his own situation. He knew things had changed. He attributed his relative equanimity to his education. But most people in the village weren't as well educated.

Much of the violence was opportunistic; people were tempted to bend the general lawlessness to their own profit. Sathy told me about a battle he'd been waging over his family's land. The value of the land had soared in recent years. He said there had been a time, not so long ago, when he went around begging people to buy it; now he was fending off ten buyers a day. But it wasn't easy overseeing two hundred acres. Sathy spent a lot of time dealing with squatters and crooks.

One man from a neighboring village, someone Sathy had known almost his whole life, had forged his ownership to an acre of Sathy's land. He'd sold it to a local bootlegger. It was prime land, right along the new highway coming up by Molasur. Sathy heard about it and confronted the man. The man came to Sathy's house and threw himself at Sathy's mother's feet. He begged for forgiveness. He said: "We are poor people, we didn't know better. You're a big zamindar, you have so much. Forgive us. Let it be."

Sathy threw him out of his house; he took the issue to court. He argued his own case. He told me he argued it "beautifully"; he wished I had been there to see. The judge upheld Sathy's rights; he declared the transaction invalid. "Now I can sit on my land, peacefully, quietly, and do whatever I want," Sathy said. "It's my land, no one can question that."

But Sathy was wrong: he couldn't relax. The bootlegger who

had bought the land was a local tough; he had his gang of *goonda*s. He sent one of them to warn Sathy that if he didn't back off, they'd deal with him. They said they knew where Sathy lived; they would come at night and finish him off.

Sathy sent a message back: "Try killing me. I'm not scared. You know where I am. I go every night to my forest land for a walk alone, at eight-thirty. Come and find me there."

I asked Sathy if he really hadn't been scared. "I've dealt with much worse, it didn't bother me at all," he said. "I've learned one thing over the years: people who warn you rarely actually do it. It's the ones who come silently at night, without warning, that you have to be careful of. Those are the dangerous ones.

"Of course," he went on, "I did take a big stick with me every night when I went walking, and I would say a deep prayer. I would recite my *shloka*s. I do that all the time when there's any danger. Because even if I'm very confident, there's always some fear. The fear is always there."

Some of the violence was opportunistic, and some of it was just senseless, a product of general chaos. But there was, too, an emancipatory element to much of it. The money pouring into the villages created new opportunities. Sometimes people had to fight to seize those opportunities. The old elite resisted, they tried to keep things in place. But the poor were no longer so meek; they stood up for themselves.

Sathy complained about "a climate of fear" that had enveloped Molasur. He talked about some of the real estate development going on in the village. He talked about young men who had worked all their lives as manual laborers, who were illiterate and who had been born into poverty. Now these men had connected with developers from the cities. They went around buying up acre after acre of farmland. Sathy said they threatened and intimidated reluctant sellers.

The men could be uncouth; they reeked of violence, a certain ruthlessness. They would sit in big groups on land they were developing—or wanted to develop—and get drunk. They'd toss their drinks when they were done, littering the fields with bottles and plastic cups and bags. Sometimes, Sathy said, he'd drive past a project, see men digging up or marking good fertile soil, and it tore at him. He felt that real estate development was killing the village.

Many farmers, Sathy said, felt the same way. The land had been in their families for generations. They didn't want to sell, but they were powerless when pressured by aggressive developers. If a farmer held out, the developers would buy all the land around him and close off his access. Sometimes, they'd bring a gang of men and threaten to attack a farmer when he came to plow his fields. The threats were usually effective; eventually, most farmers gave in.

Sathy told me about a young man who had come to him, complaining that some developers were putting pressure on him to sell. He said they had tricked his father into signing a document; he was refusing. The next day, Sathy found out, the developers shoved the young man into an autorickshaw, roughed him up, dragged him to the government land office, and forced him to sign away.

Another man, who had already put down some money as an

advance payment on a piece of land, was approached by developers who wanted the same land. When he resisted giving up his claim, they warned him: Take back your money, let us buy the land, or we'll take care of you. If we see you around the village, we'll finish you off.

This kind of intimidation had been going on for a couple years now. Sathy said it created a tense atmosphere in the village; people were unhappy and uneasy. He tried to talk to some of the developers. He told them that what they were doing wasn't right. He said that God would punish them for forcing farmers to sell their fields, for taking good agricultural land and turning it into plots. He talked to them about the crisis in agriculture, he said they were contributing to the problem of rising food prices. He warned them that if agriculture died, their families would also suffer.

In truth, though, the developers didn't seem to have suffered at all. Many of them seemed to have done quite well. Driving through the villages around Molasur, you could always tell who the local real estate magnates were. They were the ones with new, polished cars, with the expansive houses equipped with air conditioners and washing machines.

Still, Sathy was confident these people wouldn't get away with it. He said: "Till now, God has left them unpunished, but let's see what happens. Let's see, let's see. God doesn't punish immediately. He takes his own time. I'll just wait and watch. I don't think they can escape the laws of nature."

"Why don't you step in and do something about it?" I asked him. "Shouldn't you help protect the village?"

"It's too complicated," he said. "Too messy."

"Are you scared of them?"

He bristled; he laughed. He said he had nothing to fear from a couple of young rowdies. Then, when I pressed him, he acknowledged that they could "cause some damage." He said none of the young developers would dare confront him directly; they knew who he was. But they could do things like destroy his underground irrigation pipes. I had a feeling he knew they could do worse.

"It's a kind of revolution," he said. "Some of these people, they've never tasted power like this before. They've never had so much. No one can do anything about it. People who were down for so long dominate now."

One of the people from Molasur who was involved in real estate development was Das, the Dalit whose house Sathy had taken me to. Das had tied up with a couple partners to develop around fifty acres at the edge of Molasur. They called their development Kingmaker City. They divided the fifty acres into 1,700 plots. They marketed the plots with the assistance of some businessmen from Chennai. The project had been a big success: they'd managed to sell all 1,700 plots in just four months.

I asked Sathy to take me to Kingmaker City. He resisted. The development had taken place more than a year before, but Sathy said going there was still like "torture" for him. He could remember when the fifty acres were planted with rice and peanuts. It caused him "too much mental tension" now to see the land fallow, to see how the fields had been flattened into roads and cut up into individual plots.

Sathy was sure that projects like Kingmaker City would ruin

Molasur. He felt that when city people came in and built country homes, they'd bring city values with them. They would do "cinema stuff" in the village, by which he meant that they would come with women, girlfriends or prostitutes.

He worried, too, that the project would further erode his position. "Wherever I walk now, even nine kilometers from my home, people know me, they respect me," he said. "I enjoy that. But these city guys will come in and they'll ask my people, 'Why do you salute him?' and gradually the respect will fade. They'll put jealousy in my people; city people don't understand this concept of respect. It's a village thing."

Still, I persisted, and finally one afternoon we made a plan to meet Das at Kingmaker City. Sathy and I walked there from his house in Molasur. We walked across his fields, and then we walked through his forest land. It had been raining recently. The earth was soft. I saw paw prints in the soil and I asked Sathy about them. He said they were from jackals.

You had to watch out for jackals around there, he said. They could be aggressive. One time, an old man had fallen and hit his head on the forest land. He passed out, and the jackals ate him. Sathy said that was very rare.

We emerged onto a stretch of open fields. The property directly in front of us was green, sown with crops, but beyond that I could see an empty, uncultivated stretch, marked with red and green flags, and yellow stones that demarcated plots. That was Kingmaker City.

As we walked toward Kingmaker City, a white Ambassador car made its way up a tarred country road. It turned onto a dirt path that led through the plots, kicking up a cloud of dust. The car stopped and a window rolled down; somebody threw an empty mineral water bottle onto the road.

"Bloody Chennai people," Sathy said. "Every day, twenty cars come here. Look how they litter, look how they treat this place. No respect for the land.

"It's my fault," he said, and he put his hand on his forehead. "I'm the greatest fool. This was all my land. My father gave it to the villagers. I should have just taken it back, but I wanted to honor my father's memory. I let it be, and now look what's happened."

We met Das. We shook hands. I hadn't seen him in a while. I thought he looked older. He had circles under his eyes, and black marks on his forehead and cheeks. He was dressed casually, in a hanging blue-striped *lungi* and an untucked red shirt.

We searched for a shady place to talk. We found a mango tree, near a well filled with murky green water, and sat on the ground. Das said he hadn't been to Kingmaker City in a while; being there now brought back memories.

"It's a useless place," Sathy said. "Lousy dry land."

"What do you mean, dry land?" Das asked. "In winter, this is the most fertile land. It gets wet and green."

"Yes, but you killed the fields, didn't you?" Sathy said. "Nothing grows here anymore. What does it matter if it's fertile or not?"

Das told us about how he'd built Kingmaker City—how he'd joined forces with his local partners, how they'd tied up with businessmen from Chennai, and how they'd convinced farmers to sell their land. He laughed when he remembered some of those stories. He told me about a teacher who had refused to sell; they got a group of men together and chased his tractor across the fields. He told me about a man who had been rude to them, who said that he wouldn't even sell them garbage. They'd closed off his access; they refused to let him set foot in his fields. Like all the others, he ended up selling.

Das said that most people sold willingly; he wanted me to know that he and his partners always paid a fair price. What they did wasn't cheating. But it was true that in some cases, if people were unwilling to sell even when the price was right, they'd been forced to apply a little pressure.

I asked Das if he ever felt bad about the way he had muscled people out of their land. He said again that many people had sold willingly; it was only a few people who held out. Still, he acknowledged that he did sometimes feel bad. He said that when he sat there with us now, under that tree, remembering how green this land once was, seeing how dry it had become, he felt a little guilty.

He didn't feel bad about taking land away from wealthy farmers; they could afford it. But when he thought back to some of the smaller farmers, people who had lost everything they owned, it made him sad.

He talked about the piece of land we were sitting on. It had belonged to an older man. He was a simple, uneducated farmer. He hadn't needed much convincing; Das and his partners had just sweet-talked him a little, and he'd been happy, eager even, to sell.

But now, Das said, the farmer had gone "crazy." He sat around all day, depressed, not speaking to anyone, staring off into space. The land was all he had; he'd been a farmer his whole life. Das couldn't help feeling that he was depressed because he'd lost his land. Sometimes, when Das drove or walked past the farmer, when he saw what had become of him, he felt maybe what they'd done hadn't been right.

"So why did you do it?" I asked.

Das said: "When we did it, it was just business. I was thinking of the money. Now the owner of this land has fallen, he's so weak. It's a bit difficult to see him. Probably if I had been doing it on my own, I would have thought more carefully. But we were a group, and we didn't think so much. It was a group thing—we were blinded by the money.

"You know, everything has a season. Now everyone is buying gold. But when we were selling these plots it was land season. Everybody just wanted to get a piece of land. Some of the people who bought these plots never even saw them. They just put their money down. They were like gamblers. It was that kind of season, and I suppose we were a little caught up in the season."

Das talked about all that Kingmaker City had given him. He said Kingmaker City had changed his life. It hadn't just given him financial security. It had also given him respect and status—status that his father never had, that it would have been unimaginable for a Dalit to claim fifteen or twenty years earlier.

"It gave me a new direction," Das said. "Whatever I feel or say now, this project gave my family security. It made me who I am today. It gave me a kind of freedom."

Das seemed tired. His speech was halting, and he seemed to be having trouble concentrating. I thought maybe the memories of putting Kingmaker City together had upset him, but he said his blood pressure was up. His sugar levels had also been out of control recently.

He'd been to see a doctor in Chennai a few days before; the doctor told him he needed to rest. He hadn't wanted to go to Chennai. It meant missing the memorial service for a Dalit murdered in a neighboring village. It was a big service; a Dalit leader from Chennai had visited and given a speech.

The murder had taken place six months earlier, during a bout of violence in the area. One caste had prevented another from carrying a corpse through their streets. In the ensuing riots, the murdered man was captured and had his head smashed in with a stone. It was done right by his house, in front of his wife and children. It was a ghastly killing.

Perhaps Das was tired, too, because another friend of his had been murdered just a few days before, in a nearby town. The friend was part of a gang of *goonda*s that extorted free food from a restaurant owner. They'd gone to the restaurant over and over, tormenting the owner, refusing his entreaties to leave him alone. Finally, the owner had taken matters into his own hands. He'd organized another group of *goonda*s to kill Das's friend. There were around ten people in the owner's group. They waited outside the restaurant, and they stabbed Das's friend. He was rushed to the hospital, but it was too late. He bled to death.

"That's a lot of death," I said.

"We're such emotional people," Das said. "We hit without thinking, we murder without stopping."

We stood up. Sathy showed me a water tank that farmers had used to irrigate their fields. It was empty; the concrete was cracking. "Agriculture is dead," Sathy said. "The village is over. It's all gone, and I'm helpless. What can I do? There's no point in brooding. Come, Akash, let's go."

Leaving Kingmaker City, I asked Das why the restaurant owner hadn't called the police before murdering his friend. Das said that in fact, he had, a couple times, but the police didn't do anything. His friend kept harassing the owner, showing up drunk, demanding free food, driving away customers with his behavior. Several people had asked him to stop; even Das had tried to talk to his friend. He'd told him he wasn't behaving correctly.

Eventually, Das said, it had all been too much for the restaurant owner. He had felt humiliated. Das assumed he had to do something to prove himself.

"So do you think the murder was justified?" I asked.

"It's difficult to say," Das said. "One part of my mind says he shouldn't have taken the law into his own hands. But if it was me, I also wouldn't have tolerated it. I also would have murdered. He was my friend, but he did something wrong. I suppose I understand why the owner thought he had to kill him."

When the law is insufficient, when the police are inadequate, people take matters into their own hands. This is the essence of *goondagiri*—mobs taking the place of a weak state, greed and revenge and hurt pride standing in for justice.

Sathy and I were traveling along the East Coast Road one afternoon when we decided to take a break at a tea shop. Sathy recognized a man he knew from the area. His name was Dhanapal. His brother had been murdered recently. Sathy was helping the dead man's daughter, Dhanapal's niece, get married.

Dhanapal's brother's name was Kumar. He'd been a taxi driver. He had a bit of a drinking problem. Sathy said he warned Kumar many times not to drink and drive, but he never listened. One day Kumar was driving along the highway when he hit a woman getting out of a bus. She died on the spot. She was in her early sixties.

A mob from the surrounding villages gathered and started beating Kumar. He managed to get away. He ran, with the mob in pursuit, into the house of someone he knew. Kumar thought his friend would protect him, but his friend didn't want trouble. He asked Kumar to leave. Kumar ran out the back door.

The accident happened in the evening. Dhanapal heard about it soon after, and, with another brother, they went looking for Kumar. They couldn't find him anywhere. They searched in the houses of friends, they searched along the highway, and they searched in the fields. They were still searching at night when it started raining. Dhanapal went to Kumar's house, where his wife was waiting with their four children. She was crying; it wasn't like her husband to stay away at night.

Dhanapal and his brother searched for three days. They went to at least twenty villages, asking everyone if they'd seen Kumar. No one had, but one man, an acquaintance of the brothers, said he'd seen Kumar's blue shirt floating in a village tank. That got Dhanapal worried.

Finally, someone said he'd seen Kumar run into a eucalyptus forest by the road. Dhanapal and his brother went into the forest. They called Kumar's name, they searched everywhere. They found him hanging from a tree. There were flies buzzing around his head and ants crawling on his body. Dhanapal noticed how dark his brother had become. In life, his brother had been handsome and fair-skinned; in death, Dhanapal thought he was ugly.

Dhanapal started to cry; he felt a wave of anger. He was convinced that his brother had been murdered. The woman who was killed in the accident had powerful relatives. He'd heard about the mob. He started searching for clues; he wanted proof that his brother was killed. But his head was spinning, his ears were ringing, and he passed out.

When he came to, he called the police. They cut down the body and sent it to their station. From there, the police told Dhanapal, the body would be sent to the hospital for an autopsy.

I met Dhanapal more than a year after his brother died. He told me, in a husky voice, that he had yet to see the autopsy report. The police had refused to register a case. Every time he went to the station, they just told him his brother had committed suicide. But Dhanapal was convinced his brother hadn't hanged himself. For one thing, he said, people who die by hanging always have their tongue sticking out; his brother's tongue hadn't been sticking out. Also, he said, when he found his brother, he noticed that he had taken a large thorn out of his foot; he saw the thorn on the ground. "Tell me," Dhanapal asked me, "does a man intending to kill himself remove a thorn from his foot?"

There was one more thing: the man who told Dhanapal he'd seen his brother's blue shirt later admitted it wasn't true. There had been no blue shirt. Dhanapal felt he was just trying to send a message; the man knew that Kumar had been killed by the mob, but he didn't dare tell Dhanapal directly.

Dhanapal said someone he knew had seen a friend of the dead woman's family at the police station a couple times, talking to the police. He assumed they had been influenced. He felt they weren't going to do anything to make sure his brother received justice.

Sathy asked Dhanapal what he was going to do next. Dhanapal said he was still thinking about it. When his brother's body was first found he'd come to Sathy for help, and Sathy had advised him against taking any action on his own. He'd told him to go to the police, and from there to leave matters in God's hands.

But now, Dhanapal said, it was too much for him to bear, knowing that his brother's killers were walking around, free, while his wife and kids suffered, no one to support them. He felt he couldn't count on the police; maybe, he thought, God wanted him to act to ensure justice for his brother. He was thinking maybe he should hire some *goonda*s and get revenge. They were easy to find, and didn't cost much. A man's life was cheap these days.

Sathy sighed. He put his hand on Dhanapal's shoulder and squeezed it. "See, this is how it goes," he said to me. "Violence leads to more violence. People feel forced to take care of things themselves. This will become a cyclical thing. I'm afraid that many more people will have to die before this story is over."

More than the violence, more than the lawlessness, Sathy was upset about what all the real estate development was doing to agriculture. The escalating value of land was adding to the pressures on farming. Many farmers, struggling financially, heavily indebted after years of poor crops, were lured into selling. The money tided them over for a while; maybe it helped fund a daughter's marriage. But soon the money ran out, and the farmers found themselves worse off than where they had started.

Even if the money lasted, they often found themselves unmoored, cut off from a way of life they had inherited from their ancestors.

It was a treacherous bargain; people were getting rich off real estate, but they were losing their heritage in the process.

Sathy took me one afternoon to meet a man from Molasur who had sold his fields. His name was V. Puroshothaman. He was forty years old, a former farmer, a man who had grown up working on land that had been farmed, too, by his father and grandfather. Puroshothaman was one of the lucky sellers. He had started a catering business with the proceeds from his land. He had done something productive with his money; he was much better off financially. Still, he told me that since he'd stopped farming, he felt like a part of himself was missing. If he ever made enough money, he said, he'd definitely buy his land back.

I met Puroshothaman on the four-and-a-half-acre property he used to farm. Once, we would have been surrounded by watermelons, rice, and chilies. Now the land was marked only by yellow stones that defined plots for sale. When he was a boy, Puroshothaman told me, that land had kept his family alive. It had fed, clothed, and educated him and his three brothers. But by the turn of the millennium, he could no longer afford to support even his single daughter off the land.

"I was helpless," he said. "I couldn't pay for my daughter's tuition, I didn't even have one good shirt. I was ashamed to go to family functions. I worked so sincerely, for so many years. I started at four in the morning and worked all day. But at the end of it all, I had nothing."

Puroshothaman's life was changed by the highway coming up along Molasur. When word got around that the government was planning to build that highway, Puroshothaman started noticing men from the cities driving around in their air-conditioned Sumo jeeps, stopping every now and then to scout out pieces of land. One of Puroshothaman's neighbors, also a farmer, sold his property. The man who bought it sold it to another man, and then that man developed plots and sold it on again. It was a like a chain of prosperity, with each link making more money than the previous one.

Puroshothaman talked to his brother and parents about selling their land. His family was opposed at first, but Puroshothaman convinced them. He told them that sometimes you had to give up something to gain something. He said that he'd tried everything; he was prepared to lose his ancestral property if it gave him another shot at life.

Puroshothaman had benefited from Molasur's real estate boom, but he wasn't happy about the way it was changing the village. Like Sathy, he complained about a culture of violence, of intimidation and impunity. "A man who makes a little money suddenly thinks he's the boss," Puroshothaman said. "He buys a car, he fills it with ten *goonda*s, and they drive around and do what they want. They force people to sell. They think they own the village. It creates a very unpleasant feeling."

He worried about the future. He said his own family's future was brighter. His daughter was studying to be a doctor, and it made him happy to know she would never have to work on a farm. But he had to wonder: What would happen to the village, to the nation, if everyone quit farming? Like pretty much everyone I talked to around Molasur, he complained about escalating food prices. "Right now, people feel good about switching from farming," he said. "But later, they'll regret it. Rice will be as expensive as gold. Look at the price of onions! I worry that the country will go hungry."

I asked Puroshothaman if he regretted selling. Not really, he said. His life was better, more secure. But he couldn't deny that sometimes the changes in Molasur left a bitter taste in his mouth.

He pointed to a plotted piece of land next to where we were standing. He said that for years he'd rented that land from his neighbor and farmed it. It was hard, backbreaking work, in the rain and under the sun. Puroshothaman had struggled; he never really broke even. Then one day his neighbor sold the land to some people from Chennai, and they'd plotted it and made a lot of money.

"I slogged all my life on that land, and I only made a loss," Puroshothaman said. "To see a city fellow come in, put a little paint on some stones and make a fortune in three months—how do you think that feels? Of course it creates ill feeling. This village is filled with that kind of feeling."

At this, Sathy interjected, "Farmers can only be squeezed so much. People who were once huge landowners, today their children have to work in the homes of people who've made new money. Imagine that happening to me. I was the king once. Imagine if I had to work in someone's home. I don't think this can go on."

Sathy was speaking from the sting of personal grievance. For him, social change had been individual loss; new prosperity had meant a slipping of his family's status. But it was striking to me when Puroshothaman, who seemed to have benefited so much from the new order, whose daughter's horizons had indisputably widened, nodded in agreement.

He said that Molasur was changing too fast, too much, and in the wrong ways. He could remember when farming had been a noble profession. Now it pained him to see that farmers were no longer respected; they were looked down upon, considered old-fashioned fools who were missing out on India's growth. It frightened him that agriculture was dying. He felt that Molasur was losing its identity. He asked: What was the use of prosperity if the village disappeared?

He looked hard at his land—his former land—when he asked that. A few goats were grazing on it. A cow hung around, with no apparent purpose. It was all quite rural, even agricultural, except that the land was dusty and dry, and desiccated yellow grass had taken the place of Puroshothaman's crops. In the distance, I could just hear the horns from the buses and trucks traveling on the emerging highway.

Sathy said: "Farmers haven't fought back yet, but one day, I know it will happen. A frustrated farmer around here will blow up. The pressure is building and building and building. How long can it keep building? I'm sure one day something will happen. This village can only take so much. One day, things are going to blow up."

DIOXINS

Life in the country had its rhythms; it was one of the nicest things about living in Auroville. The summers were dry and quiet, with a hot wind that emptied roads and public spaces. Winters were wet, and then cool, monsoon downpours followed by a clear, clean light and crowds of tourists. The familiarity, the predictability, was comforting. The world around me was moving so fast, but the seasons stayed constant.

Then one April the summer wind brought with it an unfamiliar guest: the smell of burning plastic. It started on a Sunday afternoon, a hint of bitterness, like something rotten in the air. I barely noticed. A couple days later my wife woke me in the middle of the night and said something was burning. This time the bitterness was unmistakable, overwhelming, a chemical taste in my mouth, a trail of roughness along my constricted throat.

My older son woke up, vomiting. We nursed him through the

night. We told ourselves it was a stomach bug, something he'd eaten. But he'd eaten what we had all eaten, and as we stayed up with him, wiped his vomit and rubbed his stomach, comforted him, promised him it was nothing, it would pass, we couldn't shake the terrible feeling that it was in fact something very real—that he'd been poisoned by the air.

The smell invaded our house throughout the following weeks and months. Sometimes it blew in during the day, mostly at night. It came from a twelve-acre landfill south of my home, next to a village called Karuvadikuppam, just outside the town of Pondicherry. It was Pondicherry's main landfill. Every day, almost 400 tons of garbage—plastic bags and shoes and rubber tires and batteries mixed with rotting fruit and meat and rice—were carried there by tractors, and dumped in putrefying piles that emanated combustible methane gas.

The landfill was far from my house—across fields, a village, more fields, and then a forest and cashew plantations. It was almost two miles away. It had been there for over a decade, smoldering, throwing smoke into the atmosphere, but I had never noticed it. Now, with Pondicherry growing, its residents getting richer, buying more, discarding more, the dump had swollen.

Every day, the tractors brought their loads of garbage. Over the years, hundreds of thousands of tons had built up. The dump was running out of space. The fires, some man-made, some the result of spontaneous combustion, were getting bigger. The smoke was getting thicker, and traveling farther.

To me and my wife, the situation was bewildering. For so long, we had told ourselves that we were happy with the bargain we had made by choosing to live in rural India—happy to trade the vibrancy and life of the cities for the safety and cleanliness of the countryside. We had decided to live, to raise our children, in a place where crime was low, the water was drinkable, and the skies clear at night.

But now the world was crowding in—murder in the villages, poison in my living room. I was told that the dump was emitting dioxins and furans and other toxic chemicals. I was told that these poisons could lead to cancer, diabetes, cardiovascular and respiratory disease. And I was told, too, that children, with their undeveloped immune systems, were most susceptible.

What were responsible parents to do? We kept our children off the roads after dark. We bought a new air conditioner. On a good night, a night when the fumes weren't too thick, it filtered out the smell (though, I suspected, not the poison).

We talked a lot about moving. "But to where?" my wife would ask. Crime was everywhere, and so were the dumps, smoking heaps outside (and sometimes inside) cities, along highways, in fields and forests. In Chennai, just off Rajiv Gandhi Salai, a massive landfill spewed black smoke, making a mockery of the surrounding state-of-the-art technology complexes. I took a holiday in Goa, stayed at a high-end beach resort; every night, I choked on an all-too-familiar smell.

India produced some 100 million tons of municipal waste every year. On a per capita basis, this was still lower than most developed countries. But the problem was in the way the waste was treated—or not treated. According to the Organisation for

Economic Co-operation and Development, only 60 percent of municipal waste was even collected. A far smaller (almost nonexistent) amount was recycled. Instead, the garbage just piled up—and rotted, and smoldered, and polluted the air and water.

Sometimes, when I drove along highways lined with blazing mounds of garbage, when I passed through remote villages shrouded in acrid smoke, it seemed like there wasn't a safe (or clean) corner in the country anymore. India, I began to feel, was burning.

*India was burning—and, in a similar way, it was eroding, melt-*ing, drying, silting up, suffocating. Across the country, rivers and lakes and glaciers were disappearing, underground aquifers being depleted, air quality declining, beaches being swept away.

The numbers were astounding. According to a government report I read, almost half of India's land suffered from some kind of erosion. Seventy percent of its surface water was polluted. Half a million deaths a year were attributable to air pollution. Altogether, environmental damage cost about 4 percent of the nation's annual GDP (about the same amount the country spent every year on education or health).

Evidence of this destruction had been apparent around me for years. I had, of course, noticed how beaches and fields were being despoiled, how rivers and canals were choking on plastic bags, and how every scenic picnic spot was turning into a mire of paper plates and foam containers. I had seen these signs, registered them, but never really fit them together into a bigger picture. Auroville was green; I lived by a forest. I was shielded from—and a little blind to—the environmental calamity enveloping the nation.

But now the calamity had crept up on me, blown into my bedroom late one night, and into my children's lungs. The smoke was in my house; I could smell the fire. I could no longer overlook the scale of the problem, or the terrible human toll I suddenly understood it was exacting across the nation.

In the weeks after I first smelled the garbage, I started paying more attention to the way we had been abusing our world. The crisis in Indian agriculture, which I had thought of primarily as a social drama, a tragedy played out in farmer suicides and disruptions to village culture, now became apparent to me as an ecological crisis. The fields around me had been abused with chemicals for too long. Farmers had taken their wells for granted. Now the land was dying, and the wells were emptying.

Everyone always said India needed better roads, that without new infrastructure the country couldn't develop. I mostly agreed. Now, though, my eyes were fixed on the ancient tamarind and jackfruit trees that were being chopped down all over the place to make way for highways. Some of those trees were more than a century old; it took an excavator fifteen minutes to uproot them.

Along the beach, a twenty-minute drive from my house, the sandy stretch of coconut trees and fishing villages that lined the East Coast Road was slipping away, a victim of massive erosion. This was another man-made calamity. Some two decades ago, the town of Pondicherry had built a harbor farther down the coast. It was designed to spur development in the area. There was some debate about whether it had done that, but the harbor had indisputably blocked replenishing sand flows carried by currents from the south. Now the beaches around me were starved of nourishment.

I went to the ocean one day, to the fishing village of Chinnamudaliarchavadi. It was on a beach I used to frequent as a child. I had heard about the erosion, but I wasn't prepared for what I found. It was a shocking sight. A stretch of sand that had once extended for at least a hundred meters was now reduced to a strip of no more than ten or fifteen meters. Trees were uprooted, and fences and compound walls were breached. At least one electricity pole had come down. In the village, houses were perched precariously above the waters; some huts, I was told, had already been swallowed.

I sat on that sand, what was left of it, and I thought of just how little remained of the beach I had known as a boy. So much was being swept away. So much was being destroyed. I knew it was part of the compact of modern India: in with the new, out with the old, all in the name of progress.

I welcomed the progress. But all the destruction seemed a heavy price to pay.

The landfill outside Pondicherry occupied my mind. It was in my dreams, in my conversations, in the half hour of meditation I did every day. Every morning, I tried to clear my thoughts, find a quiet space. Visions of smoking garbage, of a country in flames, would rush in.

I found myself looking at the world in a different way. I noticed heaps of ash, impromptu burning sites, all over the place. I began to see plastic bags and discarded mineral water bottles as enemies. Their sight tightened my stomach; I thought of them as hazards, bombs waiting to explode on my children.

In the weeks and months after the smoke started entering my house, I visited the landfill over and over. I wanted to get to know my nemesis. I wrestled with him. I sent out press releases. I met activists and politicians, tried to convince them that something had to be done. Everyone was enthusiastic, everyone had ideas. People made promises. But the scale of the problem was overwhelming.

Solving India's garbage crisis, I came to see, would require whole-scale social transformation—changing the way government worked, reforming education, instilling a sense of civic consciousness in a population capable of maintaining ritualistic levels of hygiene at home, yet that dumped its garbage on the streets without compunction.

Most important, it would require altering the trajectory of India's development, nudging the country from the path of more more more it had so gleefully adopted from the West. After all, the landfill had existed for over a decade. It was only now, as Pondicherry and the surrounding villages succumbed to the consumerist culture infecting the nation, that the dump had swollen into a major ecological peril.

I took Sathy with me to the landfill one day. I thought maybe he could help. He was always talking about his connections, about all the politicians and government officials he could introduce me to. He knew how to work the system; I wanted him to work the garbage system.

We took his car. We drove with the windows rolled up, the

air-conditioning on high. We drove through bare, flat land, with goats grazing on dried-out fields and farmers taking shelter from the sun under solitary trees. We stopped and asked two farmers for directions. They were sitting under a neem tree; they were surrounded by plastic bags, paper plates and cups, the detritus of their lunch.

The fields gave way to a forest of acacia and eucalyptus. There were mansions in the forest, large country homes with high stone walls and carved wood doors. Expensive cars were parked in the driveways. The houses belonged to the rich. They were enveloped in smoke, and I couldn't help thinking they were mansions in a slum.

We parked at the edge of the landfill, by a gypsy encampment, a row of boxy concrete rooms. A yellow sign attached to one of the rooms announced the name of what I assumed was a donor organization. It was a dubious gift. The garbage came right up to and in some cases beyond the camp. As Sathy and I stepped out of the car, we were hit by the smoke. The stench was overwhelming.

A group of four or five gypsies sat on the ground in front of their homes. A woman was delousing her daughter. A newborn baby was lying in the sand, flies swarming on her blood-encrusted belly button. Pigs and chickens and stray dogs ran around. A few children chased the pigs over piles of garbage.

A woman came up to us. She was fiery, with red lipstick, and wild eyes. "What do you want?" she asked, in a gypsy dialect, a version of Tamil that both Sathy and I struggled to follow. "You people always come and promise to help, but you never do anything." When we told her we weren't from the government, that we, too, were affected by the dump, she softened. She complained about the smoke. She said the garbage attracted mosquitoes and flies. She said her children were always sick. They had sore throats, coughs, fevers. They missed a lot of school; they were often in the hospital.

"We used to live in town," she said, talking about Pondicherry. "Our people lived where the white people lived, right by the big houses and parks. But then we were brought here, promised houses, and we were dumped like we were just a piece of garbage. Look at our lives now. This is the way we live."

"Don't worry," Sathy said, in a fit of zamindar munificence. "We're working to move the dump. We're talking to people, and we'll have all this taken away."

A young man standing next to the woman shook his head and raised his hand in a supplicant's gesture. "No, no, sir," he said. He was shirtless; his *lungi* was old and dirty. "Please don't move it. It's our livelihood. What will happen to us if you move this?"

The gypsies were ragpickers. Like the people Vinod worked with in Dharavi, they earned a living extracting recyclable pieces of waste—metals, plastics, glass—from the dump. They got much of their food from the dump, too. The gypsies told me about scavenging for tomatoes, onions, and the occasional chicken bone they used to make soup. It was a hazardous life. But it was the only way they could survive.

Sathy, flustered, suggested we go to the top of one of the houses to get a better view. We climbed up a narrow flight of stairs, to a terrace blackened by smoke. There was a tattered mattress and a blanket on the terrace; they, too, were black.

We were standing, now, above the Karuvadikuppam waste dump. It was an apocalyptic sight, a sea of brown, muddy sludge,

interspersed with flakes of blue and pink and white and red—
plastic bags, the occasional computer monitor or keyboard, tubes
of toothpaste, and CDs that glinted in the sun. Municipal tractors
drove through the garbage, pulling carriages of waste like industri-
ous ants, dumping them indiscriminately, piling the garbage
higher and higher.

The landfill was bordered by denuded cotton trees and head-
less palmyras. They looked sickly; they were draped in torn pieces
of fabric. Hanging over it all was a gray pall, a dense accumulation
of smoke that lifted with every gust of wind and blew through the
gypsy settlement and the neighboring cashew plantations.

As Sathy and I stood on that terrace, we heard a series of pops;
the methane gas emitted by the tons of organic waste in the landfill was exploding. Each pop was followed by a burst of crimson
and yellow flames.

I cursed the flames. I swore at each pop, denouncing the garbage and the clouds of smoke. I grabbed Sathy by the shoulder.
"That's the shit that comes into my house every night," I said to him,
my voice raised, agitated. "People throw away all that stuff and it
ends up in my living room. People in the cities don't know where
their garbage ends up. They don't know, and they don't care. It's a
culture of 'out of sight, out of mind.' It's a culture of not caring.

"Everyone's too busy buying these days; no one thinks about
what happens to all that stuff they buy. They don't give a damn
about their garbage, and they don't give a damn about these gypsies. They certainly don't give a damn about me or my family.

"Tell me something, Sathy," I said. "I have two kids. Why
should I subject them to this poison? What am I doing to them by
living in this country?"

Sathy didn't say anything. He was uncharacteristically quiet. He just stared at the dump, his hands in his pockets, his shoulders slumped, his eyes behind a kind of glaze. I continued with my diatribe for a while, and then, finally, I asked him: "Sathy, say something. What are you feeling?"

"I feel," he said. He stopped. He turned to me. He looked at me as if from a distance. "I feel like shit," he said.

❦

Back on the ground, at the gypsy camp, I found myself talking again to the young man who had begged us not to move the landfill. His name was Raghu. He wasn't sure, but he thought he was about twenty-eight years old. He was short and broad-chested; he had rotting teeth, and matted hair pulled back in a ponytail.

Raghu was distressed. I could see he was worried that I really would manage to shut down the dump. He wanted me to understand just what the landfill meant to him and his people. He cornered me under a wilting tree. With a carpet of garbage at our feet, kids and pigs running around, sometimes bumping into each other, he told me about scavenging with his children.

He talked about collecting plastic bottles and cardboard boxes and milk cartons. He said he used magnets to fish out pieces of metal from the piles of composting waste. Life was hard, he acknowledged, but at least he and his children were alive. He said that on a good day, they made around thirty rupees. It wasn't much, a little over sixty cents, but it was enough—just enough—to eat.

Raghu told me that in the past, the gypsies had been hunters. They had guns; they were able to supplement their incomes by hunting for birds, rodents, **and rabbits** in the surrounding fields. But now the government had banned them from using their weapons. Everything they got, they got from that landfill. "If you remove this garbage, we will starve," Raghu said. "Our stomachs will be empty. We'll die."

I told Raghu not to worry. I said I didn't have the ability to move the landfill. But I asked him, also, about the wild-eyed woman Sathy and I had met when we first arrived, who had complained to us about all the health problems people in the camp suffered. She had talked about sore throats, coughs, and fevers. Another man I'd spoken to, a doctor who had done some work near the dump, had told me that the mosquitoes and flies drawn to the garbage carried diseases like typhoid, dengue, and filariasis.

"What about your health?" I asked Raghu.

"What use is health if your stomach is empty?" he asked me. "Health is secondary for us—living is the most important. This is how we eat.

"It's not a big problem," he went on. "If the children get sick we can always take them to the hospital and give them injections and medicine. They take pills, they get better. We've been here for twelve years and we're still alive. I'm strong. I don't have any big health problems, they come and go."

As Raghu spoke, a skinny man came over. He was one of the few men in the camp with a shirt on. He listened to us, he waited a bit, and then he interrupted Raghu. "My mother has heart disease, my uncle has blood cancer," he said, in a low, controlled voice. "This place is killing them. My uncle has seven children. One of them is in the hospital with jaundice right now. Who will take care of them when he dies? Of course we should move this garbage. It's certain death."

Raghu turned to the skinny man with an angry look. He made a loud, aggressive noise, almost a bark. "You shut up," he shouted, and he told me not to write what the man just said. "He doesn't know anything. He's not from here originally, he's from another village. He doesn't understand our condition. He's not one of us— he doesn't even know how to shoot a gun."

"I understand everything," the skinny man said. "Just because I can't shoot doesn't mean I don't know about this poison. I understand that the tsunami came and killed so many people, but it came only once. This comes all the time, it's like a tsunami every day. When it rains, the garbage comes into our houses. It floods us."

The skinny man said he was a "decent type." He didn't scavenge for a living; he didn't send his children to the landfill. He sold balloons in a market in Pondicherry. Raghu scoffed. He said selling balloons was an even worse way to make a living than scavenging. Sometimes, Raghu said, the balloons popped and the man lost everything he'd invested.

"He's an idiot," Raghu said, talking to me, ignoring the balloon seller. "Even if he lost his balloon business he'd probably refuse to come out here with us. He'd rather be a beggar. He would rather see his family starve. We do what we have to do to feed our family. I have four children—do you think balloons will feed them?

"Don't write anything he says," Raghu said again. "He's just a fool."

The skinny man repeated that the garbage was killing everyone in the camp. He walked away. Raghu kept talking. He was trying to convince me now; I could see he was still worried that I would move the landfill.

Scavenging was tough, Raghu said, but it had its rewards. He pointed to a freshly painted house. It was pink and green, a lively contrast to the plain concrete and drab yellow of the other houses in the camp. He said the house belonged to his brother. His brother had saved money from scavenging; he'd bought twenty pigs. He was a rich man now; he could afford to paint his house. He didn't need to scavenge anymore.

Raghu had only three pigs. He had three pigs and four children, and so he was forced to scavenge. He was a practical man, not like the balloon seller. He would take care of his family. One day, though, Raghu said, I would visit the camp and see that he, too, had a brightly painted house. He would keep working on the landfill; he would save; and then, finally, he would escape the garbage.

"It's our profession, it's like our business," Raghu said. "If they move this place, I don't know what will happen to us. Of course we don't have the power to stop it. We don't have any power. If they move it, I guess we'll have to shut down our business. I suppose we'll find something else. But I know this: I know that some of us will starve."

Raghu's dilemma—the sense that he was forced to choose between his livelihood and his health, that addressing the environmental catastrophe at his doorstep would mean losing his income—was an old one in India. Some forty years ago, Prime Minister Indira

Gandhi attended the first United Nations conference on the environment, in Stockholm, and announced to her audience that poverty was the worst form of pollution. Her words set the tone for the way India thought of the environment for decades. Ecological activism was seen as a luxury for the rich; it was something a poor country like India couldn't afford.

Today, when I talk to people who were involved in India's nascent environmental movement in the 1970s and 1980s, the sense I get is of a lonely struggle. They were up against a popular perception that environmentalists were elitists, more concerned with saving trees and animals than helping the country's poor. One veteran of the movement, in his sixties now, told me that he was accused of being "anti-development," and that he was labeled a "dinosaur" for his perceived opposition to India's progress.

A certain tension between the environment and development still exists in India (as, indeed, it does in much of the Western world: think of the United States' reluctance to impose a carbon tax for concern that it could stifle growth). But in recent years, as India has become richer, and as the state of the environment has in tandem become more precarious, it is a tension—and a distinction— that has become less and less tenable to maintain.

Men like Raghu don't live next to uncontrolled waste dumps because the nation is too poor to provide them with an alternative. They do so because India's prosperity is at least in part built on a model that keeps millions of people economically and environmentally subjugated. For Raghu, pollution is just another dimension of his poverty. His choice—India's choice—isn't between a job and clean air. It is between a model of growth built on the backs of the poor and the ruins of the environment, on the one hand; and on the other, a model that is economically inclusive and environmentally sustainable.

These were the thoughts—or variations of them, at least, because I wasn't thinking quite so clearly—that were in my mind as Sathy and I drove away from the gypsy camp that afternoon. I was angry, as I usually was after visiting the landfill. With the air conditioner on high again, and the stench slowly filtering out of the car, I continued the diatribe I had begun on the terrace overlooking the dump.

I told Sathy that when I talked to people like Raghu, so desperate to preserve the very thing that was killing him, I felt like something was fundamentally wrong in the nation. What kind of country imposed those kinds of choices on its people? What kind of economic superpower (even if it was a self-proclaimed one) allowed its citizens to live in those kinds of conditions?

I blamed consumerism, I blamed capitalism, I blamed the blindness of the middle classes and the callousness of the government. I was strident, worked up, maybe a little shrill. But I felt so helpless and frustrated. I kept returning, in my thoughts, to the night my son had woken up vomiting. I said again that I wondered what I was doing to my children; I wondered if I should move them somewhere safer.

Leaving the landfill seemed to loosen Sathy up a bit. He talked more now, first in a trickle, then in his habitual torrent. He said that, waiting for me while I spoke to the gypsies, watching as kids and pigs ran around, played with each other, he'd been possessed by a thought. For the first time in his life, he felt as if there was no difference between animals and humans. The landfill had reduced people to beasts. It was appalling, it was pitiful, and it was shameful. He, too, wondered what kind of country could treat its people that way.

He said he rarely felt hopeless, but when confronted with that landfill in Karuvadikuppam, he couldn't help feeling that India faced insurmountable problems. It's true, he said, that the government didn't care about those gypsies, and neither did society. But even if someone did care, if someone did want to help, what could they do?

Standing on that terrace, Sathy said, he felt like he was up against something larger than humans. It wasn't unlike the forces tearing apart his village: it was epochal, it was imposing, and it was beyond control. "I love this country, it's my home," Sathy said. "But sometimes I wonder what's happening to it. I come here with you and I see this kind of burning. I think: 'What's going on? What are we doing? What hope is there for India?'

"We're just too many people in this country, Akash," he went on. "This country is too big. What can we do with one billion people? Who can stop them? I really believe that this is something unstoppable. Nothing can reverse the direction of such a big country. It's like a huge machine. Once the destruction starts, there's nothing anyone can do."

Sathy talked like that the whole way back—through the cashew plantations bordering the landfill, through the mansions enveloped in smoke, through the littered fields, and then through the forest near my house. As I was getting out of the car, he did something unusual. He shook my hand. Then he said: "I'm sorry, Akash. I don't think I can help you with this. There's nothing I can do. I can introduce you to everyone I know, but the problem is just too big. It's beyond one man. Maybe it's even beyond all of us."

*Was it all really as hopeless as it seemed? In Mumbai, I had fol-*lowed the work Vinod was doing with the ragpickers of Dharavi. In the offices of his nonprofit organization, I had seen the heaps of waste, segregated into neat little bundles of plastic and metals and paper, ready to be shipped out to the informal recycling units that dotted the slum. One weekend I attended an "eco fair" that Vinod hosted in a park at the edge of Dharavi; it was a lively event, attended by movie stars and artists and musicians, and hundreds of eager children.

Closer to home, around Pondicherry, I had seen similar projects, all designed to ease India's garbage crisis. I saw school curriculums that tried to raise environmental awareness, and I saw street fairs organized with the same purpose. In a shed at the edge of a field, I saw a large concrete tank filled with pink worms writhing in a coarse brown powder. It was a vermicomposting project; the worms ate garbage, and excreted it as compost that could be used for agriculture.

All these efforts were well intentioned and, from what I could tell, mostly well run. They were not unimpressive. But they were so small when measured against the scale of the problem. We were, as Sathy had said, a nation of a billion people, all caught up in a scramble for riches, all eager participants in India's consumptive binge. There were tens of thousands, and perhaps hundreds of thousands, of steaming landfills like the one by my house. The projects I saw seemed insignificant—tiny points of light in the vast and otherwise dark firmament of India's garbage catastrophe.

A report I read estimated that India's production of waste would increase by 130 percent over the first three decades of the century. Numbers like that gave me little reason for hope. Every time I visited the landfill at Karuvadikuppam, when I saw the seemingly interminable procession of those municipal tractors, piling their poison ever higher, I was left with a humiliating mix of resignation and impotent rage.

I decided to pay a visit to Vinod. I knew a little about the work he was doing to promote recycling, and I respected it: I admired the passion he brought to what I had come to consider a hopeless task. I thought that maybe in Vinod's persistence I could find an antidote to the negativity, the sense of helplessness, that had possessed me since the dioxins started blowing into my home.

I met Vinod at his home in Bandra. He lived with his wife in a small one-bedroom apartment, off a winding lane behind Bandra's imposing St. Andrew's Church (the largest, and oldest, in the neighborhood). He lived in a waterfront building. The view from the dining table in his living room was pleasant, at least by Mumbai standards: shimmering (if blackened) waters, and a rocky promontory dotted with a few surviving mangroves.

But then, when I stood up from that table, walked to the end of his living room, and looked out at the ocean through a window, I saw that the shore was lined with a thick, compressed slab of garbage, consisting mainly of plastic bags. Vinod said the garbage was flushed out through the city's sewage system. Sometimes, people set it on fire. The smoke blew into his apartment. He, too, suffered the dioxins. His wife told me they had recently been forced—reluctantly, because it was an additional expense and put a burden on the environment—to buy an air conditioner.

Vinod and his wife had moved into their apartment in the early nineties. He said that in the two decades since then—a period of time that corresponded with India's transition from a planned economy to a capitalist one—the waste on the shoreline "had grown by feet." For Vinod, this was clear indication, visible and gruesome evidence, of the connection between the nation's economic success and its despoiled environment.

When Vinod talked about India's environmental problems, he used the same language he applied to the nation's capitalist economy. He talked about "corporate greed," "out-of-control growth," and "unequal and unjust policies that exclude the people."

Vinod told me about traveling the country, seeing rivers that had turned red from chemical effluents, and agricultural land that had become barren because industries were over-pumping the water table. He said he'd recently taken a trip to the South Indian town of Mangalore, where he'd grown up. He was dismayed by what he saw. The coconut plantations and forested hills of his childhood had all but disappeared. The hills were denuded, and entire villages were covered with a layer of red powder from iron oxide mines in the area.

In his work at Dharavi, too, Vinod saw the link between India's new economy and its troubled environment. Not only was the quantity of waste increasing dramatically, but the composition of that waste was changing, too. Whereas Indian garbage had once consisted primarily of biodegradable materials (kitchen waste, for example), now the proportion of plastic, batteries, and other nondegradable materials was rising. The volume of electronic waste, in particular, was alarming. Vinod lamented the "insatiable greed" of a new middle class that had forgotten an earlier generation's frugality. He said we were like the West now: we dumped goods as soon as they broke, and often even when they were still working, just because we wanted the latest model.

Vinod and I left his apartment, walked out to the shore. We made our way, gingerly, across the garbage. We stood at the edge of the waters and Vinod burrowed his shoe into the plastic, dug a hole that revealed black sand. He said that when he had first moved in, this had been a sandy beach.

We stood on that garbage, a few pigs running around us, and I caught a whiff of a smell I knew too well. Farther down the shore, someone had lit a fire. I pointed it out to Vinod, and he just laughed. I asked how he maintained his humor. He said there was no choice: What else could he do? He couldn't stop all the fires. He just kept working, plugging away, searching for solutions, remaining confident that the nation wouldn't, ultimately, commit suicide.

He acknowledged feeling sad sometimes. On that recent trip to his hometown, when he saw villages covered in red from the mines, he was overcome by "a feeling of loss." "Something very dear to me was being destroyed," he said. "All my peaceful childhood memories are tormented now by those horrible images." But at the same time, he returned from his trip motivated to fight harder. He said: "Seeing all of that gave me the conviction and the courage to keep campaigning, to teach children and a new generation about how precious our natural world is."

"Where do you get your hope from? Where do you get your conviction?" I asked him. I told him about my sense of hopelessness, about feeling like I was up against an unstoppable force.

"I believe that people have a strong survival instinct," Vinod said. "I've seen how they throw off tyrants throughout history, how they fight for their lives and freedom. My reading of history is that whenever repression gets out of hand, people rise up. I think we're in such a moment now. We're involved in a huge struggle with nature. We're fighting for our lives. Everything going on now will somehow come to a head. How can this city or this country sustain this kind of growth? I mean, how many more people can you fit into a single room?"

"So you think we're heading toward major upheaval?" I asked him. I wasn't sure, really, if the tyrant he was talking about was nature, or the economic system that was destroying nature. I wasn't sure if he was expressing hope that India would somehow learn to control the environment, or that it would reverse the economic path it was on.

"Who can say for certain what will happen?" Vinod asked. "But one thing I know for sure: There's going to be a huge amount of destruction. We have to accept that we're destroying ourselves. We're engaged in a dark fight with nature, and of course nature will react. This ocean is going to rise, water will take away parts of this city. There will be destruction on a huge scale."

"That's not very hopeful," I said. Vinod said his work was just to push the moment of destruction further and further away. He drew conviction from small things. When he looked around now, for example, he saw a few mangroves and coconut trees, and crows in the trees. They had persevered, they were living despite all the damage. That gave him hope.

"Look," he said, as we walked back to his apartment, pointing into the garbage. "A flower. A flower has also survived—against all odds." He was right; it was a red flower, half buried in the plastic. But then I looked closer, and I realized the flower wasn't real. It was made from cloth. No real flower could have survived the devastation on that beach.

On a hot Sunday in May, I went for a jog. I went through a forest in the north of Auroville. It was a beautiful forest, one of the biggest in the area. It was filled with silver eucalyptus, slender acacia, and ancient palmyra trees that stood like sentinels over the land. It was marked by winding dirt tracks and rows of channels that became muddy ponds during the monsoons.

I went in the evening, when the sun was low, when the harsh light of afternoon was turning yellow. I ran past houses, municipal buildings, a few schools, and then, as the development and traffic thinned, into the green. I could always tell where city ended and forest began. The air was cooler, somehow clearer. I felt a sense of upliftment, of stillness and well-being.

There is a clearing in the middle of the forest. It wasn't always there. It was created a few years after I returned to India, when a landlord from a neighboring village cut down the palmyra trees and cashew groves growing there and built a women's college.

The college was big and bulky. It had been open for while, but the building was still incomplete, a concrete block with unplastered walls, and steel rods pointing from its roof. The grounds were piled with rubble and overrun with stray dogs. I thought of the college like a gash in the forest.

As I approached the college on that Sunday in May, I felt something in my throat: the garbage reached all the way into the forest. Even there, miles from the landfill, protected (or so I had assumed) by acres and acres of green, of carbon dioxide–absorbing trees, the smell of burning plastic was strong. It was harsh, repellent, and deeply distressing.

I had to stop running. I leaned against a tree. I crouched on the ground, took a few deep breaths. My heart slowed, but my breathing was labored.

Across from the college, a village entrepreneur had set up a chicken farm. I could hear the cackle of chickens now, cooped up in their cages, and I could smell their shit. Someone was playing a radio; it was loud, Tamil disco music.

A white SUV drove past, its horn honking and its own loud music playing. A man and a woman, tourists by the look of them, sat in the back. I knew that a businessman had bought land in the forest, set up a spa hotel. I assumed the SUV's passengers were guests.

Forty years ago, there had been no forest. A group of ecologists, the first people to settle in Auroville, had planted and irrigated a barren soil. Then they'd moved out, left the earth to its own devices. It was a gift of sorts, an act of homage to nature, and over the years, a desert had turned into a lush and often wild green land.

Now humans were reclaiming the gift. The country was pushing back in, its lust to build and grow and prosper encroaching upon the territory from which it had once withdrawn. It was a form of colonization. Sitting there that afternoon, with the smell of burning plastic and chicken shit in the air, with disco music and car horns drowning out the birds and crickets, all the development struck me as violence—violence against the forest, of course, but also violence against ourselves.

A woman I knew from a local village was sending her daughter to the college. She was an illiterate mother, and her daughter was studying engineering. The mother was justifiably proud. She was convinced that her daughter would have a better future. But would she, really? I wasn't entirely convinced.

I wasn't convinced, anymore, that any amount of money, any increase in salaries or GDP or the number of cars of billionaires, was worth the damage we were causing to the country and our-selves. I wasn't convinced that the path the nation had chosen—a path I had so eagerly joined just a few years earlier—was leading to better things. More things, maybe. But not necessarily better.

Maybe I was wrong. Who was I, after all, to speak for impov-erished village women? Let them make their own trade-offs, I guess. Let them decide if an engineering degree or a forest—or breathable air—was more valuable. I knew that I was in a privi-leged position. But I knew, also, that I felt increasingly resentful about the price we (the country, my family, myself) were being asked to pay for development.

A watchman came over from the college and gave me a dirty look. He seemed drunk; he carried a stick. He asked what I was doing there. It seemed like a good question. What *was* I doing there?

I didn't say anything. The watchman was angry, a little aggres-sive. I thought I might as well be on my way. So I stood up, I ran away, I ran back home, to my children and my wife, and that night, when the smell of garbage wafted into my bedroom, when my kids started coughing and my eyes were stinging, I shut the windows and turned on the air conditioner, and I did everything to shut out my doubts, I held on to all that was good, all the reasons I had moved to India—and all the reasons I had for staying.

HARD TIMES

Later that summer, I took a trip to America with my family. We went to New York. We were escaping the smoke and dioxins of our new home, and my wife and I were revisiting our old life—the bars and restaurants we used to frequent, the bookstores we had browsed, the park to which we had once retreated, sought solace from the city, and in which my children now chased pigeons and marveled at the horse carriages.

Things had changed for us since we'd left the city. We had two sons. We'd built a new life at the edge of a forest. We'd made new friends, and I'd rediscovered the country I had known as a boy.

India felt different, too. It was tougher, in many ways harder to endure. Of course India had always been tough, a little wild; that was part of its charm. But now it was harder to keep the wildness at bay.

I felt tired. I was worn out by the grind, the turmoil and

instability of a nation perpetually in reinvention. It's hard to believe, but New York, with its eight million people and frantic pace, its grasping scramble to the top, felt soothing. The streets were cleaner, the air was easier to breathe. In Central Park, I met two friends from India. It was their first time in America. They were impressed. "Everything works here," they said. A few years earlier, I would have dismissed their reaction as a cliché. Now I identified; I agreed in a way that was painful, longing. I wanted to live in a country where things worked.

My wife and I took a trip outside the city, to a summer house on an island in Connecticut. We drove across the Triborough Bridge, and we made a side trip through the back roads of Connecticut, along the well-manicured lawns, the order and security I would have once ridiculed in suburbia. "Everything feels so clean," my wife said. I knew that the ecological damage was just better hidden, but what she said was true: there wasn't a plastic bag in sight, no stray dogs or pigs, no rotting vegetables emitting methane gas or deadly dioxins.

One night in the West Village, at a restaurant where we had once been regulars, a few glasses of wine in us and the glitter of the city exhilarating, seductive, my wife asked: "Couldn't we move back? At least for a little while? Just to recharge our batteries."

I thought about it over the next days, and, back in India, over the following weeks and months. We talked about it some more. It was tempting. India was certainly exhausting. It was exasperating, and often dispiriting. But our time in America had also soothed us, calmed the nerves left raw by a summer of breathing garbage. There was so much we still loved in India. There was so much to keep us going—just enough uncertainty, just enough movement, just enough of a sense of things still being played out, a story still unfolding, so that we wanted to be around to see where it was all going.

I had left America because I felt that the country was in many ways at a standstill. I moved to India in search of action. I wanted to feel alive, and I suppose I got a little bit more than I had bargained for. India was undeniably—sometimes terrifyingly—alive. The country was an adventure. On good days, the dust and chaos and danger could seem part of the adventure; they were invigorating. On bad days, I now decided, I would remember the good days.

On my way back from America, I had a stopover in London. I looked up Hari. I had e-mailed him a few weeks earlier, and now, from the taxi coming in from the airport, I called. He seemed happy to hear from me. In Chennai, I sometimes felt I was imposing on his busy social and work schedule; now he sounded a little lonely. We made a plan for the next day.

He told me he worked near the London Eye. He said I should take the Northern or Jubilee line to Waterloo Station, and meet him outside his office. "Ask for Elizabeth House," he said. "Everybody knows it—it's famous." But when I got out of Waterloo Station, into the thick air of a rainy summer evening, no one could help me. One man I asked for directions pulled at his maroon fedora and said, in accented English: "Young man, I don't even speak English, how can I help you find this place?"

So Hari came out to the street to get me, and together we made our way to a park bench under the London Eye. We sat just off the Thames. It started raining a little, thick drops that splattered the footpaths in intervals, with dry gaps between the wet, and I put my umbrella up. Hari, well adapted to the weather, seemed impervious. He kept talking.

He had a lot to say. He told me about the places he'd been visiting, the people he'd met, everything he was learning at work. He loved London. He visited its sights on the weekends. He had seen Big Ben, he'd been to the National Gallery, to the parks, and recently, he'd visited Madame Tussauds, where he posed with Justin Timberlake and J.Lo, but not with Britney, because she was too ugly ("Even Kylie looked better").

He'd made some friends. He talked about a Taiwanese man he had met online, and a Czech woman he had met at work. She had expressed admiration for how well Hari was adjusting to London. She said it had been much harder for her when she moved to the city. She asked what his secret was, and he told her, "It's easy, you just have to know how to mix and match," by which I think he meant you had to remain flexible.

He complained about his roommates, the two colleagues who had come with him from Chennai. He said they were immature, always fighting with each other. They gave long lectures at work about Indian tradition, and about the country's superior moral values. They praised arranged marriages, they talked about the modesty of Indian women. Hari called them hypocrites. He couldn't stand people who talked so much about tradition. "What does tradition mean?" he asked. "It's just a game, a word people use."

He liked the English. He found them open and friendly. He hadn't encountered any racism. On the contrary, he said, everyone at work admired Indians. People thought of Indians as "the brains of the world." Whenever there was a tech problem in the office, they came to the Indians for help. "We're the leaders now," he said. "It's just us and the Chinese. Who else is there?"

He pointed to an imposing gray tower overlooking the park. He said it was the headquarters of a major corporation. According to Hari, 30 percent of the employees in the building were Indian (I couldn't verify this information). It made him feel good to know that—"on cloud nine," he said. "Earlier, they used to call us 'bloody Indians,' and we used to feel bad," he said. "Now we know what to say. We just call them 'white trash.'"

An ice cream van rolled up. It was covered with cartoon characters, Mickey and Daffy and Donald, and it was playing a tinny tune from speakers attached to the roof. A group of French schoolkids ran over; they queued, arguing, shoving each other eagerly.

Hari said that when he saw the ice cream van, with the kids lined up, he thought of all the business opportunities back home. "Do you know how little money they started Infosys with?" he asked me, and I said I did. He told me about the founder of a global chain of Indian restaurants who had started with just twelve dollars.

He had decided he was going to start his own business when he went back to India. One day, he would sell his business. He would return to England and buy the company where he was now working.

"What, with the proceeds from your ice cream company?" I asked, teasing a little.

"Don't laugh," he said. "Anything is possible."

❧

Hari and I went for dinner to Leicester Square, in the West End of London. In the Tube station, he showed me how to work the ticket machines, and he led the way to our train. It was rush hour, and Hari explained the protocol to be followed on crowded trains—how you let passengers disembark before boarding, how you ceded your seat to the elderly and the disabled. He was proud to tell me these things; I thought he was showing me that London was his city.

Leicester Square glistened after the rains. It was crowded: punks with colored Mohawks and tongue studs, men in low-hanging jeans, down to their knees, and women in heart-stopping little outfits that defied the evening chill. Hari and I laughed at the goose bumps on their uncovered arms and backs.

"People here are sexy," Hari said. "When I walk down a street, there are so many good-looking people. It's not like in Chennai, where everyone is fat and ugly. Everyone here is white, and they're fit. They all work out. They all have such nice asses—both the boys and the girls."

I asked him if he'd met any men. He pointed to a red Porsche. "What a car," he said. "Expensive!"

"Expensive cars, expensive girls, expensive boys," I said. "It's an expensive country."

"Boys and girls aren't expensive," he said, laughing. "They're free. As long as you know what you want, and you know how to speak, you can get it. You just have to know what you want," he said. "And you have to know how to ask for it."

We decided to eat at a Japanese restaurant. Hari had never eaten Japanese food before. The confidence—the worldliness, the ease with city life—he had displayed on the train wavered a bit, but then he just told me to go ahead and order whatever I thought was good. "I don't mind anything, as long as it's cooked," he said.

We talked a bit about how expensive London was. Hari complained about his pay; he could barely live off the small supplement his company was giving him. He said that everyone in London seemed so rich. Earlier, he had talked about returning to India to start a business; now he said he'd like to come back to London, try living there for a longer time.

"Why, for the money?" I asked, and he said: "That, and other things. Not just the money."

His mood had changed. He seemed sullen. He wasn't talking as much as he had been in the park. I asked if he'd been in touch with his parents. He said he had. I asked if they were proud of him. "Yes, they think it will get me a good wife," he said. "But some things they can never understand. Some things about this life I can never explain to them."

"Like what?"

"Just things," he said, and he poked at a crack in the table with a chopstick. "It's difficult to explain."

I pressed him, and he looked at me as if he was trying to decide what to say. "Like maybe the way people dress," he said. "If my father saw how some people wear clothes here, especially the women, he wouldn't be too happy. He wouldn't be angry, but he might make a face."

I said I imagined that over time his father would adjust. "Yes, but there are so many other things," he said. "So many things they could never understand. Clothes, sex, money—the gaps are too big. I could never explain."

Then he reconsidered: "Maybe they could understand. Who knows? They must have had gaps with their parents."

"Right," I said, "it's not so difficult."

"I guess I won't know until I speak to them. I won't know how they really feel."

He picked at some tempura; he said it reminded him of pakoras. He ate some edamame and asked what was so special about salted peas. He said Japanese food reminded him of Vietnamese food. He'd been to a Vietnamese restaurant recently, also for the first time.

"Hari, I'm sure your parents would understand the way people live here if they had to," I said. I told him that I had many friends who had emigrated from India to America. It had been hard for some of them, but most eventually adapted.

"Yes, of course," he said. He looked down, he played with the tempura. Then he looked up: "Still, if they knew what I was, if they ever knew what I really was, they would be so ashamed."

"You mean the fact that you like boys?" I asked. "So that's what you mean is difficult to explain to your parents?"

"That's the Mount Everest of differences," he said.

He told me that one day, a few weeks after arriving in London, he'd gone to a park in front of his apartment. It was a Sunday. He woke up late, washed his clothes, and watched some TV. He ate lunch; he felt relaxed.

The park was busy. It was filled with people walking their dogs, kids on Rollerblades, and men playing football. It was a clear day. The grass was green, well maintained. Hari walked around a little, and as he was walking, an idea suddenly hit him: "What if it was actually easy? What if I told my parents, and they just understood everything? What if they accepted me?"

He had seen the way gay people lived in London. He had seen the way they went around holding hands, hugging, even kissing in public. In the nightclubs they danced together; in the parks and gardens they leaned against each other, lay side by side. All of this had made him think: "Everyone here is so free. Everyone lives however they want. People can walk down the street without being harassed. What if it could be the same for me back in India?"

He knew his father could never accept him, but he wondered about his mother. Maybe she could learn to tolerate him. He said—and now he was talking, opening up like he never had before—that he felt lonely sometimes. He corrected himself: "Not lonely, but it's like a burden, something I'm always carrying around, something that I have to hide from my parents.

"It's very strange, you know. Your parents know everything about you until you are a teenager; they know you inside out. And then it gets harder and harder. You start to have secrets; you have to hide things. It all started with me in school. I knew I was different, I knew I had to hide it. Now there are so many things my parents don't know anymore. In a way, it just feels wrong—it feels wrong that they don't know this thing about me."

He wondered how he could tell them. He'd been thinking about it a lot. Should he tell them in a single day? Should he break the news slowly, over time? He worried that they would throw him out of the house, but he felt that eventually, they'd take him back in. He was terrified that someone, maybe a family member living in Chennai, would find out and break the news to his parents before he got the chance.

One thing he knew for sure: It had to remain a secret until his younger sister got married. If people found out, it could ruin her chances of getting a good match.

I said I found that silly. He said I didn't understand: Reputation was everything. I told him about Selvi, and about her shame over Sudha's death. I said she, too, had been worried she would have trouble getting married. It seemed ridiculous to me.

"Society does that to you," he said. "You can push to be yourself, you can be so bold. But finally it gets you and makes you dumb. It flattens you."

"What about you?" I asked. "What has it done to you?"

"I can be myself, I'm strong enough for that," he said. "But no one can ever know who I am."

Hari went to London in April. He stayed there through the sum- mer. It was cold when he landed, and warmer when he left; there was more blue in the sky. He was hoping his stay would be extended, he would have enjoyed a few more months in the city. But his company brought him home, and by late July he was back at the same desk, in the same office, living in the same apartment, in Chennai.

I talked to Hari a couple weeks after he returned. He said he was still tired from his trip, jet-lagged, and I thought it was a way of holding on to his time in London, delaying his return. He was busy for a while after that, helping two cousins organize their weddings. He told me he was their "fashion consultant"; he traveled around the city to jewelry and clothes stores, helping them choose outfits.

I finally met Hari a couple months after he got back. He came down to Auroville to visit another friend, and we met at a coffee shop on the East Coast Road and went for a walk on the beach. It was the afternoon, sunny, and Hari was worried about his complexion.

He didn't want to get too dark. So we sat in the shade of a fishing boat, in the sand, surrounded by the stench of drying fish.

He complained about how boring nightlife was in Chennai; he said he missed London. He'd gone out a lot there, to nightclubs and pubs, to restaurants. His favorite pub was called The Edge; it was in Soho. He said the clubs in London were "two hundred percent" better than in Chennai.

He'd made a lot of gay friends in London. He learned a lot from them. He'd seen how they were open and proud. They didn't hide who they were; he felt he should be the same. One friend told him about his struggle to come out. He'd waited for years, afraid of his parents, but then, when he finally told his mother, she said: "You've been gay all this time and you're only telling me now? You poor thing, you should have told me earlier."

"Can you imagine that?" Hari said. "She not only accepted him, she encouraged him!"

Hari seemed to have returned with a clearer sense of identity. He told me he had decided he wasn't bisexual. He wasn't attracted to women, only to men. He knew, now, that he was homosexual. When he told me things like that, he didn't speak in euphemisms anymore. We didn't have to talk about "that thing" or "it" or "the way I am." Hari was able to call himself "gay," to speak about himself as a "homosexual."

He'd come out to seven close friends in Chennai since returning. They were all shocked. "But you're such a flirt, you're such a playboy with girls," one told him. "Why? Why did you choose to become that way?"

Hari told his friend: "Because I like it. Because I like it that way."

Coming out to his friends had been easy. Hari was still trying to decide how to come out to his family. But in any case, he said, that would have to wait. He had more pressing concerns right now. He was in financial trouble. He had big debts.

He owed more than four lakhs, a sum equivalent to almost two years at his current salary. Some of that was credit card debt accumulated from his shopping sprees. Some of it was because he'd been forced to buy a new laptop and cell phone after his old ones were stolen. Also, he'd borrowed a significant sum to help a friend whose mother needed heart surgery. The friend had promised to pay him back, but then he'd gotten into a motorcycle accident and lost a leg, and now whenever Hari visited him the friend just stayed in bed, depressed. It was terrible; Hari felt he couldn't possibly ask for his money.

Hari said he needed a new job, one that paid a lot more than his current position. He was willing to go anywhere, do anything. He said: "All I need is money, money, money. I'm broke."

He'd sent out his résumé to dozens of places. He had high hopes; after his posting in London, he expected to get good offers. But times weren't as positive as they had been. The Indian economy was feeling tremors from the American subprime earthquake, and the software and back-office companies that relied on American business were particularly hard-hit. For all the talk that India had escaped the worst of the global crisis, Indian companies were nonetheless having to cut costs and slow down on hiring. Hari hadn't been called to a single interview; only one company had even bothered to acknowledge receiving his résumé.

He told me about layoffs at software firms, and salary cuts that were hitting his friends. One of India's largest software companies, he said, had raised salaries by a mere 500 rupees. Hari was scandalized, and, I felt, a little disoriented. This wasn't the world in which he and his friends had come of age; for the first time in his working life, the future seemed uncertain.

"Sometimes I wonder why this is happening to me," he said. "All my debts, all my financial problems, and now the world economy—it feels like everything is coming in a flood. But I guess somehow I'll manage. There are always ways to manage."

One thing, at least, was going well in his life. He'd met someone, a young man, and they'd been spending a lot of time together. Hari was crazy about him. "With everything else happening to me, it's good to have this one bright spot," he said. It was his first relationship. He said he was in love.

Hari wasn't the only one having a hard time. Across the country, I heard stories like his—stories about frustrated job hunts, about layoffs and slowdowns, and projects that had to be shelved or put on hold. India's trademark optimism—its enthusiasm for capitalism, its faith in the future—was still evident. There was none of the panic or despondency I sensed in e-mails and phone calls from friends in America. People seemed confident that the troubles were just a blip. But accompanying the unabated (perhaps willful) cheeriness, I did sense a new wariness, and maybe even sobriety.

The new sobriety was most evident in the cities. In Bangalore, the fount of modern Indian business, the crucible of its new economy, there was a palpable change in mood. Nightclubs were less crowded, shopping malls less noisy, and the airport less busy. Hotel rooms, for a while among the most expensive in Asia, were affordable again.

One day Banu took me to meet her uncle, a Bangalore real estate developer. He had done well for himself in the boom years. He'd built a three-story mansion with granite floors and carved teakwood doors. Now, he said, times were tough. He took me to see one of his projects; it was a hole in the ground, with unfinished concrete columns and rusting steel rods. It was supposed to be a commercial center, but financing had dried up. He couldn't get a loan; his partners were out of cash.

Standing over that hole, the wind blowing cement powder and dust into our eyes, Banu's uncle said: "We are all just sitting around at home, nothing to do. It was so good for so long, but now it feels like it was just gambling, a dream. We all wonder: When will it end? How much longer can it take? When it will be like it was again?"

At the shopping mall where he worked in Bangalore, Arvind, Veena's husband, told me that business was definitely slower. He said only the jewelry stores were still doing well. Business was especially brisk on weekends, when middle-aged men bought earrings and necklaces for younger women. Arvind's theory was that they were buying for their mistresses; infidelity didn't slow down with the economy.

But things weren't as good for Veena, Arvind told me, and he said she was having a tough time. When I asked him what was happening, he said I'd better just speak to her myself.

Veena was, as ever, looking for a new job, but this time the conditions were different. She had quit her last job, at the software company, after getting entangled in an episode of sexual harassment. Now she was worried; given current economic conditions, she said, she wasn't sure what kind of a job she could find. "It's the worst time to have to quit a job," she said. "I don't know what's going to happen." I had never seen Veena's confidence so shaken.

The sexual harassment at work had been difficult to recover from. Veena's company had defended her, punished the alleged offender. But then, Veena said, she started feeling uncomfortable at work. She decided she didn't want to stay on.

"It's an incredible situation," she told me when I met her in Bangalore. "I've only read about situations like this. I was very surprised that this is actually true. I was surprised that men actually behave like this. I've always been a male advocate. I always defended men when they were accused of such things. You know, generally, my history is that I always go after men and get them. In the past, if someone has come on to me and I tell them to back off, they always did. If I said, 'Forget it, take the hint,' they did.

"It's hard for me to believe that a man can be so persistent. After all that I've been through, I can't believe I'm without a job. I can't believe I'm the one in trouble."

I reminded Veena of the time she told me she never believed a woman who claimed she'd been sexually harassed. She had said that women who had sexual problems at work invited them.

"Well, I've changed my mind on that," Veena said. "I've learned that women can't always be as strong as I thought. I thought we could always push back when someone tried to pressure us. Now I know: sometimes, no matter what, we end up victims."

Mostly, what I felt in India those days, for much of 2009 and parts of 2010, was a kind of stunned silence. As the global economy stumbled from crisis to crisis, stuttered in and out of recessions, the nation held its breath. There was a kind of watchfulness, a certain muted apprehension. Could the party already be over? Could the celebrations of the last decade have been premature? Or would—as the press and politicians kept assuring us, perhaps a little too stridently—the contagion soon pass us by?

There was silence in the media, where the cheerleading evident for so long was replaced by a new self-restraint. There was silence in the cities, where shops and restaurants were emptier; and silence in the tech parks and recruitment centers, where business was down and young men clutching engineering degrees, raised on the assumption of an ever ascendant job market, were shocked to find their skills no longer in demand.

There was silence, too, from Hari, who had stopped replying to my e-mails and phone calls. His phone would ring and ring without an answer. Often, I would get a recorded message saying his phone was switched off. I got this message for weeks on end. I started to worry.

Then Leo, the friend who had introduced us, told me that Hari had bought a new number. He was giving it out only to close friends. Leo said Hari's financial situation had worsened. He was trying to avoid the banks and credit card companies that kept calling him about his debt. I called Hari on his new number, and he told me that yes, things had deteriorated; he was trying to keep a low profile.

He was getting harassed by collection agencies now. They would call him at work, they would call him at home. For a while, he'd been able to roll over some of his debt by taking new loans. But as the economy got worse, banks started cracking down; no one would lend to him anymore. Hari said he was barely able to make his monthly payments.

We met a short while later, in our old haunt, the coffee shop in Chennai with cool air-conditioning and synthetic leather chairs. Hari was waiting for me when I got there, sitting at a table eating a piece of chocolate cake. He had circles under his eyes; his hair was uncharacteristically unkempt. "Are you still a regular here?" I asked, and he shook his head and said he'd barely left his apartment in a month. "I just sit at home these days," he said. "All I do is stare at the wall and wonder what happened to my life."

Hari had lost his job. It wasn't entirely clear what had happened, although I thought I could read between the lines of the story he told me. He said his manager had submitted a negative performance report. She said he wasn't living up to his potential. According to Hari, the real reason she'd given him a negative report was because they had personal differences.

Hari was angered by the report; he said he quit his job. An old friend offered him another job; he had a business that handled outsourcing projects, and he promised Hari a good salary. But the friend started having trouble getting contracts, and he couldn't pay Hari what he'd promised. Hari felt deceived. He thought the friend was being dishonest.

Hari confronted his friend, and his friend accused him of lacking loyalty. He said business was tough; Hari didn't understand his situation. He said Hari cared only about money; he called him greedy. Hari told him: "I was very clear with you when I joined you. You knew about my debt problems. You knew that I needed money and that's why I quit my old job." They had an argument; Hari told his friend to "fuck off." He quit that job, too.

Now Hari was unemployed, heavily in debt, and scared. The last two checks he'd written to his credit card company had bounced; if a third one bounced, they'd file a court case against him. He said he really had no idea what to do. He'd applied for jobs everywhere he could think of; he'd even sent his résumé in to an airline. He hadn't heard anything back.

He just sat at home staring at a wall. He wondered where he would go, he wondered what he would become. He was disappointed and shocked. He was having trouble sleeping.

I asked Hari if he'd told his parents about his situation. He clenched his jaw; there was no way he was going to turn to them. "I don't want support from them," he said. "I'm finished with them. Let them pretend we're a happy family all the time—we're just a pretend family."

I told Hari he seemed angry. He said: "I'm angry because in my street every single mother wanted a son like me. I was so perfect, I seemed so good to everyone. And now, if people come to know the things I've done in my life, if they come to know me, who I really am, they won't ever want a son like me—never, ever. Everything is blank for me. I have no future."

I brought up the topic of coming out to his parents. He laughed; he sounded bitter. He said he wasn't scared anymore. He was going to do it, as soon as his sister was married. He was going to look his parents in the eye and say: "I know what I am, and I'm not going to change. Accept it or not—I won't change."

His phone rang; he looked nervous. But it was his private number.

He picked it up, made a plan with a friend for that evening. "If I switch on my other mobile I'll be dead," he said. "They chase me all the time. 'What's happening with your payment? Why is it late? Why did your checks bounce?'"

He looked out the window, where the traffic was, unusually, moving smoothly. He said: "Even the one thing that was going well for me is gone now." He'd broken up with his boyfriend. The boyfriend had been too jealous, so Hari called it off. The boyfriend called him one night, around midnight, and threatened to jump off the roof of his hotel. Hari talked him out of it, and in the morning his boyfriend sent him a text message: "You are one A-class, third-rated bitch."

Hari replied: "Thanks for the compliment."

The story seemed to cheer him up a bit. He started telling me about all the great sales that were happening in the city. It was just his bad luck that the biggest discounts were available now, when he had no money. Benetton had a huge sale under way. It was a good thing he'd been locked away at home, depressed; if he had gone to the store, he said, he wouldn't have been able to resist.

I reminded Hari of the time we had gone shopping together in Spencer Plaza. I reminded him of the way he and Nikhil had been so sure of themselves, so certain they'd have their pick of jobs. He laughed at the way he'd flashed his credit cards around, at the memory of his easy confidence. Back then, he never imagined that things would turn out this way.

"What happened?" I asked Hari.

"That was then," Hari said. "The job market was different. Things were hot then. But the times have changed. The world has changed. Do you watch TV? Do you see what's happening? I guess we have to change accordingly. We have to go with the flow."

His phone rang again; he screened the call. "People also change," he said. "I guess I'm different now. I'm not the same Hari I used to be."

❦

I had stayed in touch with Dr. Reddy, the sexologist I visited soon after meeting Hari and Selvi. We e-mailed every now and then, and I kept track of his activities in the newspapers. He called me one day and invited me to a conference at which he was speaking in Chennai. It was a conference on homophobia. He remembered that I had asked a lot of questions about homosexuality; he thought I might be interested.

I asked Hari if he wanted to come with me to the conference. I said I'd introduce him to Dr. Reddy. He scoffed. "Why would I want to meet a doctor?" he asked. "You seem really angry," I said. "You're upset. Maybe he could help."

"I don't need a doctor," Hari said. "I need a job."

The conference was held in a concert hall with dusty cement floors and fake wood paneling. Dr. Reddy sat on a stage with another sexologist and several activists. The activists talked about coming out, about their experiences with discrimination at home and in society. Dr. Reddy talked about the difficulty of eliminating homophobia; he said it was deeply entrenched, fed by a general neuroticism in the country about sex. "We have to get this sex thing out of the closet," he said.

After the conference, I asked Dr. Reddy if he'd consider seeing

Hari. I told him a bit about Hari's situation. I said I thought he could benefit by talking to someone. A little while later, I found myself back at Dr. Reddy's office, this time with Hari, waiting while a woman and a man (a married couple, I assumed) rotated in and out of the counseling room without looking at each other.

While we waited, Hari told me his situation was getting worse. He said he'd been hit by a "tsunami of problems." His mother had consulted his horoscope and seen his bad luck. She had assured him things would be better in a few months. Hari put little faith in that; his mother didn't know the full extent of his problems. Even his scooter had broken down. The engine had seized, but he didn't have the money to fix it. He had to get around the city by public transport.

"If this goes on, I'll have to move back to Tindivanam," he said. "I'll just have to run back to where I came from."

Dr. Reddy and Hari sat at opposite ends of a black table in the counseling room. Dr. Reddy made small talk for a while. He asked about Hari's education, his family, his parents, their backgrounds, his work life. Hari told Dr. Reddy he'd come out to his friends recently. He said he had told them "what I am," and Dr. Reddy asked: "What do you think you are?" Hari, wrinkling his nose but looking straight at Dr. Reddy, said: "Gay."

He told Dr. Reddy about his first sexual experience with a male. It happened in school, when he was about fourteen years old. He said he had felt shameful and guilty after the encounter, but comfortable and happy while it was happening. Later, when he started having more encounters in college, the shame dissipated. What he was doing felt natural. It felt right.

Dr. Reddy asked Hari what he was hoping to get out of their

discussion, and Hari talked about his trip to London, about the gay friends he'd made there, and how he'd felt when he returned. He said he wanted to come out to his parents, but he didn't know how.

"Do you think they already know?" Dr. Reddy asked, and Hari said he didn't think so, but sometimes he wondered about his mother. Just the other day, she had turned to him with a sad look in her eye and asked: "Hari, why are you so different now?"

"No, Mother, I'm not different," Hari said. "I've always been this way."

"No, something's changed in you since you left home," she said.

"No, I've always been this way," he said. "Don't you remember, at school I was the only one who was able to talk to girls? I was always comfortable with girls. I've always been so comfortable with women."

"You didn't used to be this way," his mother insisted, and she turned back to the book she'd been reading. Hari wanted to pursue the conversation. He wanted to ask her what she meant. But the moment had passed.

Dr. Reddy told Hari that if he did come out to his parents, he should expect a huge scene. He warned Hari that it wouldn't be easy. First, Dr. Reddy said, his parents would probably refuse to believe him. They might try to take him to a doctor, to cure him. They'd say it was a state of mind. "It's not a state of mind!" Hari said, indignantly. "That I can tell you—it's not just a state of mind."

Dr. Reddy said Hari's parents would surely emphasize the social problems he would cause his family. They would talk about the family's reputation; they would talk about the difficulty his siblings would have in getting married.

"That's the one question I can't answer yet," Hari said. "That is the only question that's still bothering me. For them, society is so important, and I don't know what I can say to my mom if she raises that issue."

"Not just society," Dr. Reddy said. "Your relatives also won't keep quiet. That pressure is going to be there. You and your parents will have to face incessant questioning from relatives."

Hari said his relatives had already been putting pressure on his parents, asking why their son wasn't married. The questions had been going on for years. He knew the situation was difficult for his parents; he knew it made them tense, and maybe a little sad.

As Hari spoke to Dr. Reddy, I thought I saw some of the anger he had previously displayed toward his parents ease a little. He seemed more mindful of their situation, concerned about the difficulty he might cause them. Still, he said, he'd made up his mind: he was going to tell his parents. He'd been thinking about coming out for years, right since his college days, but he'd always been scared of the consequences. Now, after his time in London, he was sure who he was, and he was sure he was ready to tell other people. He just needed to find the right time, and the right words.

Dr. Reddy steered the conversation away from coming out. He and Hari discussed a wide range of issues about homosexuality in India. They talked about cultural and religious norms toward homosexuals, and they talked about Section 377, the British-era law that had criminalized "carnal intercourse against the order of nature," and that had recently been overturned by the Delhi High Court. Hari said he had a copy of the judgment on his laptop.

Sometimes, their conversation became fairly technical. Dr. Reddy spent a considerable amount of time delving into the biological differences between transvestites, transgenders, and transsexuals. He asked Hari why he referred to himself as gay rather than homosexual. He asked if there was a difference between the two words.

Toward the end of the session, Dr. Reddy asked Hari whether he had found their time together helpful. Somewhat to my surprise, because they had spent so much time talking about issues that seemed tangential to Hari's interest in coming out, Hari said he had, extremely. He said Dr. Reddy had given him a lot of new information. "You've opened new ways to consider it all, you've given me new ways to talk about it," Hari said. When he did come out to his parents, he'd be able to "categorize and tell."

Hari stepped out of the room, and I asked Dr. Reddy why his conversation had been so free-ranging. He said: "You see, there's actually not much I can do to help him. There's no way I can avoid the scene that will blow up at home when he tells his parents. One way or another, it's going to be a big trauma—for him, for his parents, for everyone involved. So all I can really do is arm him with information. I can make him confident, more sure of himself, and hope that he can stand his ground. I'm just trying to empower him."

As I was leaving, Dr. Reddy said: "You know, he's really very self-confident. I'm not sure how he ended up like this, but I can count on my hands the number of men I've seen who are so sure of themselves and so comfortable talking about it."

Outside, in the advancing evening, Hari was waiting on the road, leaning against a compound wall. He seemed contemplative, but he was in better spirits than I'd seen him in a while. He said all doctors should be like Dr. Reddy. They should listen and give their patients information. He said he felt he understood what it meant to be a homosexual, and especially a homosexual in India, much better now. He was sure it would help him when the time came to tell his parents.

"So, when do you think that will be?" I asked him.

"Who knows," he said, and his face dropped. It was like watching a shadow come over him. "First, I have to sort through my mess," he said. "No job, no money, so many debts—it's not the right time to add to my difficulties."

I lost track of Hari for a while after that. When I next heard from him, a few months later, things seemed to have turned around for him. He told me he'd come out to one of his sisters. She was the first person in his family to know, and she'd accepted him. That was a big load off his back. He'd found a new job, too. He was living in Bangalore now, marketing for a company that offered software services to American clients. He was getting paid substantially less than he'd hoped for. But it was better than nothing; it allowed him to pay off his debts.

Hari was living in a suburb far outside the city. He commuted into town on weekends. He had a wide circle of friends, many of whom he'd met over the Internet. He was enjoying Bangalore's gay life. He went to meetings and get-togethers sponsored by gay rights associations.

We met one afternoon when I was visiting Bangalore. Hari took the long bus ride from his suburb, through the city's chaotic traffic, to the center of town. He was almost two hours late.

We sat in a restaurant by Cariappa Park, not far from where I had first met Veena. The restaurant was noisy, full of conversation about venture capital and stock options and new start-ups. Hari ordered garlic bread he didn't seem too happy with, and apple pie and ice cream he liked better. He told me about life in Bangalore. He said it was like living at the center of India, the place to be if you wanted to make something of yourself. He seemed ambitious again. He had that old lightness, that joyful, carefree quality that I remembered from when we'd first met.

He told me about coming out to his sister. She sent him a text message one day asking when he planned to get married, and he replied: "I can't get married. If I do, I'll spoil a girl's life. I'm gay. I don't want to live a lie."

His heart was pounding after he sent the message. His palms felt cold. His sister wrote back almost immediately, saying she had suspected that he might be gay, and it was fine with her. They met a couple days later. She said he should live the way he wanted. But she asked him not to tell their parents.

Hari was relieved. "I was scared," he said. "She's my sister and I didn't want a gap between us. It's like a big rock has been lifted from my head. But still, I feel a lot of pressure. When will I tell my parents? One rock is gone—a whole mountain remains."

I asked Hari about his debts. "They're still there," he said, laughing. He said money was tight, but he managed to make his monthly payments. He was sure it would work out, somehow. I asked him if he was saving, and he said he had the same opinion he'd always had about that: he didn't like the concept of saving, he still didn't see why he should have to.

I asked about the job, and he said things were slow at work. He'd been at his company for several months, but he had yet to make a sale. He said no one was making sales. Things were really hard in America; no one was buying their services.

He told me some stories about approaching American customers. He could hear the tension of the bad economic climate in their voices. A man he called recently yelled at him. He told him to "get your fucking business out of my face." Hari had the man on speakerphone, and everyone in the office laughed and clapped when he hung up. Hari needed to "reset" himself after that conversation. He stepped out for a cup of tea; he played some solitaire.

As far as Hari could tell, his company hadn't signed up a single new client since he'd started working. "Things are very difficult out there," he told me. "The world economy is in a terrible situation. We're lucky that we escaped it."

"Did we?" I asked him. I pointed out that he'd gone months without a job. I reminded him that he wasn't getting paid anywhere near what he had wanted or expected when he came back from London.

I asked if he wasn't worried about the fact that he hadn't found any new business for his company. What if they decided they couldn't afford to keep him around?

"No, why should I worry?" Hari asked, smiling. He took a bite of his apple pie. "This is how I understand it. Times were bad, I went through hard times. But now they're good again. I'm back in the good times. I know my company won't fire me. I don't see why I should worry about anything."

REALITY

Veena was back at work. It had taken her a little while to find a new job. Opportunities weren't as plentiful, and, she said, she was a little more fussy. She wasn't the same woman ("girl," she called herself) who had moved to the city all those years ago. She knew her worth now. She had higher expectations.

The position she finally found paid a little less than her previous one. But she had learned that money wasn't the only—or even the best—measure of a job. She said she had a lot more responsibility at her new company. She was the head of a department at a large export business. She had more than forty people working under her. She'd grown revenues by more than 200 percent.

I talked to Veena on the phone once about her new job. She sounded enthusiastic. She said her company treated her well, and it offered a lot of scope for what she called "career development."

This time, she told me, she wasn't going to look for other opportunities. She felt like she was on a good track. She was going to keep her focus, see where that track led.

Veena was committed to her company. She talked, uncomplainingly, about the long hours she worked. But then, when I visited her in Bangalore one rainy Monday, just before five in the evening, she was already at home. These days, she told me, she left the office early. She'd just come back from six weeks off the job. She was trying to take it a little easy; she needed to slow down.

A couple months earlier, I'd woken up one morning to find the following text message from Veena on my phone:

> Friends, life has taken me by surprise yesterday. I have
> been detected with cancer in my colon. today i go for my
> ctscan to determine if there are multiple growths. Early
> next week i go under surgery. Please pray for me. your
> prayers will see me through. I regret that i had to sms you.

I stayed in touch with her and Arvind over the following weeks. I didn't want to intrude—just a text message or short phone call here and there. I heard about them from friends. I heard that the results of the CT scan were positive, and that Veena had gone into the hospital for surgery. I heard that the surgery was tough, long, but that it went well.

By the time I visited Veena in Bangalore, she had pretty much recovered from the surgery. She'd spent ten days in the hospital, and another twenty or so at home, mostly in bed. She told me the pain had been intense—more intense than anything she could have imagined. She said she'd been weak, and that she'd lost a lot of weight. I told her she looked the same to me. "Yes," she said, and she laughed. "Unfortunately, I've put it all back on."

She led me up the stairs to the third floor of the house she and Arvind were renting. It was a large house, with four bedrooms and a small garden in the front. It was an impressive building. I knew it was testament to the progress they'd both made in their careers.

At the top of the house, under a tile roof, we sat side by side on a wooden sofa. The room was dominated by a large pool table covered with a blue plastic sheet. A string of colorful Chinese lanterns hung over the table. Veena said the lights had been set up for a New Year's party, but they'd been forced to cancel the party.

She spoke a lot that evening; I felt she was unburdening herself. She talked about what she'd been through—her diagnosis, the surgery, conversations with various doctors, the emotional roller coaster she and Arvind had been subjected to. She was remarkably upbeat. She said that initially, she had felt great fear—"terror," she called it—but that now she was learning to control her mind. It was one of the best things to have come out of the experience. In the past, her mind had always been whirring; now, with the aid of yoga, with some meditation, and through sheer willpower, she was learning to focus on the present.

"Arvind and I decided early on that we wouldn't break down," she told me. "Just by pretending to be brave, we found some kind of courage. It gives me an incredible amount of peace to know that the only thing I have to deal with is just this moment."

She focused on the positives; she told me about another good thing that had come out of her diagnosis. The confusion she'd felt for so long—about her career, about the choices she'd made, and most of all about the balance between her professional and private lives—had dissipated. She said she had a new clarity.

In the past, work had always consumed her. She thought it was the only thing that mattered. Now she had a different view. It was a very new Veena who told me: "If you just go from one job to the other, your career is going well, but you're not progressing as an individual. You're pursuing your ambitions, not your dreams. I've understood now that I could be writing short stories instead of nasty e-mails at the office. An individual is capable of doing a lot of things, but we let work define us. We don't think anything else is important."

She had so many plans: she wanted to write a book, she wanted to travel. Most of all, the clarity she'd found had convinced her, finally, that she did want children. She told me that her mother had come down to Bangalore from Jaipur when she'd first been diagnosed. She'd stayed with Veena in the hospital for ten days; she hadn't gone home for even one hour during that time. Veena told me this with awe. It had made her realize what it meant to be a parent. Nothing was as important as one's children. That was a feeling—a sense of commitment, a certain purpose—that Veena wanted to know in her own life.

There was another way, too, in which her illness had convinced her she wanted kids. She said she'd been thinking more about Arvind, and what it meant to be married to him. He'd been a rock; he'd supported her so much. But she had no illusions: she knew that if she died, he'd carry on. She wondered, though, what would happen to "us"—to the joint entity they'd created by getting married and living together. That "us" meant so much to Veena. She realized she wanted it to survive her. "And that," she said, "is when I really thought we should have kids. That's the 'us' that would survive."

As Veena spoke—spoke in a torrent, as if reaching deep within herself, to the bottom of her recent ordeal—dark clouds rolled across the sky. It rained gently at first, a few patters against the tile roof, and then the clouds broke into an unseasonable downpour, a crash so loud that I had to move closer to Veena to hear what she was saying. A cool breeze blew in. I found myself hugging my knees, holding them closer to keep my body warm.

"What I'm not able to tell you, and what I've not been able to tell anyone, is how big this is," Veena said, looking outside, through the rain. I wasn't sure, but I thought she was welling up with tears. "Now you see me, and I look normal. But I can't explain the terror to you—the uncontrollable terror, the reigning terror. It was like drowning twenty-four hours a day. I think my biggest achievement in all of this is the control of the terror. I have to focus on the moment. If I project into the future, then the terror will take over."

She was quiet for a while. When she spoke again, she returned to the positives. "Maybe I'm allowed to say stupid things in front of you, maybe you have to listen," she said. "But the fact is that every time I've had a serious issue or illness in my life, it has taken me to a better thing. Every time I've had a tough period, it has been followed by a better period. It is my belief that I can come out of this thing better and stronger. It's like a rebirth."

It felt strange to be back in Bangalore. Driving to my hotel from Veena's place that evening, past the multitude of construction sites, the lit-up towers of scaffolding that were crawling with laborers even at that late hour, I could see that the city was picking up again, awakening from the slumber imposed on it by the economic slowdown. I noticed that restaurants and bars were livelier, shopping malls full of eager customers once more.

I had a couple nice meals in the city. One night, I went to a bar by myself. I sat in a corner, basked in the anonymity, the comforting privacy of urban crowds, that I sometimes longed for in Auroville.

The truth, though, was that I wasn't spending as much time in the cities. I was less attracted to them. Something in me had changed, or maybe settled. I wasn't so drawn to the confidence and optimism of urban India. That was a story I didn't fully believe in anymore. After more than seven years in the country, I knew that India's future—like its present—was a lot more complicated than the postcard version offered by the cities. I found the countryside more real, and more honest.

In Pondicherry, Sathy, who was still living in a rented house with Banu, told me that he, too, was tired of urban life. He was tired of hearing horns and his neighbors' televisions all day, tired of the washed-out, starless skies. He longed for his village; he missed the slow pace of life and sense of community, of belonging, that he remembered from Molasur.

He still kept a room in his family house, but he said Banu tried to keep him away from the village as much as possible. She wanted him to show commitment to their life in Pondicherry. She wanted him to place family first.

I had noticed a few changes in Sathy since he moved to Pondicherry. He dressed up more, in long-sleeved shirts and pants. I rarely saw him in sandals anymore; he wore closed leather shoes.

He was working part-time at a business in town. (I was one of the founders of the business, so Sathy was, improbably, working with me as a consultant.)

I noticed, also, that Sathy's stomach had grown; he no longer walked his fields. Sometimes, when I asked him about village life, when I wanted to know about how certain crops were doing or whether farmers were satisfied with the monsoon, he fumbled his responses. It was clear to me that he was a little out of touch.

Sathy's citification reached its height one January, when he missed the annual Pongal festival in Molasur. Banu wanted him to spend Pongal with her. His mother implored him to come home. Sathy hesitated. He spent one morning of the three-day festival in the village. But that year, for the first time in his life, Sathy wasn't in Molasur when the offering to the gods took place at his house.

Sathy said his mother didn't say much; he could see she was disappointed, but she didn't want to put pressure on him. The pressure, he told me, was in his own head: he worried that he was losing his roots. "When I visit Molasur, I feel like I'm a stranger, as if I'm a guest in my own house," he told me one afternoon, after we had lunch in Auroville. "I'm being pushed into that category now—pushed by other people, but mostly by my own mind. It's a psychological feeling."

Recently, he said, he'd woken up at two in the morning to take his son's dog for a bathroom walk. He looked out the window, and he saw the moon. It struck him as beautiful, something special. But then he remembered that he used to see the moon every night—that it was in fact something normal, that all his life he'd taken the night sky for granted. He said he felt just like a city dweller then, staring in astonishment at a "natural phenomenon."

City life was cut off from nature. It felt synthetic. People never went for walks. They just drove everywhere, and they never came into contact with their surroundings.

"I've seen the worst of life," Sathy told me. "I've seen the suffering of village people, their poverty, the murders, the suicides. I've been to the mortuaries, seen how they die. Once I took two bodies, a father and his daughter who had been struck by lightning in the fields. They were black, burned all over. I saw the rats tearing at bodies, I had to buy country liquor so that the people working in the mortuaries could build up the courage to cut the corpses. I've seen all of this, Akash. This is the reality of life. City people don't understand any of it. They don't understand life."

"It doesn't sound like a very pleasant reality," I said, and Sathy shook his head. "Yes, but that's the way it is," he said. "That's the truth of life around here. I don't want to be cut off from the truth."

Sathy told me that Banu let him go to Molasur only if he could come up with a valid excuse. He was forced to make up reasons—stories about his mother's health, for instance, or problems in the family fields. He was always happy when I wanted to visit the village or meet someone around there. He said my book was a perfect excuse; if I asked him to come to Molasur, Banu couldn't say no.

I asked Sathy once if he could help me find Ramadas. I hadn't seen Ramadas in a long time. The last time we'd met, his cow-brokering business was thriving. But so much had happened since then. I wondered if he had felt the impact at all of the nation's economic slowdown. I wanted to know what he thought about all the new money coming into the villages.

It was hard to track Ramadas down. He was an elusive character. I sent messages through people who knew him, but he didn't respond. I visited the lodge where he stayed when working at the cow market; they hadn't seen him in a while. Then Sathy told me he had a cell-phone number for Ramadas's son. He called, set up a meeting with Ramadas at the shandy in Brahmadesan. When we went to the shandy, Ramadas was nowhere to be found.

We caught up with Ramadas, finally, at another cow market, in a village called Madagadipet. It was about fifty kilometers from Brahmadesan. Ramadas told us it was safer for him there. He was trying to keep a low profile.

Ramadas was in a bit of trouble. He had stood guarantor for a friend who bought twelve cows. The friend had a piece of land he intended to sell to raise money for the cows. When he made the deal, he had lots of potential buyers. But then the economy had slowed, the real estate market cooled, and all the buyers backed out. Ramadas's friend wasn't able to come up with his payment.

The cows had already been shipped to the neighboring state of Kerala, probably slaughtered. The sellers were furious. It wasn't safe for Ramadas to show his face around. "If I go back to Brahmadesan, I could be in trouble," he told me, when I met him in Madagadipet. "It could turn violent, I might get beaten."

Ramadas was at the cow market with Krishnan, his friend and fellow cow broker. They were working together. When I found them, they were standing under a tamarind tree. Ramadas had shaved his beard and grown a mustache; he looked cleaner, less rough, younger.

I told him he looked good, and he shook his head and said he'd been under a lot of pressure. He said he'd been restless. He was having sleepless nights. I looked more closely, and it was true: I saw that Ramadas had deep circles under his eyes.

As we spoke, two men came up and slapped him on the back. "So this is where you are," one of them said. "Lots of people are looking for you. We should lift you from here and take you back to our village." Ramadas laughed, and the men went their way, but I could tell he was perturbed.

When the men were gone, Krishnan said: "If they lift a finger against Ramadas, they know what will happen to them. We'll never allow that. They won't dare enter the area again after that."

Ramadas and Krishnan were done with their work for the day, but they wanted to walk around the shandy a little. They studied the cows on display. They commented on each one they passed: too skinny, too old, nice horns, good teeth. Sathy and I followed them. I made sure to keep my eyes on the ground, avoiding the copious piles of feces and puddles of urine that had turned the dry earth to mud.

As they walked, Ramadas and Krishnan started talking about how dull the market was. They said business was down; it had been that way for a while now. "This is nothing compared to what it was a few years ago," Ramadas told me. "There are maybe half as many cows here." Krishnan nodded his head in agreement. "It's because they're all being eaten. The cow population is being reduced," he said.

"Nonsense," Ramadas said. "It has nothing to do with eating. If people eat them, then there's more demand—the market should be busier. It has everything to do with what we've been watching on TV. We all know what's happening in the world. Look, before, a cow skin used to be exported for six hundred rupees. Now you can't even get two hundred rupees. So of course there aren't any buyers. When the whole world is down, do you think we'll be up? It's very simple: people don't have money."

Krishnan insisted again that the problems at the shandy had nothing to do with the global economy. He said cows were being eaten faster than they could breed. Ramadas seemed kind of exasperated with his friend; he found an excuse to get rid of him.

When Krishnan was gone, Ramadas told me that things had changed quite suddenly, about a year or two before. Initially, he said, the price of cows started going down. It was the first time since Ramadas was a young man that he'd seen that. Then, he started noticing fewer buyers, especially those representatives of slaughterhouses that exported cow hides and meat.

For a while, Ramadas kept making the trip from Chennai to Brahmadesan. He stayed in his lodge, sleeping on the floor at the top of the building, with just one bulb to light the room. He went to the cow market in the mornings, hung out with nothing to do, came back to the lodge in the evenings. He wasn't making any money. He wasn't even able to cover the cost of his bus fare from Chennai.

Now, Ramadas said, he no longer held out any hope for his business. He had resisted the thought for a long time, but he'd come to an undeniable conclusion: Cow brokering was gone, and it wasn't coming back. Maybe what he'd been watching on TV had led to this situation, he said, but he thought it had only precipitated something that was already under way. "It's a hopeless line of work," he told me. "What kind of a living is it to sell cows? I don't think it will ever be the way it was again."

I tried to encourage Ramadas. I told him I was sure if he just stuck around long enough things would get better. Already, I said, the world economy was picking up. India was doing well again.

Ramadas wasn't convinced. He curled his upper lip, disgusted, and he said again that his line of work was gone. Then, unexpectedly, he started smiling. He told me he didn't really care anyway. He'd already decided to get out of the business. He was almost sixty years old. He'd been working in this field for forty-five years. It was tough work. He said it wasn't worth it anymore; Ramadas had decided it was time for a change.

"What?" I asked. I was astonished. "But you said you'd do it as long as your blood flowed. You said you'd never stop, no matter what happened."

"So what?" Ramadas said. "Can't a man change his mind? Yes, it's true I told you that, but now the whole situation has changed. An era has passed. A moment in history is gone. I grew up doing this work with my father. But you know, I don't really mind. It's fine. This business is over. I wouldn't recommend it to a young man today. The country has changed, and I'm happy to move on."

He pulled a business card from his shirt pocket. It was for a real estate developer he'd met in Chennai. The developer had told Ramadas that real estate was the future. He'd convinced Ramadas that he had bright prospects in land. He said the business needed people like Ramadas—men with energy and know-how, who knew how to swing a deal.

Ramadas was enthusiastic. He told me he'd seen for himself how land prices had jumped in recent years, how young fools, uneducated kids, had made more money in a few months than he had made in all his time as a cow broker. He wasn't interested in sticking with a dead business. Maybe he was sixty years old, but he wasn't finished; he still had a future.

"Won't you miss this business?" I asked him. "Are you sure you won't regret leaving it?"

"Not at all," Ramadas said. "I didn't invest crores and crores into anything. I just made my money and went home. Maybe if a prostitute quits prostitution, or if an arrack seller stops selling arrack, they might have regrets. They don't know how to do anything else. But I have so many skills. I can make money so many other ways."

He stopped at a vendor's stall and bought himself some juice, an onion-and-millet mix. "I won't miss any of this," he said, "nothing at all. All I'll remember is how I slogged—slogged and slogged for forty-five years, and no savings to show for it. Even my wife— she works as an unskilled laborer, but she has a fixed deposit. She asks me all the time what I have, and what can I say? Nothing."

He drank his juice, he wiped some off the tips of his mustache. Then he turned around, pointed at two cows tied to a tree, and asked Sathy and me if we had any idea how much they cost. We said we didn't. "I bet they cost around twenty-three thousand to twenty-five thousand for the pair," he said.

He went up to a group of men sitting on the ground. He asked if the cows were theirs, and one man said yes, he had bought them earlier that morning. "How much did you pay?" Ramadas asked, and the man told him he had paid 25,000 rupees.

"See, see," Ramadas came back and said. "See how right I was? After all my time in this business, I knew exactly how much they would cost." He was beaming. "I know my trade," he said. "I know it inside out."

"He'll miss it," I said to Sathy.

"He'll miss it," Sathy said.

We laughed.

"I won't miss it at all," Ramadas said. "I'm making a new start. I won't miss a single day."

On our way back from the market, past a row of scrap metal shops and rusted tractors and sugarcane fields, I told Sathy I thought it was a bit depressing that Ramadas was quitting his line of work. I said I understood that times were tough, but it didn't make sense to me that Ramadas was going to start a new career at the age of sixty.

To me, Ramadas was a victim—of difficult economic times, maybe, but even more, of changing times. I saw him as a man being forced out of the profession he had followed—and loved—for forty-five years. I saw him as yet another casualty of India's development.

Sathy said he saw it a little differently. He didn't think it was so depressing that Ramadas was going to stop working as a cow broker. For him, it was exciting that Ramadas had found a new line of work. Yes, times were changing, and Ramadas was being forced to move on. But, Sathy said, I had to admit he was entering a much more promising field. Ramadas was right that real estate was the way of the future.

"Just one deal goes through and he could make a lot of money," Sathy said. "Why should he sit around and waste his time at the shandies? He's right when he says that's the past. Those days are over, Akash. These days, if you have drive and ambition, it doesn't matter who you are or even how old you are. It's a whole new scene in this country. Who knows? Ramadas could get rich."

He started talking about his own situation. He said Banu always told him farming was history. She asked why he couldn't be more enterprising. The whole country is getting rich, she would say, and we're the only ones missing out on the action.

"For years, I told her she didn't know what she was talking about," Sathy said. "I was like Ramadas. I told her that I was a farmer, that farming was in my blood and I would never leave it. But I have to admit: When I see everything that's happening, part of me wants to start a new life also."

We turned off the main road, onto a country path that led between rice and peanut fields. The fields were green. A few water buffaloes were resting in a pond. A woman was crouched over, picking peanuts, her head protected from the heat by a faded blue cloth.

"In a few years, none of this will be here," Sathy said. "I'm sure this will all be plots and houses." He was pensive, a little rueful. Then he chuckled. "That Ramadas—you have to admit he's an enterprising fellow. It'll take him far. He'll probably figure out a way to make a fortune off these fields."

Not too long after that conversation with Sathy, I went to the beach. I went back to the fishing village of Chinnamudaliarchavadi, along the East Coast Road. It was the evening, winter, and the rains had been torrential that year. Farmers in the area were celebrating a successful monsoon. But in Chinnamudaliarchavadi, the mood was grim.

I went to Chinnamudaliarchavadi because I had heard that another stretch of the shore had recently been lost to erosion. I heard, too, that angry villagers had staged a demonstration on the East Coast Road, blocking traffic for hours. At least fourteen homes had been swept away. I wanted to see the situation for myself.

What I found was a pitiful sight. Last time I had been in Chinnamudaliarchavadi, the waves were already lapping up against the village, but only a few thatch huts had been swallowed by the ocean. Now at least three rows of houses, many made of concrete and brick, had disappeared. All over the shore, on bits of higher ground, families had set up makeshift shelters, improvised tents of canvas, thatch, and straw sheets. The village looked like a refugee camp.

A group of women sat on the ground, amid the ruins of their homes. They told me about the buildings that were lost, about the difficulty their men confronted while fishing in those turbulent waters. Many families, their livelihoods decimated, were reduced to a single meal a day. Children had been pulled from school.

Up the shore from those women, I spoke to a husband and wife outside their shelter. It was a sorry excuse for a home: waist-high, just a couple meters long, a sheet of straw and some tattered saris draped over a few branches staked in the ground. Their original home had been lost one morning when the husband was out at sea and the woman was selling fish at a market. They came back to the village, and all their possessions were gone. At least, they said, their son had been at school. He survived.

Their son was seven years old. His name was Ajit. He hung around the shelter, smiling, but with tired eyes. His mother told me that Ajit wanted to be a doctor. She laughed when she said that. "Who has the money to make him a doctor?" she asked.

She wanted her son to be a fisherman. Her father and grandfather had fished for a living, and her husband's father and grandfather had, too. Her husband, himself a fisherman, shook his head. "What kind of living can he make from fishing?" he asked. "Look at this ocean. Let him get a job. Let him become something real—something with a future."

I walked away from that family. I walked along the narrow beach, past all the debris, past a house that had been cut open, as if sliced in half, slabs of concrete suspended midair from thin steel rods. I walked and I walked. I walked fast, as if I was trying to get away from all the devastation.

I sat on a catamaran. Waves crashed at my feet. There was a strong breeze lifting from the ocean; the air was crisp.

In the distance, I could see the town of Pondicherry. Its lights were bright in the advancing evening, multicolored. I could see the outlines of a pier, and a beach promenade where I knew traffic was busy and tourists crowded into swanky hotels. Pondicherry was a thriving town. It was everything Chinnamudaliarchavadi was not: prosperous, self-confident, with a future.

Sitting on that catamaran, my thoughts turned to the shandy I'd recently visited in Madagadipet. I thought of the conversation Sathy and I had about Ramadas on the way back from the market.

I had seen pathos, even heartbreak, in Ramadas's story. I thought his decision to leave cow brokering was a modern Indian tragedy—less dramatic, certainly less painful, than the tragedy being played out in Chinnamudaliarchavadi, but not dissimilar in its sense of exile, of banishment from a way of life established over centuries.

I saw Ramadas and Chinnamudaliarchavadi as forms of collateral damage. They were the losses Indian society had to bear—was willing to bear—in order to enjoy its new prosperity.

Sathy had a different opinion. He saw Ramadas's interest in real estate as cause for optimism. Now I wondered: Which one of us was right? And, on that beach, with the detritus of an ancient village on one side and the shine of a newly rising town on the other, it struck me that, in fact, we had both been right. Ramadas's story was a quintessentially Indian story—a story of loss and renewal, of ruin and reinvention. This duality, this delicate dance between destruction and creativity, between tearing down and building up, was what defined the Indian condition at the start of the twenty-first century.

It was a small realization, something I'd been aware of—if less explicitly, as if in the background of my consciousness—for some time. But that evening, my understanding of India's duality came as a form of release. It came as comfort, a relief from all the questions and doubts and anger I'd been harboring recently about the nation. For the first time in months, perhaps in years, I was able to locate a certain equanimity within myself when I thought of India and what it was becoming.

I had returned from America full of enthusiasm. I celebrated what I saw as the rejuvenation of my home. Later, the enthusiasm started seeming naive, the rejuvenation something of an illusion. My optimism turned to skepticism, occasionally to despair. Now it seemed to me that I had perhaps rushed to judgment on both occasions—that my initial, positive reaction was as hasty as my later, negative one.

India didn't lend itself to easy judgments. The central fact (perhaps the only incontrovertible fact) of modern India was change. The nation was on a journey. It was still sorting through the contradictions of a rapid, and inevitably messy, transformation. Who could say where the journey was leading?

I realized that evening that there was only one thing, really, of which I could be certain: I was lucky to be part of the change, to be witnessing and living it every day. India was in the midst of one of the most momentous transitions (at least when measured by the number of people affected) ever undertaken by mankind. I was a privileged spectator, with a ringside seat at one of the greatest shows in history.

The show was still unfolding. I resolved just to sit back, stop trying to figure out what I thought of it—and enjoy it.

Later that evening, leaving Chinnamudaliarchavadi, I turned onto the East Coast Road. I drove away from the broken village, I drove past the yoga centers, restaurants, and guesthouses that had come up over the past few years.

It was the end of the day. The road was dark. Traffic was dangerous. Almost every day, I knew, people were hit on that road.

Many were killed. Families were destroyed. But I was trying to keep my mind off destruction that night. I was trying to hold on to some of the equanimity I had found on the beach.

I knew that if I kept going, just followed the highway, tracked the curves and angles of the coast, I would retrace (in reverse) the trip I had taken all those years ago, when I first landed back home. I would drive through villages and farms, along plotted-out developments, past mango and coconut plantations whose owners were considering selling out, trading the familiarity of farming for the riches of real estate.

If I continued, I would end up in the town of Mahabalipuram, with its shore temples and thriving tourist economy. Then, past Mahabalipuram, at the outskirts of Chennai, I would turn off the East Coast Road, onto Rajiv Gandhi Salai, where the excavators were no doubt digging up fertile soil and the cranes lifting shiny plates of glass at that very moment into the night sky.

I imagined the evening shift beginning in the office buildings along Rajiv Gandhi Salai. I pictured the rush of young technology workers as they took their seats, powered on their computers, and prepared for a night of phone calls and e-mails with Americans just waking up on the other side of the world. I thought of those young men and women—all their dreams, the way their dreams were India's dreams. They were the future; they carried the hopes of the nation on their shoulders.

I thought of the remarkable voyage those workers were on—where they were going, and where they had come from. Many, I supposed, would have grown up in places like Chinnamudaliarchavadi, communities where ancient certitudes were crumbling, where the fixity of life was being shaken. People they knew, people they'd left behind—their parents, older relatives, friends who hadn't studied or worked as hard—were caught up in the turmoil.

Many of those people wouldn't survive the turmoil. Their lives, and their way of life, would be shattered. So much was being broken in the new India. But I knew, also, that in those office buildings, in front of those computers and behind those glass panes, something remarkable—something inchoate, something full of promise yet still, in many ways, frighteningly undefined—was being built. A world was dying. I resolved to hold on to this conviction: that ineluctably, if at times haltingly, a new world was rising to take its place.

EPILOGUE

A book ends, but lives go on. Since finishing India Becoming, *I* have stayed in touch with many of the people I write about. Some of these people have become friends; I have been in regular contact with them. Others, I hear about through mutual acquaintances, or exchange the occasional email or SMS with.

Readers often ask me about these people. They want to know how their lives have developed. Here are some brief updates.

Sathy is still living in Pondicherry, still trying to figure out how to stay with his family but keep a leg in the village. Banu has had a few business ideas—one in e-publishing, the other having to do with organic products—but her main role is still as a homemaker. The highway being built by Molasur has been completed. Sathy complains that there are more cars, and more real estate plots, in the village.

Das bought himself an air-conditioned Tata Safari car. He parks it outside his house. He's started a few new real estate projects in villages around Molasur, but he says business is dull. His son graduated from engineering college and is working at a technology company in Chennai; his daughter is in her third year of college, also studying engineering.

Hari left his job, drifted through a few others, and then ended up working in a Gulf country with security concerns. He goes to work every day under military escort. He isn't allowed to leave his room or go into the neighboring town without permission. I've met him a couple times on his visits back home. He chafes under the restrictions at his new job; his social life is poor. But he's been making good money, and he's managed to pay off his debts. All his siblings have been married. He is under intense pressure from his parents. He hasn't come out to them yet.

I never saw Selvi again. Through her landlord, I heard that she'd left the city and moved back to her village. Her landlord also told me that he'd received an invitation to her wedding, which he hadn't attended.

Dr. Reddy's practice continues to flourish. He told me that many doctors, even from small towns and remote parts of the country, contact him now, looking for training in his field. Patients are less shy. Earlier they would look the other way if they saw him in public; now they acknowledge him. "The shame has gone," he said.

Ramadas's career in real estate didn't work out. I met him one evening in Chennai, and he said, with that disgusted look on his face I remembered so well, that real estate was a business for young men. He'd taken a job as a salesman at a textiles store in Chennai. He worked a regular day now. The last time I saw him, he said he never went to cow markets anymore. He said he was happy that way, but he asked many questions about life in the villages, and I thought he seemed nostalgic. I noticed that he'd lost a lot of weight.

Veena quit her job and started a business with a partner. Building her own business was a challenge, but she told me she'd decided there was nothing she could do in life anymore that would feel risky. Her health was stable. She was trying to write about her experiences with cancer. She told me: "I'm less scared as a person."

Naresh finished and published an excellent book about the history of jazz in Mumbai. He quit his job as a full-time editor. He continues to rail against the poor state of urban planning in the country. I suspect he might one day write a book about all of this.

Vinod continues his various struggles for social justice. He called me one morning to say that city contractors had shown up and cleared all the garbage in his backyard, on the beach outside his apartment. He was happy. We spoke a few months later; it had accumulated again. "We're back to square one," he said.

As I write this epilogue, I am nursing a sore throat from the dioxins in my own backyard. It's summer, and the smoke has been blowing in my direction again. The news isn't all grim, though. The government has been working with a private company to reduce the burning. So while the unsegregated waste continues to pile up, there have been fewer fires, and overall less smoke recently. The nation's garbage problems are far from solved, but the disaster in my backyard, at least, seems to merit a cautious—very cautious—optimism.

Every day, I try to live by that cautious optimism. I hold on to a degree of faith—faith that the nation's great self-confidence will prove prophetic rather than merely boastful, that the tremendous wealth of a few presages a prosperity of many, and that the great churning that is modern India will eventually settle into some kind of equilibrium.

ACKNOWLEDGMENTS

It is customary to thank one's family last but not least, but I've never understood that custom. This book could never have been finished without the support, wisdom, and generosity of my wife, Auralice, and the unstinting (if unconscious) patience of my two sons, Aman and Emil. I also owe a deep debt to my parents, Dilip and Mary; to my siblings, Vikas, Milan, and Ayesha; and to Jacqueline.

My editor, Sarah McGrath, and my agent, Elyse Cheney, had faith in this project when it was just a couple sheets of paper and a few semi-coherent ideas. They nurtured it through multiple drafts, and helped turn the sheets of paper into a book. At Riverhead, I am also grateful to Geoffrey Kloske, Sarah Stein, Matthew Venzon, and Lydia Hirt; and at Elyse Cheney Literary Associates to Alexander Jacob. I would also like to thank Kimberly Burns for all her efforts on behalf of the book. At Penguin India, a special thanks to Varun Chaudhary, Udayan Mitra, and Chiki Sarkar; and at Albin Michel, in France, to Vaiju Naravane.

Every book (especially a first book) owes a debt to certain individuals who have played a role in the author's life long before the book was begun. Over the years, I have been fortunate to benefit from conversations and correspondence with Anthony Appiah, Jonah Blank, Ram Guha, Suketu Mehta, Pankaj Mishra, Bronwen Morgan,

Amartya Sen, Ashutosh Varney, Stefaan Verhulst, and many other fine writers and thinkers and teachers. I am grateful for the time and energy they have given me, and for all I have learned from them.

I am also grateful to all the editors who have had faith in my work over the years, and who have taught me to write better, more clearly, and less dutifully. In alphabetical order, I would like to thank Jack Beatty, Alida Becker, Jason Cowley, Toby Lester, Wen Stephenson, Divia Thani, Mike Vazquez, and Bill Whitworth. At *The New York Times* and *The International Herald Tribune,* where I wrote a fortnightly "Letter from India" column, I want to thank Len Apcar, Marc Charney, Philip McClellan, David McCraw, Jeanne Moore, and especially Marty Gottlieb and Alison Smale. Jeanne Moore took time from her busy schedule to read a draft of the book, and I am grateful for that.

At *The New Yorker,* where an excerpt from this book was published, I want to thank, again in alphabetical order, Owen Agnew, Blake Eskin, Jiayang Fan, Henry Finder, Giles Harvey, David Remnick, Nick Thompson, and Dorothy Wickenden.

I would also like to thank Rohan Bagai, Roy Bahat, Jason Bush, Roy Chvat, Priyam Cornuit, Sebastian and Marcella Cortes, Mauro de Lorenzo, Darryl D' Monte, Dipen Desai, Naresh Fernandes, Jesse Fox-Allen, Nell Freudenburger, Dirk Gastmans, Luk Gastmans, Elliot Gerson, DW Gibson, Christopher Gray, Parag Khanna, V. Laxmi, Gillian Walker and Albert Maysles (and their wonderful family and cats), David Nagel, Kami and Kapil Narayan, Muniandi Radhakrishna, Janmejay Rai, Devendra Saharia, and Matt Weiland. A special thanks is due to Vlatko Balic and Gniewko Lubecki—friends, godfathers, and patient partners, who, like so many others, gave me the space to write this book.

There are many others who have helped me along the way, and I'm sure I'm forgetting some. The people I could never forget are the ones who allowed me to write about them. I am humbled by the patience, generosity, and friendship shown to me by my "characters" (the word fails to do justice to their humanity). None of them knew what they were getting into when they signed on to this project. None of them ever showed any signs of resentment or impatience.

I have changed some names and identifying details, in order to protect the privacy of a few of these characters. In certain cases, I have also compressed or edited quotes, usually for clarity, but sometimes in order to protect the speakers. In the interest of full disclosure—and because the standard practices of narrative nonfiction have suddenly become so contentious—I should also say that I have sometimes moved events and scenes around in time, or compressed them, in order to form a coherent narrative. Occasionally, a statement or event from one scene may have been inserted into another, usually, again, in the interest of narrative coherence.

This is a work of nonfiction. There are no composite characters or invented "facts." In moving things around, I have always tried to remain faithful to the original intent of speakers and meaning of events. In the rare cases where I have had any doubts, I have shown the passages in question to the speakers or characters to make sure that I was not distorting their statements.

GLOSSARY

Beedi: An unfiltered, hand-rolled cigarette, consisting of tobacco rolled in a leaf.

Crore: A numbering unit used to signify 10 million.

Goonda: A rogue or a hooligan, often (though not necessarily) violent.

Kurta: A long shirt (often knee-length) worn on the Indian subcontinent, usually with pajama pants.

Lakh: A numbering unit used to signify 100,000.

Lungi: A long cloth wrapped around the waist, usually worn by men. Similar to a sarong.

Pakka: A Hindi word (though widely used in other languages, too) signifying good, proper, or wholesome.

Pakoras: A dish consisting of various vegetables (e.g., potatoes, eggplant, onion) dipped in chickpea-flour batter and deep-fried.

Panchayat: A traditional village assembly that serves as a local court or body for dispute resolution; *panchayat*s have existed for centuries, often as unelected bodies consisting of village elders or wise men, but recently have been formally incorporated into the Indian Constitution, and many are now elected bodies. Often, too, traditional unelected *panchayat*s exist in villages alongside more modern, elected bodies.

Pongal: A harvest festival observed primarily in South India and Sri Lanka; occurs in mid-January.

Pooja: A religious ceremony marked by the worship of deities, and often by the burning of incense or a candle and other rituals.

Roti: A flat bread made from flour; a staple of much Indian cooking, especially in the north.

Salwar kameez: A two-piece outfit, consisting of shirt and pants, worn by women; traditionally from North India and seen as somewhat less conservative than a sari.

Sambar: A brothlike dish, common in South India, made of lentils and vegetables.

Sari: A dress worn by women on the Indian subcontinent, consisting of lengths of silk or cotton fabric wrapped around the body.

*Shloka*s: Sanskrit verses, usually in praise of the gods or otherwise sacred in nature.

Tabla: A percussion instrument, like a drum, played with the hand.

Zamindar: Dating from the precolonial and colonial eras: a land-lord with authority to collect taxes and rent from tenants. The authority of zamindars was legally abolished in India after independence, but many zamindar families retained large landholdings and influence.

Akash Kapur is the former writer of the "Letter from India" column for the *International Herald Tribune* and the online edition of the *New York Times*. He has also written for *The Atlantic*, *The Economist*, *Granta*, the *New Yorker*, and the *New York Times Book Review*. He holds a BA in social anthropology from Harvard University and a doctorate in law from Oxford University, which he attended as a Rhodes Scholar. He lives outside Pondicherry, in southern India.